MYTHOLOGY
OF THE
BRITISH ISLES

Three scenes from the
Tristan story: his
voyage from Ireland
with Isolde;
his drinking of the
love-potion; the return
of the lovers.

MYTHOLOGY
OF THE
BRITISH ISLES

GEOFFREY ASHE

Methuen London

By the same author

King Arthur's Avalon: The Story of Glastonbury
Land to the West
The Finger and the Moon (fiction)
The Quest for Arthur's Britain
The Virgin
The Ancient Wisdom
Avalonian Quest
The Discovery of King Arthur
The Landscape of King Arthur

First published in Great Britain 1990
by Methuen London
Michelin House, 81 Fulham Road, London SW3 6RB
Reprinted 1991
First paperback edition 1992
Copyright © 1990 by Geoffrey Ashe

Design by Christopher Holgate

A CIP catalogue record for this book
is available from the British Library

ISBN 0 413 62990 2 (hardback)
ISBN 0 413 66540 2 (paperback)

Printed in Great Britain
by Clays Ltd, St Ives plc

Contents

en lestour · la ueissies ces cheualiers
gesir parmi laigue · qui la estoit
toute rouge del sanc des mors ·

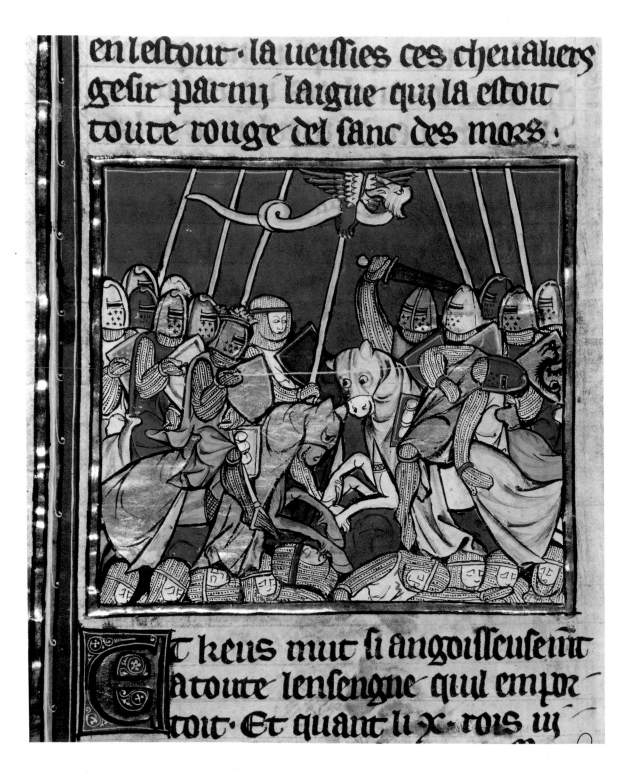

T keus mut si angoisseusemt
a toute lensengne qu'il empor
toit · Et quant li · X · rois iij

1. Arthur unhorses
one of the rebels who
claim his throne.

List of Illustrations

Picture research by Deborah Pownall

2. A page from a
manuscript of Geoffrey
of Monmouth's
Historia, telling of
the marriage of the
Emperor Claudius's
daughter to a British
king.

Preface

This book follows the arrangement admirably devised by Robert Graves for his *Greek Myths* and *Hebrew Myths*. Each section deals with its topic first as presented in legend or story-telling or speculation. Then a commentary discusses the sources, the facts, the underlying ideas, the rehandling in subsequent tradition and writing.

Is 'mythology' justified here? Much of the material is unlike myth in the classical sense, being more miscellaneous and often closer to history or literature. Yet when all these things are assembled and considered together, it seems clear to me that they have an interrelatedness which is seldom realised, and that their significance goes beyond entertainment or the weaving of individual yarns. Whatever their precise nature, they have a mythic dimension. They express ideas about a certain territory and how it came to be as it is: about its place in the world, its landscape, its inhabitants, their society and government.

The time-span of the survey extends from prehistory to the ninth century AD. It ends where it does, not because there are no myths applicable to later times, but because, with the movement into better-recorded history, their character alters. We get tales that simply embroider the well-known lives of well-known persons, such as the heroes of Scottish independence, and Francis Drake. We get conscious fictions, such as *Frankenstein* and *Dr Jekyll and Mr Hyde*. The difference is sometimes one of degree rather than kind, and with Robin Hood, for example, the older type of myth-making is still at work. But a line must be drawn somewhere, and I hope the ninth-century ending will be seen as a logical conclusion, beyond which it would be difficult to go without a loss of consistency.

It may be objected that most of the matter is retrospective. It is what has been believed or imagined long afterwards, not what was believed or imagined at the time or anywhere near it. But the same is true of the Greek myths as well, or any other. Mythology is a long-term creation. Where this book seeks to break new ground is in its attempt to show that a mass of diverse material does amount to a British mythology with something like the coherence of the Greek, if less opulent because so much has been lost.

It does, however, have a very peculiar feature. Not only is a good deal of it quasi-history, but a good deal of the quasi-history is due to a single author, Geoffrey of Monmouth. A cleric of Welsh or possibly Breton family, he taught at Oxford between 1129 and 1151. Towards 1138 he produced one of the most important books of the Middle Ages, and one of the most misleadingly titled: the *Historia Regum Britanniae* or *History of the Kings of Britain*. Using Latin, the learned and international language, he professed to trace nearly two thousand years of Britain's past, giving the truth about King Lear and King Arthur and many others. After an interval he followed it up with a narrative poem, the *Vita Merlini* or *Life of Merlin*, augmenting what he had said already about the famous enchanter.

Throughout the Middle Ages, and even the Tudor period, his account was widely accepted as factual. Before it fell into disrepute it had generated a large part of the mythology in the form now known to us.

However, this was not mere invention on Geoffrey's part. He claimed that his material was long prior to himself and that he got it from an ancient work 'in the British language', meaning Welsh or Breton. If this existed, it might have had something like the character of Homeric epic, with similar mythic value. There is no firm evidence that it did. Where Greece had its Homer, Britain, so far as we know, did not, and that is one reason why the shape of its mythology is different. Still, Geoffrey's claim is valid to the extent that he did make use of real history and authentic tradition . . . some of the time. It is often hard to tell what the earlier versions were, or what they said. Nevertheless he had them before him and he drew on them. His work has countless external links and references. There is no question here of contriving a mythology out of one writer's irresponsible fancies; though that writer, perforce, is encountered rather frequently.

Geographically the British Isles include Ireland, and the proper treatment of Irish matter, in a context dominated by Britain, is a manifest problem. Ireland's own heritage is so vast, so rich, and so largely independent, that it would be presumptuous and insulting to force it as a whole into such a frame. There could be no true unity in the result, which would be an unhappy combination of two books. The course followed here is to introduce Irish stories when they are clearly related to British ones. Where this is so, they sometimes bring illumination that would be lacking without them.

Note on References

Citations in the notes at the end of each section refer to headings in the bibliography, usually names of authors, sometimes titles of works. The numbers in most cases refer to pages. With a few early works having an accepted book-and-chapter division, they may apply to this. For example, 'Bede, I, 4' means 'Bede, book I, chapter 4'.

From a purist point of view each statement in the text should be supported by one note. To a large extent this is the case. But quite often a paragraph, or a major part of it, is based on several passages in several consulted works, and a point-by-point breakdown would be complicated and even impracticable. Readers of such a passage who wish to explore further may, I believe, find it more enlightening to consider it as a whole, and follow up the references together, than they would if they tried to analyse it. Graves gives similar multiple references in his *Greek Myths*, and, indeed, much more regularly.

The Peoples and Their Origins

1 The Giants

It is said in Wales that the first name of the island now called Britain was
Myrddin's Precinct. That was before it was even populated. The earliest
inhabitants on whom traditions agree were giants. They are reputed to have
been descendants of Noah's son Ham, and to have come from Africa in the
second millennium before Christ and taken possession. A few English
chroniclers maintain that they were preceded by descendants of Noah's son
Japheth. But these people, if they ever existed, were conquered by the giants
and all trace of them disappeared.

The giants' king was Albion. He was begotten by the sea-god whom the
Greeks called Poseidon, the Romans Neptune. 'Albion' is the island's oldest
acknowledged name, presumably taken from the giant. Some, however,
derive it instead from a princess Albina. They say she sailed to this country,
which then had no human inhabitants, at the head of a band of women –
perhaps as many as fifty – who had been banished for killing their husbands.
They were all sisters, on the paternal side at least. Their father is sometimes
named as Diocletian and described as a king of Syria. In their new home they
mated with demons, and the giants were the result of these couplings, not
migrants from outside. However, the only recorded ruler called Diocletian
was a Roman emperor many centuries later, and the tale of the husband-
killers is little favoured.

To revert to Albion the giant, after a long reign he went to the south of
Gaul (now France) to aid his brothers in a fight against Hercules. The tenth
of that hero's famous labours had taken him to Spain to fetch a unique herd
of cattle. On the way home he and his companions came under attack by
Ligurians living near the mouths of the Rhône, who tried to take the cattle
away. They were led by two other sons of Poseidon. Albion had had
warning of the clash and arrived to help. Hercules was hard pressed. When

3. King Arthur
encounters a giant on
Mont-St-Michel,
roasting a carcase on
a spit.

he ran out of arrows he prayed to his father Zeus, who dropped a shower of stones from the sky. The hero and his men used them as missiles, routed the Ligurians, and slew the giants. Thus Albion's career ended. The giant race, however, continued in his island for six hundred years, though their numbers dwindled till few were left, mostly in Cornwall.

'Myrddin's Precinct' occurs cryptically in a Welsh text, the *White Book of* 6
Rhydderch. 'Myrddin' has a more celebrated form, Merlin. It must be supposed that the enchanter bore the same name as an earlier figure, possibly a god of the island.

'Albion' is documented quite far back. Greeks writing two or three centuries 7
before Christ apply it to the larger of the two British Isles, Ireland being Ierne. Its meaning is uncertain. A derivation from *albus*, Latin for 'white', in allusion to the cliffs of Dover, is dubious because of the unlikelihood that a Latin name would have been widespread so early. Another etymology relates it to 'Alp' and interprets it in Celtic terms as 'high ground', referring not only to cliffs but to hills and mountains on other parts of the coastline.

Geoffrey of Monmouth introduces both the name and the giants without much detail. More can be found in the sixteenth-century chronicler Holinshed 8
and the poet Spenser. Albion as a person, the principal giant, was matched with the island because of a mythic coincidence. The fight of Poseidon's sons with 9
Hercules is mentioned by several classical authors. Inspiration for the story came from a geographical feature, the Plaine de la Crau between Marseilles and the mouths of the Rhône, where Greek travellers noticed stones strewn everywhere: these were explained as missiles out of the sky. The Greek account calls the relevant son of Poseidon 'Ialebion', but variant readings include 'Alebion' and (if doubtfully) 'Albion', so the connection was an easy one to hit on, though it is not certain who first did so. It appears in a work by Perottus 10
in 1489.

The tale of the husband-killers is a literary fancy traceable to the fourteenth 11
century. It is adapted from the Greek myth of the spouse-slaying Danaids, daughters of Danaus, king of Argos. Some chroniclers try to make out that these women who gave birth to the giants actually were the Danaids; Holinshed, who does not accept the notion, makes a distressed attempt to deal with it. The original hint, drawing attention to people with a name beginning 'Dan', may have come from a race of 'Danaans' who reputedly settled in ancient Ireland. The giants themselves are rather more than literary. Geoffrey gives an account of Stonehenge showing that they are fictionalised versions of the megalith-builders, who created Stonehenge as their supreme achievement. Folklore, having no record of them, assumed that the stones must have been set up by beings of more than human stature. This inference was mistaken. The real megalith-builders were not particularly large. They flourished in Britain in and around the third millennium BC. The final concentration of giants in Cornwall reflects the abundance of standing stones in that county.

Popular legend tells of Cornish giants surviving much later. One is Cormo- 12
ran, the lord of St Michael's Mount, who was slain by Jack the Giant-Killer. Another is Bolster, who was outwitted in an attempt on the virtue of St Agnes. Cornish giants are depicted as stupid, and given to aimless fighting with boulders. The same traditional motif creates colossi in other places and later still. Such are Ascapart, slain by Bevis and buried under the tumulus Bevis Mound

4. Lanyon Quoit, a
megalithic dolmen.

5. St Michael's Mount,
Cornwall.

near Southampton; and Tom Hickathrift of Norfolk in the reign of William the Conqueror, who was well liked for his protection of his neighbours against robbers, against a more sinister giant at Wisbech, and against the Devil himself at Walpole St Peter's, where the church has an effigy of Tom. But these later giants are generally regarded as freaks, not survivors of the old race.

Whereas the giants have a basis of sorts in prehistory and folklore, the descendants of Japheth are artificial. They were tacked on at the beginning by Tudor antiquaries for the sake of harmony with the Bible, which was read as implying that Japheth was the ancestor of all post-Deluge Europeans and therefore, necessarily, of those in Britain. The giants, being monstrous and African, had to be of the stock of Ham, Noah's 'bad' son, whose progeny spawned the more disreputable nations. So they were made intrusive, with acceptable Japheth people before and after. The author mainly responsible for the latter was John Bale in 1548. He introduced them by way of a non-scriptural son of Japheth named Samothes. Here he was led astray by a faked 'ancient history', the work of an Italian, Annius of Viterbo, in 1498. The Samotheans figure in Holinshed but have no real legendary roots. [13]

With the giants, a natural question to ask is how big they were. Geoffrey says one of the Cornish tribe, Gogmagog, was twelve cubits tall: say eighteen feet. Yet he apparently forgets this a moment later when he tells of an ordinary-sized man defeating him in a wrestling match, and even lifting and carrying him. A similar query arises from Bolster's proposition to St Agnes. To add to the doubt, the giants are sometimes spoken of in terms implying a vastness out of all proportion to normal humanity. Bolster himself could stand with one foot on St Agnes Beacon and the other on Carn Brea, six miles apart. Spenser seems to indulge an even wilder fancy, that Albion crossed the Channel in one bound – he 'did on dry-foot pas Into old Gall' (*Faerie Queene*, IV, xi, 16, lines 3–4). However, as an earlier passage shows (II, x, 5, line 5), Spenser is following Thomas Twyne, who acutely maintained that Dover Strait was once bridged by an isthmus, so that Albion and his fellow-giants simply walked across and there is no inference as to stature. Their country, though very nearly an island, became completely insular only long afterwards when the sea broke through. Twyne in fact derives the name 'Britain' itself from an alleged word *brit* meaning a separated piece. [14] [15]

In the upshot, the impression is that these giants, though very tall and strong, cannot have been absolutely enormous, but that poets and yarn-spinners have had a recognised licence to give them a fairy-tale quality and enlarge them for the sake of a story. The same elasticity applies to some giants outside Britain, even some who are products of fiction rather than genuine legend, such as Gargantua and Paul Bunyan.

1. Bromwich, 228–9, 231.
2. Geoffrey of Monmouth, hereafter abbreviated as GM, (1), 9, 13–14, and (2), 65, 72; Holinshed, 6–9, 432–4.
3. Holinshed, 428–31.
4. Ibid, 434–6.
5. Ibid, 7, 433.
6. Bromwich, cxxvi–cxxvii.
7. Ashe (2), 25; *Brewer*, art. 'Albion'.
8. Holinshed, 6–9, 432–4; Spenser, II, x, 5–11, IV, xi, 15–16.
9. Graves (1), par. 132k; Rhys, II, 550.
10. Kendrick, 71, fn 2.
11. Ibid, 24.
12. *Folklore, Myths and Legends of Britain*, hereafter abbreviated as FML, 34–7, 124, 132–3, 152–3, 183; Hole, 138–9.
13. Kendrick, 69–74.
14. GM (1), 14, and (2), 72.
15. Kendrick, 105–7.

2 The Ancient Britons

1　Albion became Britain in the long aftermath of the Trojan War. When the city fell to the Greeks, Aeneas, one of its nobles, escaped with a large party of companions and made his way to Italy. So Virgil relates in his *Aeneid*. After many adventures the Trojans founded a settlement, and the Romans were descended from them. Virgil introduces Aeneas's son Ascanius. He takes the family no further, apart from a brief foreshadowing, but in Britain it is told how Ascanius had a son Silvius. Soothsayers predicted that *his* son would be the death of his parents, though later he would rise to high honour. This son was called Brutus. His mother, Silvius's wife, died giving birth to him, and when he grew up he accidentally shot Silvius with an arrow while hunting.

Banished from Italy, Brutus went to Greece. The Greek king Pandrasus had several thousand slaves descended from Trojan prisoners of war. Brutus organised a revolt and captured Pandrasus, who allowed him to lead the Trojans away wherever he would. They assembled a fleet and set sail. On a deserted island they discovered a temple of Diana. Brutus ritually consulted the goddess, and she appeared to him in a dream and told him of another island, a far greater one, out in the ocean towards the sunset. She mentioned the giants who had been in possession of it, but assured Brutus that they were now extinct or nearly so. There he could establish a new Troy, and father a dynasty of kings who would be the most powerful on earth.

Much encouraged, the Trojans coasted along Africa to Gibraltar, where they met another party of their own kinsfolk, whose leader was Corineus. Joining forces, the whole company passed through Gaul, where they founded the city of Tours. But Gaul was no abiding place. They came at last
2　to Albion, sailed up the Dart, and disembarked at Totnes. Brutus stepped ashore on a rock and announced:

> Here I am and here I rest,
> And this town shall be called Totnes.

That, at any rate, is the English version of what he said. The rock is the Brutus Stone, now removed to the High Street near the East Gate.

Brutus renamed the island 'Britain' after himself, and his companions were consequently Britons. Their form of the Trojan language became 'British'. The giants had indeed almost died out, and, as already mentioned, most of the handful who remained were in Cornwall. Some of these came over to Brutus's encampment and made an attack which failed with great slaughter. One, Gogmagog, was taken alive, and Corineus, who was extremely strong, wrestled with him and threw him off a cliff into the sea. Cornwall takes its name from Corineus, whom Brutus made its overlord.
3　Spenser, in his account of the giant Albion, says he was an ancestor of the Britons and thus implies that there was not a complete break between the peoples. Possibly the larger Trojans married the smaller surviving giants.

6. (opposite) The Trojan Horse, a Greek contrivance that brought about the fall of Troy and the wanderings of Aeneas's descendants.

The Trojans, or rather Britons, explored the island and built a capital, Troia Nova or New Troy, at the confluence of the rivers Fleet and Thames. 'Troia Nova' was later corrupted into 'Trinovantum'. Later again, the city

4 became London. London Stone in Cannon Street was an altar set up by Brutus in honour of Diana, his divine guide. So long as the stone of Brutus is safe, so long shall London flourish. Brutus, as king, built his palace on the

5 future site of the Guildhall, where effigies of giants were one day to stand. His capital was completed at the time when the priest Eli ruled in Israel.

Thus began the Britons. After more than a thousand years they were to lose ground, but their descendants exist today, the Welsh and Cornish.

Some claim that even apart from hypothetical demi-giants, the Trojans were not the sole constituent of the old British population. More important were immigrants who arrived centuries afterwards, in waves, after traversing the length of Europe; and these were none other than the lost tribes of Israel, dispossessed from the Holy Land by the Assyrians. They reached Britain with providential guidance, and accepted the kingship of

6 the royal line founded by Brutus. The composite British nation is a branch of the Chosen People of God, as surely as the Jews.

7 Brutus is first documented – if that is the word – in a confused Latin work of Welsh provenance, the *Historia Brittonum*, History of the Britons. This dates from the early ninth century AD and has commonly been ascribed to Nennius, a monk of Bangor. The ascription is open to doubt, but, with that clearly understood, the author may be called 'Nennius' for convenience. Properly speaking he is a compiler, and an artless one, so he is unlikely to have invented the story himself. He gives the hero's name in two forms, Brutus and Britto, with the implication that he has heard alternative versions. But there is no previous evidence in writing, though speculations of the same type were current

8 among the Franks on the continent.

'Nennius' safeguards biblical ethnic views by giving Brutus, or Britto, a pedigree going back to Japheth. However, he is brief. The full quasi-historical account is a vast expansion by Geoffrey of Monmouth. In the Middle Ages it was seriously believed. Chaucer addresses Henry IV as 'Conqueror of Brutus' Albion'. Further details are fanciful offshoots from Geoffrey or from chroniclers copying him. The Brutus Stone, for instance, probably got its name and legend

9 from wishful thinking. It may be a fifteenth-century boundary marker actually called the Brodestone.

Brutus's saga is literary rather than popular. Some unknown reader of Virgil, impressed by what he says about the Trojan ancestry of the Romans, had the notion of taking the story further and giving the Britons the same honourable origin. The Britons in question are the inhabitants of the island during the last centuries BC. Celtic in language and culture, they were akin to the Gaelic people of Ireland, but unlike the Irish they were brought into the Roman Empire. They maintained control for a while after ceasing to belong to it, and were then partially supplanted by Anglo-Saxons. Their separated descendants – the Welsh in Wales, Cumbria, Strathclyde; the Cornish; the related Bretons – preserved vague traditions of a glorious unity in the past. One of Geoffrey's main purposes is to substantiate these traditions with a splendid national history. He picks up the Brutus tale as an excellent beginning.

There does not seem to be any factual basis, even in the sense that the Trojans' advent could echo a real one from some other quarter. Celtic Britons, in the pre-Roman Iron Age, have a recognisable identity from about the sixth century BC. An opinion which long prevailed, with archaeological grounding, was that they entered the island in a series of immigrations from the continent. 'Halstatt' Celts came first, then 'La Tène' Celts, then 'Belgic' Celts. Phases can undoubtedly be distinguished, but the mass invasions, like earlier ones by 'Beaker Folk' and others, are now somewhat discounted. Celticity, as it may be called, was probably more linguistic and cultural than ethnic, a cumulative product of a variety of developments, economic, social, technological, and artistic. There need not have been a sharp break in actual population, and the roots of Celticity may lie far back. Still, there were radical changes and long-drawn transitions. A gap does yawn between the world of the megalith-builders and the world of the Celts. 10

Geoffrey's giants are the megalith-builders so far as they are anything real. The need for a swift and exterminatory contact may have been his motive in bringing the Trojans ashore near Cornwall, where the standing stones suggested a lingering presence; though further on in his *History* he shows a continuing fondness for Totnes as a port of entry. While he is dimly aware of an earlier people and a later people, megalith-builders and Celtic Britons, chronology is against him. The conventional date for the fall of Troy, 1183 BC, is one he has to respect. His synchronisation with Eli, taken from 'Nennius', makes Brutus build his capital somewhere about 1100. The transition from giants to Ancient Britons is too late for the end of the megalithic age, too early for the beginning of the Celts, in any clearly defined sense.

As often, names are meant to supply etymologies, which are quite erroneous. 'Britain' is on record in many different spellings. Greek and Welsh writers indicate that the initial letter may once have been *P*, in which case a connection can be traced with Celtic words meaning 'figure' or 'picture', and the reference may be to the natives' custom of tattooing themselves with designs in woad. The same image is thought to underlie the naming of the Picts in the north. 'Cornwall' goes back to a British tribal name. With Brutus's city, the proto-London, Geoffrey is ingenious. Roman authors tell of a British tribal grouping in Essex, the Trinovantes. 'Nennius' and Henry of Huntingdon, a historian writing in 1129 or thereabouts, thought this name was derived from a city, Trinovantum. Geoffrey adopts 'Trinovantum' and makes out that it is really Troia Nova, thus arriving, as he desires, at a New Troy. 11 12

For the giant Gogmagog, whose name he spells variously, he may have taken a hint from a Cornish word. Plymouth Hoe has been claimed as the scene of the wrestling, on the strength of a giant figure that was formerly cut in the turf. Gog and Magog appear in the Bible (*Ezekiel* 38:2, *Revelation* 20:7–8) with an air of evil mystery. The first of the giant effigies set up in the London Guildhall, in the fifteenth century, represented Gogmagog and his opponent Corineus. They were destroyed in the Great Fire of 1666 and new ones were set up in 1708. By that time the knowledge that Gog and Magog were distinct was too strong, and the effigies were said to portray giants so named whom Brutus employed as servants in his palace. Gog and Magog were also wiped out, by bombing, and new effigies replaced them. As for the London Stone, a remnant of which is in the wall of St Swithin's Church, it may have been a Roman marker from which distances were measured. But there is serious evidence for a City temple of Diana. 13 14 15

Alexander Pope, towards the end of his life, planned a narrative poem centred 16

on Brutus. This is an instance of a feature of English literature, the national epic that has never got written. Pope's poem was to be modelled on the *Aeneid*, and would have expressed his ideas of good government and true religion. He seems not to have paid much attention to Geoffrey. In his scheme for the epic, Brutus and his followers depart from a Troy ruined by its own corruption, to found an ideal commonwealth in some foreign land. Having doubts about the known world, they sail out into the Atlantic and land at Tenerife, where some elect to remain. The rest, more dedicated, reach Britain after adventures that tax Brutus's benign leadership, and come ashore at Torbay. The island is inhabited not only by the giants but by a normal-sized population, whose priests and sorcerers are hostile. Brutus insists on good conduct towards the natives, and finally founds his community, which unites and civilises the country.

After a lifetime of brilliant heroic couplets, Pope turned to blank verse for his epic, perhaps with a reminiscence of Milton. Only the first eight lines have survived, and he may have written no more:

> The Patient Chief, who lab'ring long arriv'd
> On Britain's shores and brought with fav'ring Gods
> Arts Arms & Honour to her Ancient sons:
> Daughter of Memory! from elder Time
> Recall; and me with Britains Glory fird,
> Me far from meaner Care or meaner Song,
> Snatch to the Holy Hill of spotless Bay,
> My Countrys Poet, to record her Fame.

Dr Johnson thought the whole project misguided.

The British-Israel theory is the principal modern myth in the style of the older ones, and worthy of note as such. It belongs to a class of speculations arising out of the history of ancient Israel, God's Chosen People. According to scripture the twelve Israelite tribes, descended from the patriarch Jacob, escaped from Egyptian captivity under Moses's leadership and shared out Canaan, the Promised Land. Under David and Solomon they were united, but soon afterwards they split apart. A southern kingdom of Judah, centred on Jerusalem, was made up of the tribes of Judah and Benjamin, plus some Levites. A northern kingdom, taking the name of Israel for itself, comprised all the rest. Both endured for some time, but in 734 BC the Assyrian king Tiglath-pileser III invaded the north and deported many of its people. In 721 Sargon II carried off many more, destroying their capital Samaria and leaving only a leaderless peasantry, soon swamped by settlers from other parts of the Assyrian empire. Judah survived, but fell to the Babylonians in 587. Here too there was a mass deportation, though some of the exiles were allowed to return after Babylon itself fell to the Persians.

The descendants of the southern deportees are the Jews, who continue to be a portion of Israel, in its proper comprehensive sense. But who are the descendants of the northern ones, the Lost Ten Tribes? According to Jewish traditional belief, which British-Israelites accept in this instance, they must still exist somewhere, because God's covenant applies to all twelve and cannot be rendered void. In a future Messianic age the lost tribes will be reunited with the Jews in the Promised Land. In *Ezekiel* 37:21–4 the Lord says: 'Behold, I will take the people of Israel from the nations among whom they have gone, and will gather them from all sides, and bring them to their own land; and I will make them one nation in the land . . . and they shall be no longer two nations, and no

7. and 8. Effigies of the giants Gog and Magog in Guildhall, London.

9. Brutus and the Trojans encamped on the Loire, before their arrival in Britain.

longer divided into two kingdoms. . . . My servant David shall be king over them.'

On this logic, there is no need to prove that the lost tribes still exist, because they must. Otherwise the prophecies could not be fulfilled. The problem is to identify them, and they have been 'identified' as the Japanese, the ancient Mexicans, and others. British-Israelites assert that they made their way to Britain in several waves and all the natives of the island today (those, at least, ancestrally rooted there) are of Israelite stock. This idea prospered in the heyday of the British Empire, because the prophecies promise the Chosen People widespread power and glory of a kind the Jewish branch has never enjoyed.

The only scriptural clue to the northerners' movements is in the apocryphal book *II Esdras*, which says (13:40–6) that they left the lands where the Assyrians had settled them, and went by way of the upper Euphrates to Arzareth, taking a year and a half on the journey. 'Arzareth' means simply 'another land', but British-Israelites claim that it was north of the Black Sea. They draw attention to geographic and ethnic names, and note, especially, that early authors locate the Cimmerians here. Working backward, they point out that Assyrian inscriptions call the northern Israelites the people of Omri, after one of their best-known kings. 'Omri', it is argued, could become 'Khumri': and thence, 'Cimmerians'. Working forward, they identify 'Cimmerians' with 'Cymry', the name which the Welsh, who are the principal remnant of the Celtic Britons, apply to themselves. Thus, etymology traces a folk movement all the way, via southern Russia. ('Cymry' in fact means 'fellow-countrymen' and is not used till a comparatively late date, when the Welsh wanted to affirm solidarity against the English.)

20 As will appear, further Israelite movements are traced by similar arguments; and Brutus is woven into the scheme. Being Aeneas's great-grandson, he would have been descended from Dardanus, the founder of Troy. Dardanus, British-Israelites explain, is the same person as Dara or Darda, a grandson of Judah, whose descendants by other lines formed the Israelite tribe of that name (*I Chronicles* 2:6, *Genesis* 38:30). This pedigree gives Brutus, and his Trojans in general, a collateral kinship with the Chosen People, which would have qualified them to prepare Britain for the reconstitution of the Israelite stock whenever the northern waves arrived.

British-Israel reached its apogee in 1936. After the First World War, Palestine had come under British rule, and one of the British policies was to establish a Jewish homeland there. Ezekiel's prophecy of reunion in the Promised Land seemed to be on the road to fulfilment. Edward VIII, known to his intimates as David, was a monarch of the right name. But after his abdication, followed by the end of the British regime in Palestine and the British Empire generally, the prophetic arguments – at least as presented – came to grief. Though British-Israel goes on, little is left of its old basis. It has been suspected that the idea began in a pun. The word 'British' suggests the Hebrew *b'rit ish*, meaning 'Covenant Man'.

1. GM (1), 2–15, and (2), 54–74.
2. Brown, 7–8; FML, 165.
3. IV, xi, 16, Cp. Ashe (2), 36.
4. Brown, 7.
5. Ibid, 6–7.
6. Sargent, 66–7.
7. 'Nennius' (1), chapters 10, 11, 17, 18.
8. Tatlock, 427–8, n. 22.
9. Brown, 13–14; Kendrick, 101.
10. Ashe (7), 19–20; Renfrew, 211–49.
11. Ekwall, 66, art. 'Britain'.
12. Henry of Huntingdon (1) I, 14, and (2), 14; 'Nennius' (1), chapter 20.
13. Brown, 10–11; Marples, 209–12; Tatlock, 53–6; Westwood, 23–4.
14. Brown, 6–7; FML, 216.
15. FML, 220.
16. Mack, 771–4.
17. Ashe (8), 185–9.
18. Sargent, 141–4.
19. Lloyd, I, 111.
20. Sargent, 139; Stuart-Knill, chart of asserted royal lines (no pagination).

3 The Picts

For many generations, under rulers in succession to Brutus, the Britons held the island unchallenged. At length, however, they lost the country beyond the Clyde-Forth line. This became the domain of the Picts or Painted Men. The original Picts came from Scythia, now Russia, in the first century AD. (Some say much earlier, but as nothing further is heard of them before the Christian era, it seems unlikely.) Their leader was Sodric. They occupied the Orkneys, then crossed over to mainland Britain and probed southwards. A British king named Marius managed to intercept and defeat them. Sodric himself was among the dead. His surviving subjects accepted a treaty confining them to Caithness, which was not then inhabited by anyone else.

Barren as their holding was, the Picts increased in numbers and vastly extended it. One of their kings, Drust son of Erp, reigned for a hundred years – mainly during the fifth century – and fought a hundred battles. They made repeated forays against the Britons, sometimes in alliance with other raiders. Though their aggressions died away, they maintained their northern ascendancy till they succumbed to another people, the Scots.

10. Remaining portion of a Pictish bronze pin from Golspie, Scotland, probably made in the eighth century.

Picts, as such, appear historically near the close of the third century AD, during the Roman period in Britain. At that time they were surging out of the north on pillaging expeditions, and making curragh-borne raids on the Yorkshire coast. Constantius Caesar strengthened the defences, and organised patrols by scout-ships which were nicknamed *Pictae* because they looked like the curraghs.

Very little is certain about the Picts. The name was applied vaguely to Caledonian tribes, and more specifically to one major group. So far as its heartland can be defined, this lay north of the Firth of Forth, but Picts, in some sense, existed far outside. No one knows how long the Picts had had an identity before the first documentation, or whether they can be counted as Celtic. The Irish called them *Cruithne*, meaning strictly 'picture people', in allusion to their custom of tattooing with woad, which inspired the epithet 'Pict' itself – a Latin term bestowed by Romans, not a native one. They may have been simply Britons who remained outside the Empire, diverged further and further from the Romanised south, and were eventually seen as aliens and enemies. Some of them, at least, spoke a British dialect. However, inscriptions in another language, which appears to be pre-Celtic, suggest continuity from remote times. The Pictish law of inheritance was matrilinear, tracing rights through the mother and not the father, and that too has an air of antiquity and deep-seated difference.

11. Picts as perceived
(on insufficient
grounds) by an
imaginative antiquary.

Though 'Nennius' refers to the Picts coming from outside, he does not say
5   where from. The legend of a Scythian origin may belong properly to the Scots.
Henry of Huntingdon gives it before Geoffrey does. It is Henry who puts the
Picts' advent far back. Geoffrey's first-century date may stem from an awareness
that early records of them are lacking.

6   Drust's martial exploits and immense age are poetic hyperbole, but the
attachment of this hyperbole to a fifth-century king reflects a real crescendo of
Pictish energy, short-lived but with profound consequences.

1. GM (1), 45, and (2), 123; 'Nennius'
   (1), chapter 12.
2. Morris, 186.
3. Alcock (1), 270–7; Campbell, 13;
   Morris, 186–9; Renfrew, 226–7.

4. Morris, 192.
5. Henry of Huntingdon (1), I, 9, and
   (2), 9–10.
6. Morris, 188.

4 *The Scots*

The Scots, who displaced the Picts as the dominant power in northern Britain, had established their national character long before. According to their own account they began their career in Greater Scythia, though they were not then known as Scots. One of their nobles, who had been banished, went to Egypt with many companions about the time of the Exodus. He married Pharaoh's daughter Scotta. When the Egyptians' army was drowned in the Red Sea pursuing the Israelites, they feared that the Scythian would seize power in the weakened kingdom, and compelled him to leave. He assembled his followers under a new name taken from his wife, and led them on forty-two years of wandering. Passing through the Mediterranean, and along the African coastlands, they reached Gibraltar and settled in Spain. Their descendants lived for over a thousand years among savage tribes, without ever being subdued, and at last travelled on to Ireland. From Ireland some of them made their way to the country destined to bear their name. Their first home there was in Argyll and was called Dalriada. The Scots of Dalriada were independent under kings of their own. However, it was a long time before they were numerous or powerful enough to challenge the Picts.   1

Some dispute all this, maintaining that it was the Picts, and they only, who came from Scythia, before the Scots even existed. They landed in Britain as a warrior host. After the treaty that allotted them Caithness, they tried to attract British women as wives. When their overtures were rejected, some of them crossed to Ireland and married Irish women instead. The Scots were the result, a nation of mixed blood descended from Picts and Irish, who eventually returned to their forefathers' homeland. If so, the tale of their wanderings is a fable spun out of the Scythian origin of those forefathers.   2

Others, again, say that the Scots are Israelites like the Britons, that their phase of Russian domicile is a fact, and that they too previously came from the Middle East after the Assyrian deportation.

The Scots can be traced back to an earlier home, but only as far as Ireland. During the Roman period, and for some centuries after, *Scotti* was a normal if imprecise synonym for the Celtic Irish. The Briton St Patrick employs it. As Roman power declined, 'Scots' from Ireland made frequent raids on Britain, and sometimes settled there. They brought the ogam script, which appears on monuments in Cornwall and Wales, and in some of the more mysterious of the Pictish inscriptions. Most of the colonists were expelled or absorbed, but in the latter half of the fifth century a group said to have numbered 150 men – women and children unspecified – planted itself in Argyll. Its leaders were the three sons of a chief named Erc, headed by Fergus.   3   4   5

12. Manuscript illustration in a verse chronicle telling of the Scots' invasion of Britain.

Their settlement was the nucleus of the realm of Dalriada. Its kings ruled from the rocky citadel of Dunadd, in the Kintyre peninsula near Crinan. Some were military adventurers, without much lasting effect; most were not. Their kingdom first became important when St Columba founded the monastery of Iona, from which Christianity spread among the Picts, and later the northern English.

The Scots' reputed prehistory is given in an early version by 'Nennius', and, more weightily if with less detail, in a medieval state document, the Declaration of Arbroath. This was drawn up in 1320, probably by Bernard de Linton, Arbroath's abbot. Eight Scottish earls and forty-five barons affixed their seals. The Declaration is addressed to Pope John XXII, who was reluctant to recognise Bruce as king of Scotland, and appeals to him to think again, and oppose the pretensions of the English. Its preamble summarises the legendary story to prove that the Scots are an ancient nation and should be subject to no one. It asserts that they have had 113 kings of their own royal blood, and have lived in Scotland since 1200 years after the Exodus, a backward extension of at least half a millennium. The alternative legend, that they were a Picto-Irish stock of comparatively recent growth, is due to Geoffrey.

13. Dunadd, the first residence of the Scottish kings in their new country.

The Scythian part can of course be combined with 'Cimmerian' claims about the Britons, pointing to the same background for this other constituent of the eventual United Kingdom. British-Israelites cite it in support. It may, however, be based merely on a fanciful etymology deriving 'Scot' from 'Scythia' as 'Britain' was derived from 'Brutus', with the princess coming in merely as an afterthought – and indeed she is absent from the earliest text. The British-Israelite view is open to an even graver objection. If the migration from Scythia happened at the time of the Exodus, the migrants cannot have been Israelites deported from the Holy Land several centuries later. For the British-Israel theory to be true, at least part of the Scottish prehistory must be false, and without corroboration from outside sources, the grounds for accepting any of it crumble.

7

1. 'Nennius' (1), chapter 15.
2. GM (1), 45, and (2), 123–4.
3. Alcock (1), 253–4, 262–3, 265–70; Morris, 42, 64.
4. Alcock (1), 125–6; Blair, 5; Chadwick (1), 174–6; Lloyd, I, 96–8; Sheldon, 27.
5. Alcock (1), 130–1; Morris, 180.
6. Prebble, 112–4.
7. Sargent, 144–6.

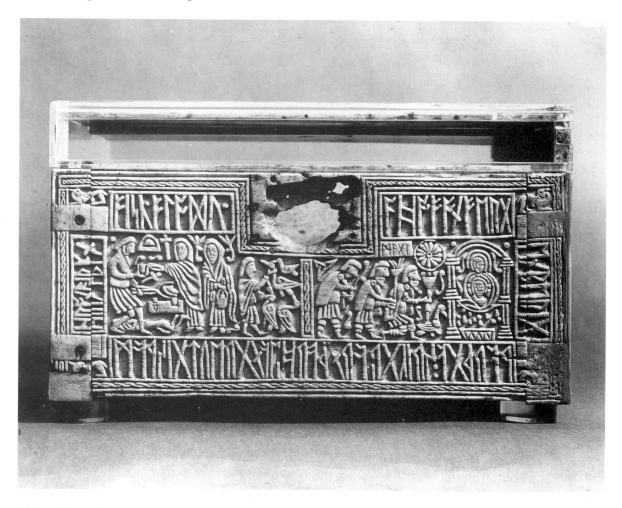

14. Detail from the
Franks Casket, a
whalebone box made in
the Angles' kingdom of
Northumbria between
650 and 750, depicting
soldiers with spears
and shepherds with
crooks.

5 *The English*

The ancestors of the English were the Saxons, who arrived in the Britons'
part of the island long after them, as will be told in its place. They came from
Germany. Some say that they had previously migrated from more distant
lands, and that they too were Israelites, so that their advent completed the
reconstitution of the Lost Tribes in the island.

No ancestral English appear, even in legend, till long after the Britons. At their
début in the Christian era, 'Saxons' is the name commonly given to them, but
this is a loose term covering Saxons proper, Angles, Jutes, and minor groupings.
The earliest verifiable homeland of most of them was Schleswig-Holstein,   1
from which they expanded. After their settlement in Britain, the area which
they overran became England – that is, Angle-land – and their language,
Anglo-Saxon, evolved slowly into English. The Britons, however, were not
displaced or exterminated, and the British-descended Welsh maintained their
independence.

British-Israelites accept the later part of the story, as attested by documents
and archaeology, but trace a prehistory before it. They regard the Saxons as   2
another of the bodies of Israelites that passed from the Middle East into Scythia
or southern Russia, and thence, after an interval, westward. Their movement
across Europe was a later instance of the same drift that had brought other
Israelites – Britons, Picts perhaps, Scots undoubtedly – to a divinely appointed
home in Britain. (Though some of the final wave never got there, but settled in
Holland and Scandinavia.) The chief evidence is a statement by Herodotus that
the Persians called the inhabitants of Scythia *Sakai*. In Persian inscriptions the   3
word is *Saka*. British-Israelites point to place-names in support. The Crimea,
they say, has a town called Sak, and Armenia has a mountain Sakh, a river Engl, a
town Angl.

These supposed clues, so far back in the alleged migration, really strengthen
an objection to the whole British-Israelite position. How could the Hebrew
spoken by the Ten Tribes have spawned new languages so different from itself
and each other, so quickly? Actually it is hard to see how it could have done so at
all, even over millennia, because the Celtic and Anglo-Saxon languages are
Indo-European. Hebrew, which is Semitic, cannot seemingly be a parent to any
of them. One British-Israelite work resorts to deriving *Angl* or *Engl* from a   4
Hebrew word for a calf, such as those which Jeroboam, when king of the
northern tribes, set up as sacred images: surely an unhappy idea, since the calf
cult was condemned as idolatrous (*I Kings* 12:28–30, *Hosea* 8:5–6). As for
Sakai, that, we are told, comes from 'Isaac'.

The Saxon-Sakai equation as such is not a British-Israelite fantasy. It was
suggested long before by Sharon Turner in his *History of the Anglo-Saxons*   5
(1807). Turner notes variants of the name *Sakai* in classical geographers, who
describe these people as – to be precise – not Scythians in general, but a branch

of them living in the Crimea and the neighbourhood of the Caspian. However, there are no traces of a migration bringing them *en masse* to the North Sea.

6   'Saxon' is thought to be derived from *seax*, meaning, in Anglo-Saxon, a short-sword, this being a characteristic weapon.

15. A dark-age sword; the Saxons took their name from the *seax* or short-sword.

1. Alcock (1), 278–9; Blair, 9–11;
   Campbell, 11; Hodgkin, I, 1–17;
   Morris, 106, 261–6.
2. Sargent, 146–55.
3. See Herodotus's *History*, VII, 64
4. Sargent, 147–8.
5. Cited in Sargent, 148–9.
6. Alcock (1), 329.

Excursus I

Upheaval versus Gradualism

Mythologies tend to picture the past in terms of conquests and mass migrations, with a succession of ethnic stocks supplanting their predecessors. Geoffrey of Monmouth shows that up to his time, Britain had avoided extremes in this respect and its legendary origins remained fairly simple. England and Wales were accounted for ethnically in three steps (giants, Trojans, Saxons) and Scotland in two (Picts and Scots); and the last stages even had a certain historical substance. Ireland supplies a parallel and also an enlightening contrast. The other island attained complexity sooner. No fewer than five invasions were reckoned before the present Gaels' ancestors appeared on the scene.

Just before the Flood came a party of fifty-three led by a woman, Cessair. Only three were men, one of them being her father Bith, a son of Noah. Another was Fintan and the third was Ladra, the pilot. These three shared the women, Fintan obtaining Cessair. When Ladra died from excessive sexual activity, Bith and Fintan re-apportioned his women, so that they had twenty-five each. But Bith also died and the Flood swept over Ireland. Fintan alone survived, hiding in a cave which the waters never reached. He lived on afterwards as a shape-shifting immortal, witnessing all the later vicissitudes, a permanent mine of information.

Next came a descendant of Japheth named Partholon, a banished outlaw, bringing a company of a thousand. They practised agriculture, cooking, brewing, architecture. They are mentioned in the *Historia Brittonum*, and stated there to have come from Spain. Geoffrey has the story too. He puts their migration in the fourth century BC and asserts that a British king found Partholon wandering in the Orkneys with thirty ships, looking for a place to settle. The Briton conducted the fleet to Ireland, then still uninhabited, and the present Irish are descended from Partholon's host. How-

16. Noah and family in the Ark during the Flood, which was fatal to the companions of his non-scriptural son Bith, in Ireland.

ever, the Irish themselves disdained such short cuts and put Partholon much earlier. They said his colonists multiplied and cleared some of the wild country, but were harassed from the north by a race of demons or goblins called the Fomoire – later, Fomorians – and finally all succumbed to a plague.

Next came Nemed, a descendant of a brother of Partholon who had stayed in Spain. He led a second party to Ireland, and won battles against the Fomorians, but died in another plague. The Fomorians continued to raid from a base on Tory Island off the Donegal coast. When few of Nemed's settlers were left they dispersed in three groups. From two of these, two new nations arose, and together re-conquered Erin.

The Fir Bolg were first. Returning from a self-imposed exile, reputedly in Greece, they divided Ireland into provinces and established kingship. Then the other nation arrived. The Tuatha De Danann, or Danaans, were not (as British-Israelites claim) the tribe of Dan; they took their name from Danann, the Mother of the Gods, and had been living in a mysterious north, or maybe in Denmark, whence that country's name and the word 'Dane'. At any rate they landed in Connacht. They surpassed other humans in beauty, wisdom and all the arts, especially magic. Some say they expelled the Fir

Bolg, who went away to Arran and other islands, though they returned later. A better-liked account is that after a battle at Moytura, in County Sligo, the two races lived in friendship and the less numerous Fir Bolg were allotted Connacht as their homeland.

17. **Dun Aengus, a place associated with the Fir Bolg.**

The Tuatha De Danann had their own troubles with the Fomorians. They succeeded in crushing them, but themselves yielded in the end to the ancestors of the present Irish, who came from the Mediterranean and were then known as Milesians, being led by the Sons of Mil. Some of the Fir Bolg survived and kept their identity. As late as the seventeenth century, families in Connacht claimed to have Fir Bolg blood. The Tuatha De Danann did not quit Ireland either, but they used their magic to retire into an unseen realm interfused with the visible. Several were worshipped as gods (having actually been gods all along; story-tellers' retrospect disguised them somewhat).

So Ireland, with six populations plus the Fomorians, vividly illustrates the tendency. Because the series is not only fanciful but utterly different from Britain's, it reveals how little such imaginings have to do with prehistory. Sometimes they embody a real attempt to interpret facts, such as megaliths, but they are not factual themselves. It should not be thought, however, that the tendency is simply naive or pre-scientific. In Britain its force was far from spent when historians discredited Geoffrey. On the contrary, it was only in a better-informed age, and after the advent of archaeology, that this type of thinking made Britain truly complicated. The nineteenth century

brought a major throwback, the notion that the Saxons not only moved into Britain in massive numbers but drove out or exterminated the Britons, so that their English descendants are a pure, non-Celtic race. Then archaeologists announced a series of invasions in earlier days: Beaker people and Beaker-Battleaxe people and 'warrior' people and three instalments of Celts, even four.

Invasions and radical displacements, it may be repeated, are now out of favour as the prime causes of changes that undoubtedly happened. This is an issue that arises on a vast scale in the Indo-European question, which sets the peoples of Britain alongside many others, in a context extending thousands of miles. Most of the languages of Europe, and several in Asia, are related in ways that imply a common ancestry. The list includes the Celtic, Germanic and Slavonic, together with Latin and its derivatives, and Greek, Hittite and Sanskrit; but not Hebrew and the Semitic groupings – we are dealing with specifics, not generalities that would fit anywhere. Proper names and geography tell the same tale. For instance, the British river name Don is akin to 'Danube' and to the Russian 'Don' and to the Sanskrit *danu*, a word for water. The Irish goddess Danann herself comes in here, and with her a distant Indian cousin called Danu.

6

All these languages may be supposed to have their source in a body of 'Indo-European' speakers occupying a single area, more than six thousand years ago. Competing theories have located this in many places, and accounted for the spread along time-honoured lines, by migrations and conquests. Russia and the Balkans have been front-running candidates, with Marija Gimbutas as a noted upholder of traditional views. Her Proto-Indo-Europeans are macho, horse-using adventurers from the steppes, who overran large parts of the Eurasian land-mass and imposed their speech. But so many conjectures have been aired, none of them with a proved basis in archaeology, that any would-be solution at all is apt now to be met with scepticism.

18. (opposite) One of many memorials of the ancient Irish; a standing stone near Rossknowlagh, County Donegal.

19. The Paps of Anu near Killarney; Anu, or Annan, was a mother-goddess, and the hills are a dwelling of the Tuatha de Danann.

Fresh light may have been shed by a conception which has the merit of being less dramatic and less mythological. Its proponent is Colin Renfrew, whose work in the megalithic field we shall be encountering shortly. He accepts that there was a starting-point, but rejects most of the rest. In Professor Renfrew's opinion, Proto-Indo-European was the language of Anatolian farming communities, about 7000 BC. The primary spread was an unspectacular drift of farming peoples from Asia Minor, farther and farther into a Europe then very sparsely peopled, with branches of linguistic influence extending over a huge expanse of Asia: a spread carrying Indo-European languages to the western limit, and perhaps to the eastern one as well, at a much earlier date than previous models have suggested. Within this process, and after it, different groups would have had ample time to diverge and develop, to change their life-style and, for that matter, to migrate. Later movements suspected hitherto, such as an advance into India from the north by 'Aryan' chariot-riders, remain perfectly credible. But the initial expansion was early, quiet, and agricultural rather than nomadic or military.

While Britain had inhabitants tens of thousands of years ago, they were very few and without cohesion. On Renfrew's showing, the first real population was the one bringing Indo-European speech, still a long way back. Once established it grew, but it was not fundamentally altered for many centuries. There were changes – economic, social, political, cultural, and of course linguistic. There were comings and goings, and local colonisations by influential groups. But, as others have concluded on other grounds, there were no violent breaks during the millennia BC, and there was much continuity. That essential point remains valid, that essential judgment remains unaffected in the face of attacks on Renfrew's ideas from other angles (notably by J. P. Mallory).

1. Cross and Slover, passim; Rees, 28–41, 108–17; Rolleston, 94–145.
2. 'Nennius' (1), chapter 13.
3. GM (1), 31, and (2), 100–1.
4. Sargent, 88–9.
5. Rees, 38–9; Rhys, II, 52–3.
6. Ekwall, 147, art. 'Don'; Rees, 52–3.
7. Renfrew, especially chapter 7.
8. Ibid, 242, 245, 249. Cp. Zvelebil, 574–83, especially conclusions.

Mysteries of Early Britain

6 Stonehenge

In the far-off times before the Trojans, when the giants came from Africa, 1
they settled in Ireland as well as Albion's isle. The finest monument of their
whole race was the work of its Irish branch. These had brought with them a
cargo of immense, long-shaped African stones, which they stood upright in
a circle on a hill in County Kildare. The stones had healing properties. A
giant who fell sick was placed in a bath below the stone appropriate to the
ailment, and water was poured over it, running down into the bath. The
stone's magical virtue, plus herbal infusions, often effected a cure.

When the giants were extinct, ordinary-sized Irish called the structure the
'Giants' Round-Dance' or 'Ring', a name preserved in Latin as *Chorea
Gigantum*. They treated the stones with religious reverence. The Ring stood
on its hill until the fifth century AD, when the enchanter Merlin moved it to
Britain and planted it on Salisbury Plain, to mark the grave of some British
nobles who had been massacred by Saxons. Later again it received a new
name in English, by which it is known to this day: Stonehenge.

According to the best report, Merlin used his arts only to dismantle the
circle and re-erect it. The stones were conveyed from Ireland to Britain by
ship. But some who prefer a more spectacular tale assert that he employed 2
the Devil. At that time, the land in Ireland where the Ring stood belonged
to an old woman, who had enclosed it as part of her extensive garden. The
Devil visited her in the guise of a gentleman, and poured out a heap of coins
of strange denominations – four-and-a-half pence, nine pence, thirteen
pence. He told her that he wanted the stones, and she could have as much
money as she could count while he removed them. She agreed, assuming
that the operation would take a long time and she would do well out of it.
However, he quickly bound the stones in a willow withy and flew to
Salisbury Plain, delivering the bundle to Merlin complete, except for a small

one which had worked loose and fallen in the Avon near Bulford. (To judge from the map, the Devil must have been circling to land.)

Many, however, have dismissed Merlin and attributed Stonehenge to the Druids, the priesthood recorded among the Britons by Caesar and others, with their occult powers, their wild sanctuaries and sacred groves, their rumoured human sacrifices. A stone that lies on the ground inside the Ring is, they contend, a druidic altar. There are those who claim that the Greeks demonstrably knew of Stonehenge at a time when the Druids flourished.

3   They cite Hecataeus of Abdera, in the fourth century BC. He writes of a large island north of Gaul, inhabited by a nation whom he calls Hyperboreans. Their chief god is Apollo, and every nineteen years, when the heavens are in a certain position, the god visits the island and plays on a harp, an instrument popular with his worshippers. They have a city sacred to him, and a 'remarkable round temple'. Britain? Stonehenge?

It is said that the stones cannot be counted.

4   Stonehenge is a composite, created in stages over a long period. Its English name is related to the Anglo-Saxon word *hengen*, which meant 'hanging' or 'gibbet'. The reference is to the cross-pieces on top of the larger uprights, either because these stones were 'hung' there or because, with the uprights, they give the impression of a group of colossal gibbets. Much of the monument has gone, but the essential plan remains. Sited in a part of Britain that was once populous and advanced, as shown by barrows, artefacts, and other evidence, it began as a circular enclosure about 300 feet across. The boundary was a bank of chalk rubble which is still there, though lower than it once was. This enclosure, in archaeologists' parlance, was Stonehenge I. After a lengthy interval, a double ring of standing 'bluestones' was arranged within it, constituting Stonehenge II. Next, probably not long after, this was dismantled and replaced by the huge system of uprights and cross-pieces – Stonehenge IIIa. Lastly, some of the discarded bluestones were set up again inside, in two phases, labelled IIIb and IIIc. The 'altar stone' may be a fallen pillar.

5   The big stones weigh twenty-five to fifty tons and are known as sarsens, a word derived, cryptically, from 'Saracen'. They are blocks of natural sandstone, extremely hard. Quarried twenty miles away on the Marlborough Downs, and transported on rollers, they were artificially smoothed and shaped, a very slow, laborious process with the stone tools available. The cross-pieces or lintels, which weigh about seven tons, have sockets on the underside fitting on to knobs on top of the uprights.

So striking is the architectural effect, unparalleled in the megalithic world, that it has prompted suggestions of outside influence. For some years, Stonehenge IIIa was dated 1600–1500 BC, allowing the conjecture that it was designed by someone familiar with Mycenae in Greece, where very large stones were used in sophisticated buildings. However, a revision of carbon-datings by

6   Colin Renfrew pushed it back several centuries. The main phase of construction, producing II and IIIa, is now thought to lie between 2150 and 2000 BC, i.e. before Mycenae.

Since it does not look residential, Stonehenge has usually been explained either as a memorial over a burial site – Geoffrey of Monmouth's idea in the Merlin story – or as a temple of Neolithic religion. While the second view has

20. (opposite) Stonehenge at sunset.

prevailed, direct evidence is scanty. There are no grounds for the name given to the altar stone. Just inside the bank forming the perimeter are fifty-six pits, called Aubrey Holes after John Aubrey, who discovered them in the seventeenth century. Some, when excavated, were found to contain cremated human bones, but it cannot be inferred that these were remains of sacrifices. Stonehenge II and III seem to be oriented towards the place where the sun rises at the summer solstice. For practical purposes, that is all.

21. Merlin setting up the stones, in an illustration to a French verse paraphrase of Geoffrey.

7   The much-favoured theory about the Druids will be discussed in its place. A myth in its own right, it originated with Aubrey and William Stukeley. The short refutation is that we have no evidence which would put the Druids anything like early enough. While they may have been spiritual descendants of an older, pre-Celtic priesthood, it would be misleading to stretch the meaning of 'Druid' a long way backwards in time. If Hecataeus's round temple were proved to be Stonehenge, that could suggest that Druids at least made use of it, because he writes in a period when they probably did exist. Despite many purely mythical details his island is certainly Britain, and by 'Hyperboreans' he means Britons. The Hyperboreans, dwellers-at-the-back-of-the-North-Wind, were a semi-mythical people whose real home (so far as they had one) was in Asia; but Greek speculation shifted them westwards, confused them with the Celts, and
8   even toyed with a notion that the Druids were Hyperborean sages. Also, the nineteen-year cycle agrees with what is known of the druidic calendar. The problem, however, is with the round temple itself rather than the Druids.

While the mention of Apollo seems to link up with Stonehenge's solar aspect, this is a false clue. Apollo was not originally a sun-god, or widely viewed thus till very late. A Greek in Hecataeus's time would not have identified him with a foreign solar deity. He is brought in because he was supposed to have a special relation with the Hyperboreans. One Celtic god did come to be counted as a British Apollo, but he had nothing to do with the sun. He was Maponus, the 9 'Divine Youth', who eventually passed into Welsh legend as the hero Mabon. Maponus was a musician. An altar at Hexham equates him with 'Apollo the Harper', and the harp-playing of Hecataeus's 'Apollo' indicates that the god he is thinking of may be Maponus . . . for whose cult, however, there is no evidence at or near Stonehenge.

A worse obstacle is that the word here translated 'round', *sphairoeides*, means 10 'spherical'; not 'circular' in two dimensions. Since the Britons did not have the technology for a spherical building, the temple must, on the face of it, be fictitious. The only way to give it even a potential reality would be to find another word that might have become *sphairoeides* through textual corruption. A credible candidate is *speiroeides*. In Greek the difference is of two letters only. It means 'spiral' and could suggest a ritual labyrinth. In one or two places Apollo is 11 associated with such a labyrinth, and its pattern occurs in Britain as a rock carving and a turf maze. But even if this idea were accepted, a spiral sanctuary could not be Stonehenge.

The Merlin story, as told by Geoffrey (its satanic variant is due to John Wood in the eighteenth century), is more fantastic than the druidic theory yet, oddly, more interesting. While Merlin's *floruit* is obviously too late, the previous pseudo-history of the stones and giants shows a vague awareness of megalithic fact. Britain's reputed primeval style, Myrddin's Precinct, may point to some god or demigod in remote antiquity, retrospectively named by the Welsh. Such a being might have been Stonehenge's mythical builder, and the feat might have been ascribed to the enchanter because, doubtless for a magical or religious reason, he bore the same name. He is 'Myrddin' in Welsh. The literary form 'Merlin' is an adaptation.

This too would be merely a fancy if it were not that the Merlin episode apparently preserves factual tradition, not only about the spread of megaliths, but, specifically, about Stonehenge. Geoffrey portrays the stones as being brought by sea from the west. Wildly improbable as his story sounds, the 12 bluestones did at least travel from the west. Geology discloses a region of origin in the Prescelly Mountains in Dyfed. They could have been transported up the Bristol Channel on rafts, and then perhaps up the Bristol Avon. This explanation has been disputed, but is upheld by Renfrew and other authorities. For some reason the Prescelly area was sacred, and stones from there embodied a vital magic. There are Welsh bluestones at Boles Barrow, which is 13 earlier than Stonehenge. The 'altar stone' is likewise from Wales, probably from near Milford Haven. On past assumptions about the Celtic Britons, implying displacements of population and cultural breaks, it might sound unlikely that a tradition could have been handed down so long, to re-surface in Geoffrey's book three thousand years later. But, as remarked, there was probably much more continuity than past prehistorians would have allowed.

Stonehenge's specific purpose must be acknowledged as still obscure. The implication of sun-worship raises the issue of a cult of other celestial bodies. But Gerald Hawkins's view, that the entire structure is a kind of computer for 14 predicting such phenomena as eclipses, stretches the conception so far that it has failed to convince. The enthusiasms of so-called hippies, as exhibited during the

1980s, were grounded more on feelings than on any precise interpretation. Renfrew stresses the importance of Wiltshire and neighbouring areas in the third millennium BC, as having the potential in organisation and labour for such a vast work. Stonehenge would have been a sacred capital. That, however, still says nothing about what happened there.

15   The legend that the stones cannot be counted is part of the general sense of mystery. Sir Philip Sidney mentions it in a poem. The diarist John Evelyn, and Jonathan Swift, both tried with different results. Defoe tells of a baker who arrived with a cartload of loaves, and placed a loaf on each stone as he counted it. Alas, he was a meticulous man and checked his figure by making the count again, and again . . . and each attempt contradicted the last. H. G. Wells glances at the impossibility in a short story, *The Door in the Wall*. Most of the early would-be reckoners ended up with a figure in the low nineties. They were not far out, and the discrepancies were due chiefly to uncertainty over what to count as a stone.

Stonehenge, druidically viewed, plays a conspicuous role in the imaginings of William Blake. Thomas Hardy and other authors have touched on it. Byron in *Don Juan* (XI.25) is the most succinct, and as much to the point as any of them:

> The Druid's groves are gone – so much the better.
> Stonehenge is not, but what the devil is it?

1. GM (1), 90–2, and (2), 195–8; Grinsell (3), 5–9; Tatlock, 81–2.
2. Chippindale, 40; Grinsell (3), 14–15.
3. Ashe (1), 172–3; Rutherford, 133–4.
4. Atkinson, 13–28; Westwood, 64–7.
5. Chippindale, 38.
6. Ibid, 208–9, 267.
7. Chippindale, 70–86; Grinsell (1), passim, and (2), 19; Piggott (1), 122–31.
8. Ashe (1), 208–10; Piggott (1), 79–83.
9. Chadwick (2), 107; Ross, 276–7, 463–6, 477.
10. Ashe (1), 173–5.
11. Ibid, 188–92.
12. Atkinson, 21; Chippindale, 185; Grinsell (3), 9–11; Piggott (2), 306–13; Westwood, 66.
13. Chippindale, 267.
14. Hawkins, passim.
15. Chippindale, 44–6; Grinsell (3), 16–17; Westwood, 67.

7 Avebury and Silbury

Avebury, west of Marlborough, is one of a cluster of major prehistoric works. It is a more or less circular enclosure, 1,400 feet across, with arrangements of standing stones inside. Other stones, in rows, form an avenue leading away from it to a smaller site called the Sanctuary. Not far off to the south is Silbury, an artificial hill 130 feet high, flat-topped, with a moat. Beyond that is West Kennet Long Barrow, a mound 350 feet in length with a stone-lined burial chamber.

The plan of Avebury, plus some of the outlying features, has been explained as representing a partly coiled snake. Silbury is the reputed burial-mound of King Sil, otherwise unknown, or of a knight in golden armour. It may even conceal a solid gold statue of a horse and its rider. Or it may be a load of earth which the Devil meant to drop from the air on Marlborough, but had to let go, thanks to the prayers of priests at Avebury. More attractive, perhaps, is the view that these places are interrelated sacred sites, all concerned with the worship of the Earth Goddess.

1
2

Avebury is somewhat older than Stonehenge. While also much bigger – so big that part of Avebury village is inside – it lacks the architectural quality that has made Stonehenge such a source of fascination. All around the enclosure is a ditch, now partly filled up. Chalk dug from this was piled outside to make a bank forming the boundary, still very impressive, with gaps in it for entrance and exit.

3

22. Stukeley's diagram of his 'serpent' theory connecting Avebury, the Avenue, and Silbury.

23. Some of the Avebury standing stones, comparable in size with those of Stonehenge, but not similarly dressed to shape.

Just inside the ditch there were once a hundred or so upright sarsens all around the perimeter. These were not dressed to shape as in Stonehenge IIIa. Fewer than half of them remain; what is left may suggest an octagon rather than a circle. The largest of the survivors weigh at least forty tons. The rest were broken up and removed long ago, partly for use as building material, partly to clear the ground for cultivation. Dislike on the part of the Christian clergy doubtless encouraged this process. About 1320 a man who was helping to smash one of the stones was crushed to death when it keeled over on top of him. In 1938 his skeleton was found, with tools of his trade – he was a barber-surgeon.

Two smaller circles formerly stood near the centre of the enclosure. These also are much depleted, one of them almost to nothing.

Avebury's order of construction was the reverse of Stonehenge's. It proceeded from the centre outwards. The circles in the middle came first, the outer ring (or octagon) later, together with the ditch and bank. The lines of stones constituting the Avenue began near the south entrance, and ended over a mile away at the Sanctuary, which then had another ring. As at Stonehenge, the main structure can hardly be anything but a temple, and as at Stonehenge, its nature is obscure. Even astronomical clues are lacking. A past guess at serpent-worship had no basis but the fancy that the Avebury-Avenue-Sanctuary formation was serpentine.

Silbury is puzzling in ways of its own. It is the largest artificial mound of old Europe, and belongs to the Neolithic era of great ritual works, the same that produced Avebury. Its purpose, however, is equally opaque. It is not simply a heap of earth, but a carefully contrived structure, built in stages with some remodelling. In its present form, it is bound together by internal walls and layers of chalk, some of it rubble, some in the form of blocks. It would have required an enormous amount of labour, and was clearly of unique importance. While its legendary character as a burial-mound may be the true one, excavation has never detected the burial.

Speculations connecting Avebury, Silbury and neighbouring features as a

24. Silbury seen across the water near its foot.

single system have failed to establish anything positive. The serpent idea began
in the eighteenth century with Stukeley, who not only developed the Druid
theory of Stonehenge but decided Avebury was druidic as well. Again, William
Blake followed his lead and, in the prophetic book *Jerusalem*, depicted a Serpent
Temple combining Stukeley's reconstructions of the two principal monuments.

The notion that the whole area is a single religious complex, embracing the
West Kennet barrow with the rest, was proposed by Michael Dames. According
to this, rituals were performed at the sites in a seasonal cycle. The starting-point
of Dames's ideas was his belief that Silbury, with its moat, forms a shape which
recalls prehistoric figurines representing a goddess, the Earth-Mother.

This theory has its place in modern myth-making as part of a more general
claim about ancient religion, put forward widely and seriously. In 1961 Sibylle
von Cles-Reden argued that the megalith-builders were devotees of a Great
Goddess, or rather *the* Great Goddess. On many grounds beside this it has been
contended that divinity was once female, or predominantly so, and the rise of
male gods was a major change, perhaps due to a shift in the sexes' relative
importance. Robert Graves and others have claimed that numerous Greek
myths are recastings of older ones with a 'goddess' orientation, in the interests of
a male-governed Olympus. Britain has less literary matter to subject to this kind
of analysis. However, when its pre-Christian cults emerge into view, female
elements are certainly conspicuous. Archaeology supplies evidence for a Triple
Goddess and other figures, and several heroines of Welsh legend are Celtic
deities humanised. When the 'British Apollo' Maponus becomes the Welsh
character Mabon, he has a mother Modron who is ultimately the river-goddess
Matrona. Modron in her turn may well be the original of the enchantress
Morgan le Fay, in whose isle of Avalon female power presides.

Many feminists regard all goddesses as aspects of the one Great Goddess. As a
step in her restoration, some have adopted Dames's theory, at least to the extent
of revering Silbury as hers.

1. FML, 171.
2. Ibid, 183.
3. Atkinson, 38–45.
4. Ibid, 52–3.
5. Piggott (1), 127, 131–3, 150, 184.
6. Dames (1) and (2), passim.
7. Ross, 242, 267, 293.
8. Ibid, 270, 453.
9. Chadwick (2), 107; Loomis, ed., 42,
   49, 66; Ross, 372 n. 57.

8 *Great Stones in General*

Megalithic circles and cromlechs are found in many parts of Britain. The latter are formed by a large stone resting on top of smaller ones, giving the impression of a very rough table. In Cornwall, some are said to have treasure buried beneath them. These are protected by the ghosts of the giants, still lurking unseen in their ancient country, under the name of spriggans. Other cromlechs are credited with other functions. Kit's Coty House in Kent is the tomb of a British chief, Catigern, who fell fighting Saxons at nearby Aylesford in the fifth century AD. Wayland's Smithy, on the Ridgeway (formerly in Berkshire, now in Oxfordshire), houses an invisible living occupant. If a traveller with a horse that has lost a shoe leaves it at this place with a coin, and returns after a reasonable time, Wayland will have shod the horse, and the money will be gone.

25. Wayland's Smithy and its approach.

4 The stones of several circles are alleged, like those of Stonehenge, to be impossible to count. The Merry Maidens, at St Buryan in Cornwall, can be counted by a woman but not by a man. These monuments are apt to be dangerous as well as bewildering. When a nineteenth-century landowner

5 tried to shift Long Meg and her Daughters, in Cumbria, a violent storm put

6 his workmen to flight. At Stanton Drew in Somerset, a survey in 1740 by John Wood, the same who told of the Devil and Stonehenge, was enough to produce terrifying thunder.

26. Long Meg and her Daughters in Cumbria, said to have been witches.

Standing stones may be human beings transformed for their sins. Long Meg and her Daughters were witches; they were condemned for their black arts, or, according to one writer, for 'unlawful love'. Stanton Drew used to

7 be called 'the Wedding', in the belief that a bride and bridegroom, a fiddler, and guests were turned to stone when their revels profaned the Sabbath.

8 The Merry Maidens also danced on a Sunday, and so did the Nine Ladies at Stanton in Derbyshire. Stones such as these may come back to life at certain times and resume their dancing.

27. Wayland at work in an illustration to Kipling's *Puck of Pook Hill.*

In Cornwall, as might be expected, the giants linger on . . . just. In most places the mythology of the megaliths does not reach so far back. Structures such as Kit's Coty House and Wayland's Smithy are burial-chambers, formerly under mounds that have disappeared, and sometimes they are known to be such, but they are Neolithic and their supposed occupants are later, like Catigern.

Wayland is a Saxon character, the same person as Völundr, a wonder-working smith of Norse myth who is captured by a king, lamed to prevent him

9

from escaping, and forced to work. He avenges himself on the king's family and uses his magic to fly away. Wayland's connection with the burial-chamber is on record as early as the ninth century. The craft of the smith is often associated with magic, and very widely: according to a Siberian proverb, 'The blacksmith and the shaman are of one nest.' Various Germanic legends introduce craftsmen dwelling in caves or hollow hills, and Wayland, or Völundr, may have been domiciled in the burial-chamber for that reason. It is interesting, however, that Völundr is also connected with labyrinths, perhaps because his air-borne escape recalls Daedalus's from Crete. An Icelandic manuscript has a picture of the Cretan Labyrinth with the caption 'Völundr's House, that is, the house of Daedalus'. Wayland is mentioned in the Anglo-Saxon epic *Beowulf* and in Geoffrey of Monmouth's Latin poem *The Life of Merlin*. Sir Walter Scott brings him into *Kenilworth* as a human being, Kipling into *Puck of Pook's Hill* as a dethroned god.

With all the stone circles – or rather, as a rule, ellipses – there is the same doubt about the purpose as there is with Stonehenge, and folklore expresses the same feeling of uncanniness. That shows in the difficulty of counting them, and in other ways, as with the storms at Long Meg and Stanton Drew. Christianity contributes the notion of the stones being sinners, transfixed by a curse or divine judgment. The petrifaction of Long Meg and her Daughters is like the change of the witch of Wookey Hole into a stalagmite. (Female bones and accompanying relics, found in the Somerset cavern in 1912, suggested that its witch existed, but there is no similar evidence for Long Meg.) The motif of revellers turned to stone for sabbath-breaking is medieval and, of course, Christian, leaving the older world behind.

A more modern opinion is that some of the circles were observatories, used for tracking the moon and other bodies. The pioneer of the megalithic observatory was Alexander Thom, who propounded the idea on the basis of much painstaking study and measurement. Arrangements of stones, and lines of sighting along them, are said to correspond to celestial movements. Professor Thom's work has gained some acceptance by archaeologists, but only as applying to certain sites, not as an all-purpose explanation.

1. FML, 117.
2. FML, 196; Westwood, 89–91.
3. FML, 35, 187; Westwood, 228–31.
4. Grinsell (2), 10–11.
5. Westwood, 310–1.
6. Ibid, 32.
7. Grinsell (2), 5–10; FML, 165; Westwood, 409.
8. Westwood, 201–2.
9. Ibid, 228–31.
10. FML, 167.
11. Thom, passim.

9 *Hillside Figures*

Here and there about this island, predominantly in the south, great images have been made by cutting away the turf on a hillside and exposing the surface underneath. Usually that surface is chalk, and the image shows white against the surrounding green. About fifty such images exist. Horses compose the largest group. There are also human figures, crosses, and military insignia. Very few have any serious claim to antiquity or mystery. But three or four have.

Most famous of them all is the White Horse of Uffington, high up by the Ridgeway, east of Swindon. The Vale of White Horse takes its name from this figure, which can be seen from more than fifteen miles off, and is seen best from a distance, though not from as far away as that. Unlike the rest this is non-realistic, being traced with a few disjointed lines: a shorthand horse, 374 feet long. Tradition attributes it to Alfred the Great. He was born at nearby Wantage and, on this view, had the figure cut to commemorate a victory over the Danes at Ashdown, in 871. But stranger tales are told. Below is Dragon Hill, small, with a bare, flat top. Here St George slew and buried the dragon – its blood made the hill-top sterile – and the figure portrays the saint's horse. Or perhaps it is not a horse at all but the dragon in person. However, it has been on record as a horse for more than eight hundred years. The local Lord of the Manor formerly had to ensure that it was cleared of grass and weeds every seven years, and the ritual 'scouring' enlisted the populace. It was a kind of fair, with feasting, sports, and general jollification at the lord's expense.

Five miles from Westbury in Wiltshire, on the face of the Bratton Downs, is another well-known horse. This one is a solid figure 166 feet long, and realistic. Alfred has been mentioned here too.

In Dorset, just north-west of Cerne Abbas, is the Cerne giant, an outlined male nude, frontal, though the feet are turned in semi-profile. The giant is 180 feet tall, with slightly bent knees, suggesting that he is walking rather than standing still. Inside the outline are a face, nipples, ribs, and a huge erect penis pointing upwards, with testicles below. In his raised right hand the giant brandishes a club 120 feet long, executed with care. Legend tells of a real giant, a Danish one, who terrorised the district till he ate a number of sheep in Blackmoor and lay down on the hillside to sleep. The peasants beheaded him, and cut the outline around the body as a warning to other giants.

It used to be rumoured that the figure itself had life in it. Sometimes the giant would detach himself from the hill and drink at a stream below, or, more alarmingly, devour a village maiden. It was believed also that if a girl slept on the figure she would bear many children, and that a barren woman could be cured by having sexual relations on it. Well into the nineteenth century, maypole dancing took place in a neighbouring earthwork called the Trendle or the Frying Pan. Courting couples are still said to visit the giant at night. A scouring ceremony was formerly held every seven years, as with the

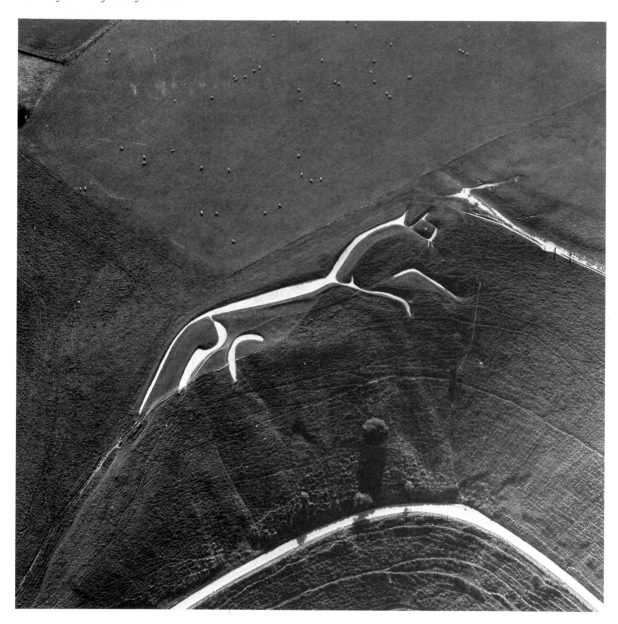

28. Aerial view of the Uffington White Horse, the oldest surviving hillside figure.

7

Uffington horse, but a vicar put a stop to it because these gatherings 'tended to practical illustrations' of the folk-beliefs.

On the north face of Windover Hill in Sussex is the Long Man of Wilmington, also known as the Lanky Man and the Lone Man. He is frontal like the Cerne giant, again in outline, but in this case there are no visible features inside. The figure is a silhouette about 230 feet tall. For many years this was the world's largest representation of a human being. The man's arms are partly extended sideways, and he holds two staffs in a vertical position, one in his right hand, one in his left. They are slightly longer than himself. In 1874, when grass had nearly effaced him, the Duke of Devonshire paid for the outline to be made permanent with whitewashed bricks. Faint traces of eyes, nose and mouth were not marked.

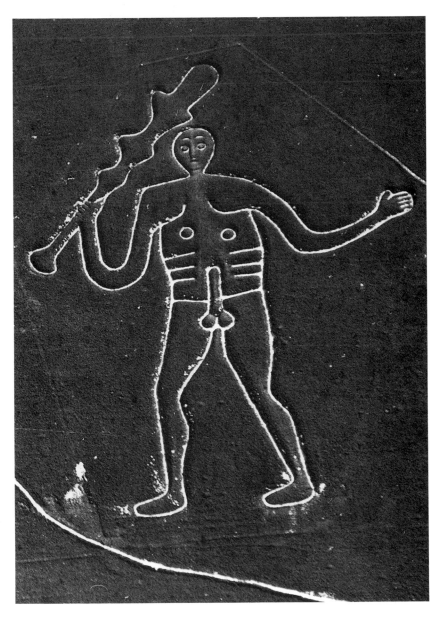

29. Aerial view of the Cerne Abbas giant and the Trendle earthwork.

Long ago, local legend relates, a giant living on Windover quarrelled with another on Firle Beacon across the valley. They pelted each other with boulders, a common practice of giants, familiar among their Cornish brethren. The Windover hill-top became pitted. At last that giant was killed and the Long Man is the outline of his corpse. Perhaps the indentations ascribed to boulders are only the remains of old flint-mines. But on the crest of the hill is a large Neolithic barrow, and some say that this is where the giant was buried, and the Long Man is a commemorative effigy. No explanation is forthcoming for his two staffs.

30. A coin of the Atrebates in the Silchester area, with a horse facing right.

31. King Alfred directing the original cutting of the White Horse, ascribed to him, probably erroneously, in legend.

While hillside figures exist in several countries, Britain has the most, and their creation by turf-cutting may be reckoned a British art. The chalk downland of the south is the main reason, though a now-vanished horse at Tysoe, between Banbury and Stratford, is described as red. How many figures there have been altogether is unknown, because, if they are not scoured or otherwise retrieved, the grass may grow over them and make them virtually invisible. With the Long Man of Wilmington it almost happened.

Few of those extant now can be earlier than the seventeenth century, and most are more recent. All the horses derive from the Uffington horse. That, at least, is certainly old, and distinguished from the rest by its ultra-simple style and by the fact that, unlike most of them, it faces right. It can be documented as far back as Henry II. The first antiquaries who studied it judged it to be Saxon. Aubrey thought it was cut at the order of Hengist, the legendary founder of Kent, who was believed, owing to the lingering influence of Geoffrey of Monmouth, to have briefly conquered much more of Britain. Hengist means 'horse', and a white horse is a Kentish emblem, but it stands on its hind legs and faces left. The recurrent Alfred idea is the same Saxon theory in a more popular and durable form.

G. K. Chesterton, in his poem *The Ballad of the White Horse*, accepts the traditional connection but has Alfred only institute the regular scouring, to retrieve and safeguard a figure that was much older. On the last point, archaeological opinion has come to converge with poetic insight. Celtic coins of the last centuries BC, imitating a coin of Philip II of Macedon, portray horses that face right, and, in some of the poorer issues, are debased or simplified into something like the Uffington horse. While the likeness is not exact enough to prove it contemporary with them, the only other parallels are Bronze Age engravings older still.

The figure's purpose is obscure. Designed to be seen from far away, it may have depicted the totemic animal of a tribe spread over a large area. Or it may be related to the cult of a deity in equine form. A horse-goddess Epona was prominent in Celtic Gaul, and she had a British guise or counterpart, who finds her way into Welsh legend . . . as will be told in its place. Wayland's Smithy is only half a mile or so off, and there are other hints at sacredness in this piece of country. Thomas Hughes described the regular ritual cleansing in his novel *The Scouring of the White Horse*.

The Westbury figure is not ancient, but there is testimony to an earlier horse, if perhaps not much earlier. The historic exploit supposedly recalled is Alfred's victory over the Danes in 878, won at Ethandune, probably the nearby village of Edington. The notion seems to be quite unfounded. Francis Wise, author of the first printed account of this horse in 1742, heard that it had been cut within living memory. Gough, an editor of William Camden's *Britannia*, thought Wise had been misinformed and held to the Saxon theory. He surveyed the figure in 1772 and published a picture. If this is accurate, the horse was a grotesque creature, facing right and more like a dachshund. It may have been a comparatively recent fake, a bad imitation of the Uffington horse. Anyhow it is no longer there. In 1778 Lord Abingdon's steward decided to replace it. By a great deal of turfing and re-cutting he blotted it out and created the present horse, facing left.

The Cerne figure is first mentioned in 1751, but its artistic style, and its blatantly phallic nature, do not suggest a date anywhere near that. The popular

15 legends have an air of antiquity; Thomas Hardy mentions the rustic belief in the
16 giant's cannibalism. In 1872 an archaeologist, W. A. Black, proposed a Roman
date, and may well have been right. Unfortunately he grounded his case on very
far-fetched arguments. He claimed that the figure marked a point used by
Roman surveyors, and that lines could be drawn relating it to known Roman
sites. Also, that some of the more mentionable dimensions, such as the giant's
height and the length of his club, recorded key distances. Black's fancies
foreshadowed a type of thinking that has come to the fore in more recent
speculations concerning leys and sacred geometry.

Yet attempts to maintain the alternative of a 'dark-age' or medieval date have
been ineffectual. They depended on guesswork about the monastery at Cerne.
17 There is a record of monks in 1268 – though not here – making an image of the
fertility god Priapus to calm peasants worried about diseased cattle. Presumably
those at Cerne might have done something similar. It is unlikely, however, that
any monks would have been allowed to complete such a huge, prolonged, and
scandalous work as drawing the giant on the hillside, whether as an essay in
magic or as a joke.

Legends of Cerne Abbey's foundation emphasise stubborn local paganism,
18 centring on a god called Helith, Helis, or Heil. St Augustine, on a (fictitious)
mission to Dorset, is said to have smashed Helith's idol and founded the Abbey
on the site. Explicit equations of the god with the giant are speculative, but the
evidence for a strong pagan cult, before the local Christianisation, is good
enough to carry some weight. It may have been strong enough to persist
afterwards, beneath a Christian veneer. The monks clearly judged it prudent not
to try expunging or bowdlerising the giant.

That could bring us back to Black's dating, though not to his fantasies. A view
19 originating with Stukeley, and revived with modern academic approval,
explains the giant as a picture of Hercules made during the Roman period,
perhaps in the second century AD. British worship of this club-wielding deity,
or of a god likened to him, is proved by various remains, such as an altar at
Whitley Castle and a sculpture at Corbridge, the latter portraying him nude
with upraised club in a pose like the giant's. The name 'Helith' is related to
others that may derive from a corruption of 'Hercules'.

The Long Man of Wilmington is very puzzling indeed, partly because he has
only looked as he does now since his reconstruction in 1874. His two staffs may
once have been more complicated, may even have been implements. In a sketch
dating from 1779, the year of his documentary début, they are a rake and a
scythe. Guesswork has put him in several periods, and identified him with a
20 medley of characters – Baldur, Beowulf, Woden, Thor, Apollo, Mercury; even
the Hindu god Varuna; even St Paul and Mohammed. Thor has more to be said
for him than the rest, but only a little more. Again, the Long Man may be a
memorial of some chief, dimly recalled as the slain giant on the hill-top. He
may be a prehistoric surveyor or 'dodman'; or a Roman soldier; or the military
badge of King Harold; or a pilgrim drawing attention to the whereabouts of
Wilmington Priory. If the last, he dates from before 1414 when the Priory was
dissolved. On the basis of place-name etymology and a Saxon artefact, a case has
been made for Waendel, a mythical warrior, possibly a war-god.

Other attested giants are gone for ever. One on Plymouth Hoe, already
21 noted, was called Gogmagog and was said to mark the site of that monster's
wrestling bout with Corineus. The figure is first mentioned in 1486. Plymouth
Corporation's audit book lists payments at intervals for Gogmagog's 'making
clean' or 'new cutting'. In 1602 there were apparently two figures, distinguished

as Gog and Magog, though one writer calls them Gogmagog and Corineus. Neither survived beyond the reign of Charles II.

A figure at the earthwork fort Wandlebury Camp, near Cambridge, is 22 mentioned early in the seventeenth century. At that time the students called these hills the Gogmagog Hills. The giant could still be seen in 1724, and the students' name for the hills has remained to this day, but the giant has not. Quite possibly he was cut by the students themselves. 'Wandlebury', however, sounds like 'Waendel' at Wilmington, and there may have been some pre-Christian tradition of a god or hero. There may even have been a previous figure. Another Wandlebury story, recorded much earlier, tells of a combat between a knight and a colossal phantom. In the 1950s the archaeologist T. C. Lethbridge carried 23 out excavations and probes, and claimed to have found not merely one but three ancient figures under the topsoil, including an earth goddess. His reconstruction, however, has not proved to be persuasive.

32. Cross-country view of the Long Man of Wilmington.

1. FML, 187; Marples, 28–66.
2. Devereux and Thomson, 101–2; FML, 102; Marples, 29–30, 50.
3. Marples, 53.
4. Marples, 55–65; Westwood, 23.
5. Marples, 67–76.
6. FML, 101–2, 123–4, 152; Marples, 159–79; Westwood, 46–50.
7. FML, 102, 209; Marples, 180–203; Westwood, 92–4.
8. Marples, 16–17.
9. Ibid, 108–18.
10. Ibid, 40–1.
11. Marples, 42–6; Ross, 404.
12. FML, 102–3; Ross, 287, 406–7, 419.
13. Marples, 55–60.
14. Ibid, 68–72.
15. Westwood, 48.
16. Marples, 170–3.
17. Westwood, 48.
18. Marples, 166–8.
19. Marples, 175–9; Ross, 477–8.
20. Devereux and Thomson, 95–6; Marples, 188–202; Westwood, 92–3.
21. Marples, 209–12; Westwood, 23–4.
22. Marples, 204–6; Westwood, 167–70.
23. Bord, 164–5; Devereux and Thomson, 163–4; Westwood, 169.

10 *Ley Lines*

According to some, prehistoric sites are not scattered at random about the landscape. Many are arranged in straight lines, called leys. This fact was

1   discovered by Alfred Watkins, a flour miller, who noticed such alignments during his business journeys. On Watkins's showing, megaliths, burial mounds, and so on, were often placed as landmarks to guide travellers along the shortest cross-country routes. Moreover, a feature which is not pre-historic, such as a church, may still have 'evolved' from something else that is, so that sites of that kind may carry the same significance, and can be taken into consideration when tracing a ley line.

Revivalists of the theory, who describe themselves as ley hunters, have

2   plotted various instances. They reckon that five or more sites in a row establish a ley. The average length is about ten miles. Some have drawn comparisons with a Chinese system of landscape-magic called *Feng-Shui*. However, many reject Watkins's 'old straight track' idea, partly or wholly.

3   They interpret leys as lines of terrestrial force or channels of energy, existing whether humanly marked or not, so that the megaliths, etcetera, were put there merely to plot their course. It follows that points where two or more intersect are foci of power.

4   Among the cases regarded as convincing are the Old Sarum ley, going through Salisbury Cathedral and the Old Sarum hill-fort, and near enough to Stonehenge to count; the Cambridge ley, going through the alleged Gogmagog figures, Sidney Sussex College, and Cambridge's Church of the Holy Sepulchre; the Corfe Castle ley, going through a series of Dorset earthworks and, naturally, Corfe Castle; and the Bamburgh ley, going through several Northumbrian earthworks and a well near Bamburgh Castle. The longest ley – not perfectly straight, but good enough to be

5   significant – is the St Michael Line. This begins at St Michael's Mount, off Marazion in Cornwall, and continues through St Michael's Church, Brentor, in Devon; then through St Michael's Church, Burrowbridge, St Michael's Church, Othery, St Michael's Church on top of Glastonbury Tor, and Stoke St Michael, all in Somerset. If the line is extended it also goes through Avebury and Bury St Edmunds.

While alignments exist, and a few may be deliberate, the ley theory as a whole is a modern myth. It has no real affinity with *Feng-Shui* or any other relevant system. Moreover, the ley hunters' shift of ground, from trackways to lines of occult force, threw it into confusion. If leys are ill-defined 'somethings' which are there anyway, and ancient monuments only draw attention to them, the requirements can be less rigid. The monuments need not be close enough together, or visible enough, to be usable as landmarks along a route, because they are not. Ley hunters of the lines-of-force school have spoken of leys crossing the sea, with nothing marking them at all; of leys twenty-five miles wide, 'corridors' rather

Frankenbury
Camp

Clearbury
Ring

Salisbury
Cathedral

Old Sarum

Stonehenge

tumulus

N

33. Three points on the six-point ley claimed to traverse part of Wiltshire: Old Sarum, Salisbury Cathedral and Clearbury Ring.

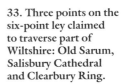

34. (right) Diagram of the Old Sarum ley, reckoned as eighteen and a half miles long.

than lines; and of leys that are not even approximately straight . . . because dowsers who claim to detect straight ones by means of rods and pendulums also claim to detect curved ones, with equal confidence. The topic has been absorbed 6 into a wider-ranging body of speculation known as Earth Mysteries, and has become a matter of faith rather than verifiable fact.

Even to the extent that ley hunters follow the Watkins scheme, as set forth in his book *The Old Straight Track* (1925), their claims are open to serious criticism. First, they show far too little regard for chronology. Sites of very different ages are freely counted as belonging to one ley. It seems dubious to line up alleged markers four thousand years old with others that have been there only four hundred. This problem arises in an acute form when churches are brought in, as they often are. Indeed, alignments of churches are apt to be the best. Believers argue that church builders before the Reformation frequently chose pre-Christian sacred sites. Sometimes they did, but a church, in itself, is not evidence for such a site.

A second criticism is probably fatal. Ley hunters allow too many types of 7 feature. Watkins listed seventeen, in descending order of evidential value: mounds (meaning chiefly burial mounds), stones (covering various kinds of megalith), circular moats, castles (as 'evolved sites'), beacons, traditional wells, pre-Reformation churches, crossroads, road alignments (stretches of road that coincide with a ley), fords, tree groups, single trees (if ancient and named), notches (dips in a hill profile), track junctions, camps (i.e. hill-forts), ponds, and square moats. Watkins's successors have added further classes of evidence. 8 These include hillside figures, dowsing as noted, UFO sightings (on the grounds that UFOs follow the ley lines), and ghost stories. Given such a glut, alignments could be expected to happen by chance. It would be surprising if they did not. Attempts to computerise have failed to prove that the distribution is other than random.

The ley hunters' only really good exhibit is the St Michael Line. Since the same saint occurs in six places, the linkage is more impressive than most, and while churches are not prehistoric, a Michael dedication makes a pre-Christian presence likelier than it usually is. The St Michael Line is absurd, of course, on Watkins's terms: the churches, or whatever was there before, could not have been used for guidance along a straight track. It has one very curious feature: it passes on through Avebury, and Avebury is at the point where it cuts a parallel of latitude distant from the equator by exactly one-seventh of the earth's circumference – 51° 26′ north, to the nearest minute.

1. Devereux and Thomson, 9–32.
2. Ibid, 72, 85.
3. Ibid, 68–71.
4. Ibid, 107–8, 126–9, 163–6, 202–4.
5. Ibid, 36.
6. Ibid, 53–71.
7. Ibid, 31.
8. Ibid, 53–4, 62–5, 85.

11 *The Temple of the Stars*

There are those who say they can trace the outlines of astrological figures on the face of Somerset. The Glastonbury Zodiac, as the system is often called, is formed by features of the landscape and covers a circle ten miles across. The figures vary in length from a mile to five miles. They are in roughly the same relative positions as the constellations are in the sky.

Aries, the Ram, covers most of Street and the fields between that town and the Polden Hills. Taurus, the Bull, is a horned head only, plus a hoof, and extends along the same line of hills and over an area on the south side. Gemini, the Twins, comprise Dundon Hill and its neighbourhood. Cancer, the Crab, is not actually a crab but a ship, partly surrounding Gemini. Leo, the Lion, is at the south of the circle near Somerton. Virgo, the Virgin, is round to the south-east, alongside the Fosse Way. Libra, the Scales, is another substituted image like Cancer, being a dove, close to the centre of the system at Barton St David. Scorpio, the Scorpion, straggles over the Fosse Way north of Virgo. Sagittarius, the Archer, is a huge mounted man around the Pennard Hills. Capricorn, the Goat, is a unicorn on the circle's north rim, his single horn being the earthwork of Ponter's Ball. Aquarius, the Water-Carrier, is represented by a phoenix, its head at Glastonbury Tor. Pisces, the Fishes, lie between Glastonbury and Street, one of them being the ridge of Wearyall Hill, the other less definite. There is also an extra, a Dog outside the circle, stretching from Langport to Athelney.

Katharine Maltwood, who discovered the Zodiac, called it the Temple of the Stars. She was led to it by clues in a medieval romance, *Perlesvaus* or *The High History of the Holy Grail*. Its anonymous author claims to have used a document at Glastonbury Abbey, and his story has episodes located in Somerset. Mrs Maltwood explained allusions to lions, and other unlikely creatures, by detecting them as shapes in the landscape. She suggested that the Zodiac was the work of Sumerians, about 2700 BC. In view of two palpable difficulties – its gigantic size, and the fact that many of the features cannot be ancient – later advocates have preferred to invoke terrestrial forces, which have moulded the figures and impelled human beings to add to them, unconsciously, in the course of making roads and fixing field-boundaries. Believers are agreed that the Zodiac is demonstrable because it can be seen from the air, and that it has been of vast importance in myth-making. The mounted Archer, for instance, who carries no visible bow or arrows, is the original Arthur, and the circle itself is the original Round Table.

The Glastonbury Zodiac is best viewed as another modern myth like ley lines. One of the major objections is the same: that it involves too many different kinds of feature. It is not formed by contours or water-courses or in any other consistent way. Zodiac-finders make use of hills, woods, streams, ditches, roads,

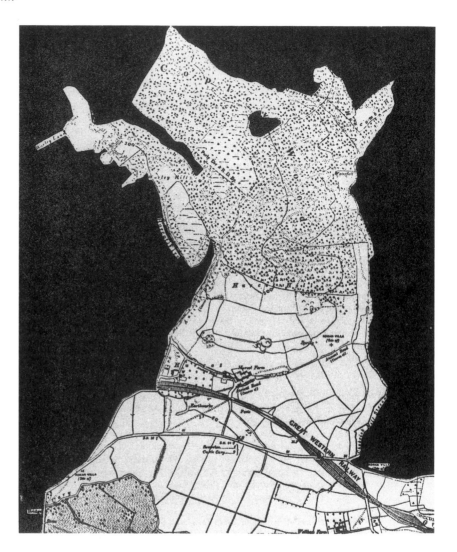

35. Part of the 'Leo' figure reconstructed on an old map.

hedges, anything that helps. A large-scale Somerset map shows such a profusion of possibilities that the selection of Zodiac outlines is plainly quite arbitrary. Other outlines could be constructed, equally convincing, or unconvincing.

Since the size of the figures, and the recency of many of the features composing them, rule out Mrs Maltwood's Sumerians, superhuman earth-forces seem to be the believer's only resort. Such tremendous entities might doubtless have created these forms that can only be seen from a great height, and, therefore, could not have been seen by human beings before aviation; after all, who knows what they had in mind? But they ought to have been able to do better. Even with all the licence which the believers allow themselves, few of the figures are good pictorially. Four of them are simply wrong, and it is not much use to argue (as enthusiasts have) that in some symbolic manner a ship is better than a crab, or a phoenix is better than a water-carrier. Assertions that place-names show traditional knowledge of the Zodiac are no more persuasive. It hardly advances the case to claim that the tumulus Wimble Toot is the Virgin's nipple, because 'toot' is really 'tit', or that the tail of the Dog – not a Zodiac character anyhow – is marked by a hamlet called Wagg.

The argument that the figures correspond to the star map might be strong if they could be proved to exist at all. If they could, all objections would have to yield, but they cannot. Many have looked at the aerial photographs in which they are alleged to be obvious, and seen nothing. Repeated challenges to Zodiac-finders to show the photographs to people unaware of what they are meant to see, and have them report on what they do see, have never been taken up. [7]

In fairness, it must be said that many who examine the photographs after being told what to look for see the Zodiac quite sincerely. Some have expanded their vision into whole sagas of mythology. The phenomenon is akin to the Rorschach ink-blot test, or to seeing pictures among the coals in an open fire. It does happen. In terms of Jungian psychology, it might be said that those who see are projecting imagery of the Unconscious on to the landscape. The fact that they do is part of the spell which Glastonbury, for whatever reason, exerts.

A question not completely resolved is whether Katharine Maltwood, who published her findings in 1935, was the first to talk about this Zodiac, or whether anyone did before. Proof of an earlier reference would at least show that some such notion was in the air, and that allegations about a tradition are not wholly baseless. The *Perlesvaus* passages can be dismissed. No reader, without prompting, would see the meanings in them that Mrs Maltwood saw. The Elizabethan astrologer John Dee has been quoted as writing of astrological earthworks around Glastonbury, but the passage has defied verification.

Only one text of any interest remains arguable, in the Prophecies of Nostradamus (VI, 22):

> Dedans la terre du grand temple celique
> Nepveu à Londres par paix faincte meutri.

> In the land of the great heavenly temple
> A nephew at London is murdered through a false peace.

Nostradamus's reference to London shows that England is 'the land of the great heavenly temple'. Since he plainly sees this as unique and distinctive, it is not a church. Stonehenge was hardly known in his time, the sixteenth century, and was not thought of as a ritual structure. Somerset's Temple of the Stars would therefore be a candidate, at least as a pre-Maltwood fancy. The second line would be impressive if we could admit the possibility that Nostradamus did see the future. The nephew could be the rebel Duke of Monmouth, who was put to death in 1685 by his uncle, James II, and the 'peace' or pacification was deceptive because James's agent in repression, Judge Jeffreys, sowed bitter resentment that helped to dethrone the king only three years afterwards. Moreover, Monmouth would call Somerset to mind, because Somerset was the heart of the rebellion, and his army twice camped at Glastonbury.

1. Caine, 19–26.
2. Caine, 43–152; Maltwood, passim.
3. Caine, 31–4; Maltwood, 1–7.
4. Caine, 35–40.
5. Caine, 22, 44, 111–7; Maltwood, 37–46.
6. Caine, 84, 85, 148.
7. Ashe (1), 121.

12 *The Maze*

For many centuries a distinctive maze has been known in Britain: not a maze in the modern sense of a puzzle, but a convoluted track going round and round, back and forth, till it reaches the centre after making seven circuits. This maze is ancient, magical, and widespread. It occurs with slight variations in shape and orientation, but its essential pattern is always the same. In Greece it was a symbol for the Cretan Labyrinth, and that meaning was known in Pompeii, where it was scratched on a pillar, with a caption. The maze is found among the Etruscans, and in India, once as representing the fortress in Sri Lanka where Rama's abducted wife Sita was imprisoned. Ireland has an instance of it inscribed on a stone from Hollywood in County Wicklow.

In Britain it is carved twice on a rock near Tintagel. However, it is best known among the Welsh. Shepherds used to mark out its complex spiral on the turf, as a pastime. In Cumbria, and near Brandsby in Yorkshire, it is likewise known as a turf design. Its traditional Welsh name is *Caerdroia*, meaning the City (or Fortification) of Troy. Allegedly, the maze is a plan of

36. Rocky Valley near Tintagel: the recurring septenary maze pattern, carved on stone at an unknown date; the path is between the lines.

Troy's defences, with seven walls and a laborious way through them. Welsh schoolboys used to challenge other schoolboys to draw the walls of Troy correctly. This 'Troy Town' motif is repeated in the naming of Scandinavian mazes which are similar, though not identical.

A huge instance in three dimensions is believed by many to encircle   7 Glastonbury Tor. All around the hill are terraces of unknown age and purpose. They can be interpreted as the remains of an earthwork system on the same septenary pattern. A maze-threader would start from a large stone at the foot of the longer path of ascent, climb the path as far as another stone, turn left, and proceed clockwise along the terrace at that level.

The maze is not a myth in the sense of being a fancy or a literary invention. Some of the instances, such as the Cornish ones, are there to be seen, and the maze on the Tor is demonstrably possible if unproved. The mythic quality is a matter of implication, in the light of occurrences outside Britain, and these point in more than one direction.

To look first at the Cretan Labyrinth, this seems to have begun as a dance   8 rather than a building. A file of dancers performed it on a ritual floor, following the septenary backtracking spiral. Cretan coins reproduce the pattern. According to the Minotaur legend, Theseus put in at the island of Delos on his way home from Crete, and instituted a ritual dance there in commemoration, which was still being danced in classical times. Delos was Apollo's birthplace among the Greeks, and the dance circled his altar. The god was involved in other ways, though perhaps not originally. Coins portraying the Labyrinth have his profile on the obverse. According to Virgil's *Aeneid*, the Labyrinth was depicted outside the cave of his oracle at Cumae, in Italy.

The Trojan link is something else. An Etruscan vase and other clues show this   9 to be very old and not purely British or even northern. The *Aeneid* describes the Trojans, supposedly ancestors of the Romans, as performing an equestrian exercise called the Game of Troy, in part of which the riders filed round in interlacing circles compared by the poet to the Cretan Labyrinth. A manoeuvre of the same name was still staged as a cavalry display in Virgil's time, and later. As to whether the Welsh *Caerdroia* owes anything to the *Aeneid*, or to some offshoot of the Brutus legend, documentation is lacking.

Far back, the Trojan connection may have arisen from an association of the   10 maze, and others somewhat like it, with a goddess. There is a Cretan allusion to such a figure, as the Mistress of the Labyrinth. Ariadne, for whom, Homer tells us, the Labyrinth was devised, is doubtless a form of her. At a later stage a more masculine theology seems to have reduced her to a woman at the centre who, like Sita, has to be reached by a hero. That recalls the Homeric story of Helen, who is carried off to Troy, and whom the besieging Greeks try to recapture. It may be thus that the Trojan link was forged. A fifteenth-century visitor to Crete, the Seigneur de Caumont, indicates that in popular lore the Labyrinth and the   11 city of Troy were so far confused that they were spoken of as the same.

This motif gives an added interest to the theory of the Glastonbury maze. An early Arthurian legend tells of Guinevere being carried off by a local king and   12 held by him at Glastonbury, so that Arthur has to come with an army to retrieve her. Archaeology attests buildings on top of the Tor, at the heart of the proposed maze, in roughly the 'Arthur' period.

37. Glastonbury Tor,
on which the terraces
may be remnants of
a prehistoric maze
making the seven
circuits that are found
elsewhere.

Attempts have been made to account for the Tor's terracing in other ways, or at any rate to refute the maze, but they have been inconclusive. While hills elsewhere in Somerset are shelved in some degree, there is no true parallel. The maze explanation was first offered by Geoffrey Russell. It is taken seriously, though without commitment, by Professor Philip Rahtz, who excavated the   13 Tor's summit area during the 1960s. In Rahtz's view the maze, if real, should probably be assigned to the Neolithic era of great ritual works, though it might have continued in use long afterwards. A 'disproof' based on a dubious allusion to the Tor being heavily wooded in the twelfth century, in which case the terracing would have to be later and follow a clearance, fails to hold water. Large trees do not grow on the Tor proper where the terraces are. It is too exposed and the soil is too shallow. Any forest would have been on the lower slopes around it. The chief rival explanation, that the terraces are agricultural strip-lynchets, is rendered unlikely by several factors, one of them being a sharp downward bend or kink in the system, effecting certain joins that would be required for the maze but not for lynchets, or indeed for anything else that has been suggested.

Unlike the Glastonbury Zodiac, the Tor maze theory does not depend on arbitrary constructions or selectivity. The entire pattern is present except in steep places where weathering or erosion would obviously have wiped it out, and, with minor and explicable exceptions, it uses all the terraces. If the apparent track is followed it makes the seven circuits. The only query arises from the last, which is not quite completed on the surface. Conjecturally, the maze-threading ended with entry into a tunnel leading to an underground chamber, an idea favoured by persistent local lore about the Tor being hollow. While the purpose of the Tor maze (if it exists) can only be guessed at by analogy with other cases, it would amount to a strong argument for a pre-Christian sanctuary. Theological feminists, who claim such sites as Avebury and Silbury for the Goddess, have also claimed the Tor.

1. Ashe (1), 155, 180, 182; Matthews, 45–6.
2. Ashe (1), 180, 186–7; Matthews, 158.
3. Kraft, 24.
4. Ashe (1), 181, 189; Hadingham, 98–9.
5. Ashe (1), 181, 189–90; Hadingham, 99–100.
6. Ashe (1), 188–9; Matthews, 92–4.
7. Ashe (1), 153–79, 256–65, and (4), passim.
8. Ashe (1), 183–6, 191–2; Hadingham, 100–1; Matthews, 157–62.
9. Ashe (1), 186–8.
10. Ashe (1), 186, 191; Kraft, passim.
11. Matthews, 156.
12. Bromwich, 381–2; Carley, 5; Lacy, ed., art. 'Glastonbury'.
13. Ashe (1), 156; Rahtz, 132–3.

A MYRROVR
for Magiſtrates,
wherein may be ſeene by eram-
ples paſſed in this realme, with
howe greueous plagues, vyces
are puniſhed in great princes and magiſtrates,
and how frayle
and vnſtable worldly proſperity
is founde, where Fortune
ſeemeth moſte highly
to fauour.
Newly corrected and augmented,
Anno 1571.

Fœlix quem faciunt aliena pericula cautum.

Imprinted at London by
Thomas Marſhe dwellynge
in Fleetſtreete, neare vnto
S. Dũſtanes Churche.

Dynasties

13 *Brutus's Kingdom*

For some centuries Britain's royal succession ran lineally through descendants of Brutus. After that, despite changes, he was still named as the ultimate ancestor. Welsh princely houses in later ages have pedigrees going back to kings and queens of the true Trojan stock. Even the monarchs of England are linked to it, through marriages made a long time ago.

There is no real reason to think that Britain was a political unit, or that a single ruler was even paramount, at any time in the centuries BC. 'Britannia' as an entity covering most of the island was created by Roman power, continued for a few decades after its withdrawal, and survived as an idea, but only as an idea, through subsequent fragmentation. Welsh tradition refers to Celtic Britain as the Island of the Mighty, with a rooted oneness that is more than a matter of insularity. But this is in retrospect, and the ancient kingdom depicted by Geoffrey is likewise retrospective, a figment projected by imperial and post-imperial unity, nothing genuinely prior to that.

Geoffrey of course wants to uplift the Celts – Welsh, Cornish, Bretons – by glorifying their ancestors, the supposedly united Ancient Britons. To do this he adopts the ready-made Brutus legend, giving the Britons a glorious background of their own and a collateral kinship with the Romans. But to complete the picture and give it verisimilitude, he has to do more. He has to bridge an immense gap between the aftermath of the siege of Troy and the beginning of genuine British history. So he fabricates a long regal succession, with a profusion of names and details, as will appear.

Britain's legendary monarchs, in Geoffrey's work and indeed outside it too, are drawn from a variety of sources. Some are fictitious characters alleged to account for geographical names. Brutus himself is the obvious example, in-

38. (opposite) Title-page of the 1571 edition of *A Mirror for Magistrates*, which, when expanded further by John Higgins, introduced a number of Britain's legendary rules.

vented to explain 'Britain', long before Geoffrey. Others are taken from genealogies of Welsh princely houses and relocated backwards in time. Others 4 are pure creations of Geoffrey's fancy. He enjoys multiplying characters, and brings in more than he needs, many of them as names only, without even the pretence of a biography.

A few of the royal Britons have a special interest as survivors from a pre-Christian pantheon. While Celtic Christians could not admit pagan deities directly, their attitude to them was unusual. In most of the former Roman world, Christians had been persecuted by pagan authorities, encouraged by pagan priesthoods. As a result they tended to view the gods and goddesses as evil – demons masquerading to lead humanity astray. In Britain, however, the persecution was slight, and in Ireland it never happened. Hence, while clerics might fulminate, the Celtic people of the islands could regard the myths of the old order in a relaxed manner, and domesticate its deities in their story-telling, disguised as kings, queens, enchanters. That is where some of the legendary rulers, and their companions, come from. So likewise – and more palpably – with some of the Tuatha De Danann in Ireland.

Geoffrey's characters are adopted in all seriousness by chroniclers right through to the sixteenth century. They also figure in two very unequal Elizabethan poets, the second of whom, if not the first, did much to keep his mythology alive. The earlier of the two was John Higgins, who contributed to the growth of a famous composite work, *A Mirror for Magistrates*. The *Mirror* is a series of 'tragedies' in the medieval sense – cautionary tales in verse about the misfortunes of various historical persons, held up to instruct and warn powerful contemporaries. It was published in 1559 and enlarged in later editions. Most 5 distinguished of its authors was Thomas Sackville, a cousin of the Queen. The chronicler Holinshed, whose book Shakespeare used, was also involved. Hig- 6 gins entered the scene in 1574 with a series of his own, offered as an extension of the 'official' one, though it seems he wrote more or less independently. It comprised sixteen of Geoffrey's rulers. He put a few more of them in a second edition. After Higgins came the incomparably greater Spenser, who, in 1590, wove long summaries of Geoffrey's *History*, with added touches from chronicles, into the vast allegorical structure of *The Faerie Queene*. The early period is surveyed in Book II, Canto x, stanzas 5–45.

39. (opposite) Head of Celtic god (Maponus).

1. Moncreiffe, 10–13; 'Nennius' (2), 101–14.
2. Rhys, I, 280.
3. Tatlock, 431–2.
4. Piggott (2), 274–5.
5. *A Mirror for Magistrates*, Introduction.
6. *A Mirror for Magistrates*, *Parts added*, 29–222.

14 *The Stone of Destiny*

1 Scotland was formerly called Albany. During the heyday of Brutus's kingdom, while under the suzerainty of his heirs, it sometimes had its own princes. Later, most of it became fully independent as the kingdom of the Picts, with the smaller realm of Scots in Argyll, Dalriada, intermittently and imperfectly under Pictish control. The Scots grew more numerous and powerful. Eventually, at a time when the Pictish succession was in dispute, the Scottish king, Kenneth MacAlpine, lodged a claim through Pictish blood of his own. He met the Pictish nobles at Scone, their sacred centre near Perth, where their kings were crowned. By a stratagem to be described in its place, Kenneth became king. Henceforth the northern land was united under the Scots, presently drawing in Strathclyde – still a kingdom of British-descended Welsh – and territory as far as the present Border.

Its rulers affirmed their legitimacy by carrying on the practice of enthronement at Scone. They looked back, like the Welsh, to a remote past.

2 The magic of the place was now said to inhere in a large stone on which the king sat to receive his inheritance. This, reputedly, was the stone on which Jacob's head rested, when he had his dream of angels and the Lord's promise about his Israelite descendants (*Genesis* 28:10–22). Calling the place Bethel, the House of God, Jacob anointed the stone with oil and set it up as a monument.

Thus far the Bible. The Scots added that the stone was brought to Ireland

3 by a princess from the east, Tea. She married an Irish king, and the hill Temair, since familiar as Tara, was named after her. At Tara the high kings held court, and the stone figured in coronation ritual as *Lia-fail*, the Stone of Destiny. Fergus, the prince who founded Dalriada, brought it over from Ireland to Iona. Kenneth himself transferred it to Scone.

The Stone was to play a part in the final intertwining of all the threads of royalty. In 1296 the victorious Edward I removed it to Westminster, where

4 it was built into the throne used for English coronations. Scots maintained that Scottish kings would reign wherever the Stone was, and their belief was vindicated in 1603 when the Stuart James VI became James I of England. James, moreover, was descended through Henry VII from Welsh kings and the original royal Britons.

Some say that the sovereigns of the United Kingdom are descended from Jacob through the patriarch Judah, and that their biblical forebears include David, so that they are the heirs to his divinely-established throne.

Scotland's tale of the Stone is another instance of the mythological treatment of sovereignty which appears, differently, in Geoffrey of Monmouth.

5 'Albany' is an authentic early name for Scotland, though not as early as Geoffrey makes out when he includes that country in the original British realm.

40. Aerial view of Tara showing the circular raths or earthworks, the largest of which, the King's Rath, contains the *Lia-fail*.

41. Westminster Abbey: the Coronation Chair incorporating the Stone of Destiny, as a token of the right of the sovereigns of England to reign over Scotland also.

**42. Edward I
enthroned after his
annexation of the
Stone.**

Still preserved in 'Breadalbane', it is a form of 'Albion' applied to a part instead
of the whole – to Scotland in a general way, and more specifically to the lands
beyond the Clyde-Forth line, which Roman Britain, Britannia, never annexed.
The Picts did not, as Geoffrey imagines, burst in from outside and detach the
north from a united island. They were simply there since no one knows when,
with the Scots on their flank from the late fifth century onwards. The shift from
Pictish to Scottish ascendancy occurred in the ninth. Kenneth did adopt Scone,
and the legendary career of the Stone of Destiny was meant to give the new
kingdom an august, even holy ancestry and a supernatural sanction. Such stones
had a role in Irish kingship ritual and Tara had its *Lia-fail*. In fact it still has; if the

Scottish stone was the original, and was removed from Tara, the present stone is a replacement. Geologists, however, claim that the one at Scone need not have [8] come from Ireland. It is a block of lower old red sandstone which could have been quarried not far away.

By his act of seizure Edward I sought to annex the mystique, or at least [9] deprive the Scots of it, but he failed to extinguish the local aura. Robert Bruce was crowned at Scone even though the Stone was at Westminster, and when Edward III recognised him by treaty as king of Scotland, he apparently did not ask for it back. Perhaps he did regard it as a sort of time-bomb that would some day cut off the English royal line and put a Scotsman on the throne. When James acceded, his partly Welsh great-great-grandfather, Henry VII, had already [10] drawn in the ancient British strand, supposedly descending from Brutus's people via the Welsh kings Maelgwn and Cadwaladr (both mentioned by Geoffrey, and real) to the Tudors. There would doubtless have been connections by marriage earlier.

Modern royalty's biblical pedigree is expounded by British-Israelites, and depends on the union of the crowns under James. They trace it by two routes. [11] One goes back through James and Henry VII to Brutus, who, as Aeneas's great-grandson, was a descendant of Dardanus, the founder of Troy. As already observed, British-Israelites make out that Dardanus is Dara or Darda (*I Chronicles* 2:6); and Darda's father was Zarah, one of the twin sons of Judah (*Genesis* 38:30).

The other line goes back, again via James, through many Scottish and Irish kings to Eremon or Eochaid, the one who married the princess Tea – Tea-Tephi [12] as British-Israelites call her. According to legend she arrived in Ireland in 585 BC with the Stone of Destiny and two companions. British-Israelites assert that she was a daughter of the biblical king Zedekiah, himself a descendant of David and, through him, of Pharez or Perez, Judah's other twin son. They further suggest that her companions were the prophet Jeremiah and his secretary Baruch. In *Jeremiah* 43:5–7, the prophet and secretary are stated to have gone to Egypt with a group that included Zedekiah's daughters . . . unnamed. Nothing is said about any of them going farther, and Jeremiah is usually thought to have died in Egypt. The alleged Irish connection seems to rest on a coincidence of dates.

1. GM (1), 15, and (2), 75.
2. FML, 448; Prebble, 22; Westwood, 418–20.
3. *Brewer*, art. 'Scone'; Rees, 167, 187.
4. FML, 448.
5. Morris, 42, 187, 219.
6. Ashe (7), 204; Mackenzie, 207–8; Morris, 196–7.
7. Rees, 146–7; Westwood, 419.
8. Prebble, 22.
9. Ibid, 76, 89, 117–8.
10. Moncreiffe, 10–11.
11. Stuart-Knill, chart of asserted royal lines (no pagination).
12. Sargent, 134–6.

15 *Gwendolen*

1   To revert to Brutus: he had three sons, Locrinus, Kamber, and Albanactus. When he died, in the twenty-third year after the Trojans' coming to Britain, he was buried in New Troy and his sons divided the island among them. Locrinus ruled over the country now called England, Kamber over Wales, Albanactus over Scotland. Thus arose the old names of those countries: Loegria, Cambria, Albany. Under succeeding reigns the British kings always ruled over Loegria or most of it, and the lesser regions were subject to them, though sometimes with princes of their own. So Britain remained united.

Albanactus was slain in battle with Huns who had invaded his territory. Locrinus, aided by Kamber, defeated the Huns in the northern part of his own kingdom, and their chief, Humber, was drowned in a river, since called Humber after him. Among the prisoners taken was a beautiful German girl, Estrildis. Locrinus wanted to marry her, but he had already promised to marry Gwendolen, the daughter of Brutus's second-in-command Corineus – the same who wrestled with the giant. Corineus, brandishing a battle-axe, persuaded him to honour his word, but when Gwendolen was his wife he kept Estrildis as his mistress, housing her in New Troy in a hidden dwelling below ground level. For seven years he used to pay visits to her, saying he was going to sacrifice privately to his gods. After some time she bore him a daughter, Habren. His wife Gwendolen meanwhile bore a son, Maddan.

When the formidable Corineus died, Locrinus deserted Gwendolen and made Estrildis his queen. Gwendolen raised an army in Cornwall, her late father's domain, and fought Locrinus close to the River Stour, where he was killed by an arrow. He had reigned only ten years. Gwendolen now reigned in her own right. She ordered Estrildis and her daughter Habren to be thrown into a river. While thus putting both to death, she still wanted the girl to be commemorated, as Locrinus's daughter, so she decreed that the river should be called Habren: a name that became Sabrina in Latin, and Severn in English. Gwendolen reigned for fifteen years and then retired to Cornwall, handing over the crown to her son Maddan. At that time the prophet Samuel flourished among the Israelites.

2   Throughout this episode, Geoffrey is inventing characters to account for geography. 'Loegria' in fact is simply a Welsh name for England, Lloegr or Lloegyr. 'Cambria' is derived from *Cymry* meaning 'fellow-countrymen', the name given by the Welsh to themselves as an assertion of solidarity. 'Albany', as an old term for Scotland, is derived – it will be recalled – from 'Albion'. No Huns ever invaded Britain, even when they were really in Europe many centuries later. 'Humber' is British and probably means 'the goodly river'. As for

3   the Severn, 'Habren' and 'Sabrina' are both found early, but the etymology is uncertain.

The Stour, near which Gwendolen's husband perished, is either the Dorset   4
Stour or a tributary of the Severn that flows into it above Worcester. In view of
the sequel, the latter seems more likely, but the poet Wace, who wrote a
paraphrase of Geoffrey in French verse, prefers Dorset.

Besides Gwendolen, Geoffrey has two more British queens who reign in their
own right, Cordelia (of Shakespearean fame) and Marcia. When he wrote, this
was a surprising thing to think of and to portray happening without comment.
England was torn by civil war precisely because many of the baronage refused to
accept Henry I's daughter Matilda, on the ground that a woman could not rule.
Geoffrey may have had some real if remote knowledge of Celtic sovereignty and   5
read it back into Britain's extended past. Celtic queens could truly reign in their
own right, and even lead armies as he says Gwendolen did. While kings were the
usual rulers, their wives could claim to be equal and even, in a magical sense,
superior, being symbolic of the land.

These attitudes had a background in goddess cults of immemorial age.
Habren, or Sabrina, is a reminder of these. She becomes the tutelary spirit of the
river and is introduced as such by Milton in his masque *Comus*, with slight
amendments to the story, and the addition of the water-god Nereus:

> The guiltless damsel flying the mad pursuit
> Of her enragèd stepdam Guendolen,
> Commended her fair innocence to the flood
> That stay'd her flight with his cross-flowing course,
> The water Nymphs that in the bottom plaid,
> Held up their pearlèd wrists and took her in,
> Bearing her straight to aged Nereus' Hall,
> Who piteous of her woes, rear'd her lank head,
> And gave her to his daughters to imbathe
> In nectar'd lavers strew'd with Asphodil,
> And through the porch and inlet of each sense
> Dropt in Ambrosial Oils till she reviv'd,
> And underwent a quick immortal change
> Made Goddess of the River.

43. (overleaf) **Hafren Forest: the Severn near its source on Plynlimmon.**

Invoked with a song beginning 'Sabrina fair', she appears as protectress of the
bewitched lady in the masque, and frees her from enchantment. The periods of
time given in Geoffrey's story imply that Sabrina was a child. Perhaps her
transformation into a river-spirit was accompanied by a change in form: a 'quick
immortal change'.

Here, as elsewhere, Geoffrey's references to the Bible are meant to give
verisimilitude by lining up the reigns of his kings and queens with the sacred
history, assumed in his time to be factually reliable. The trouble is that the
scriptural chronology cannot itself be made exact. All that can be said of the date
of Samuel is that he flourished somewhere about the middle of the eleventh
century BC.

1. GM (1), 15–17, and (2), 75–8.
2. Piggott (2), 277.
3. Ekwall, 256, art. 'Humber', and 413, art. 'Severn'.
4. GM (2), 77, fn 1; Tatlock, 29.
5. Kightly, 38; Markale, 78, 123–9, 188; Tatlock, 286.

16 *Bladud*

After Gwendolen and Maddan came several kings who raised the level of Britain's civilisation by founding more cities: York, Edinburgh, Carlisle, Canterbury, Winchester, Shaftesbury. Ebraucus, the founder of York and Edinburgh, had twenty wives, twenty sons and thirty daughters. He married off the daughters to Trojan-descended nobles in Italy, but the ancient ties of blood were fast weakening, and when the Italian Trojans founded Rome, the British ones were a clearly separate nation.

Bladud, fourth in line from Ebraucus, was king for twenty years. He reigned when the prophet Elijah was denouncing the apostasy of the northern Israelites. As a youth, heir-apparent to the crown, he had contracted a skin disease assumed to be leprosy. His parents were forced to send him away, and he became a swineherd, over the Avon from the future site of Bath. One day he was horrified to find that he had infected the pigs. To avoid their owner while he considered what to do, he drove them across a ford and climbed on to rising ground. The pigs, propelled by some obscure instinct, galloped downhill and plunged into a muddy morass where hot springs welled from underground. Bladud managed to lure them out with acorns, and drove them home. When he wiped the mud off he noticed that their skins looked much healthier. He returned to the hot springs and washed in the water himself, with the same result.

Cured, he resumed his place at court. On becoming king, with a consort named Alaron, he constructed baths where the sick could be immersed in the healing water, and founded the town now known as Bath. He dedicated

44. Swineherds gathering acorns as food for their pigs.

the springs to the goddess Minerva – in the British pantheon, Sul – and built a temple with fires perpetually burning, which were never choked with ash, because the fuel, when consumed, hardened into lumps that were easy to clear away. A plaque above one of the baths commemorates him.

Bladud was an active patron of learning. He studied in Athens himself, brought Greek scholars to Britain, and set up a university at Stamford. Unhappily he also practised the arts of magic. He made himself a pair of wings and flew over New Troy, but crashed on the temple of Apollo and was killed.

3 Bladud's name has been explained, very conjecturally, as meaning Light-Dark and implying that in his priestly role he officiated in a cult with a dual aspect. The two-faced Roman god Janus has been cited. But Minerva had no such quality, and it is not known that the British deity Sul had, either.

Geoffrey includes Bath's founder not only in his *History* but in his later work, the *Life of Merlin*. He does not mention the leprosy cure in either. This is a legend of uncertain origin, likelier to be Welsh than English, because pigs are prominent in Celtic mythology. Elijah, who disturbed the reign of the datable Ahab, puts Bladud around the middle of the ninth century BC. The plaque at Bath gives 863 for his activities there.

4 Sul may have had a sacred spring before the Romans arrived in Britain, but the main work of construction followed their discovery of the natural hot water

45. Bronze head of Sul-Minerva from Bath, dating from the Roman period.

with its mineral content. Calling the place Aquae Sulis, in effect 'Sul's Spa', they built spacious baths and a temple for Minerva, to whom Sul was assimilated. A city grew round the central complex, and the spa drew visitors from a large part of the Empire. In post-Roman times the Avon was liable to flooding, and the buildings fell into disrepair and were partially buried. However, as Geoffrey implies in his account, the thermal springs were frequented during the Middle Ages, especially by lepers hoping for Bladud's cure. The Church maintained baths on a charitable basis. Bath's revival as a fashionable resort began through royal patronage in the late seventeenth century. The full rediscovery of the Roman site is more recent. Archaeology has not revealed any trace of a previous establishment.

Geoffrey refers to Bladud's magic, but not to his academic enthusiasm. The latter appears in Higgins (for whom the final disaster supplies a good moral) and briefly in Spenser. Bladud's devotion to the erudite Minerva may have suggested it. Athens, however, had no relevant reputation at the time of his reign.

46. One of the Roman baths (the statues above are comparatively recent).

1. GM (1), 17–18, and (2), 78–80.
2. GM (1), 18, and (2), 80–1; FML, 149; Sitwell, 23–5; Westwood, 4–5.
3. Stewart (1), 127, 176, 203.
4. Jolly, 6–13.

17 *King Lear*

1. Bladud's flying accident – the first ever, unless one counts Icarus – transferred the crown prematurely to his son. This was Leir. He is remembered as King Lear; but the original story calls for the original spelling. Owing to his early accession he reigned sixty years, a record for the old British monarchy. Throughout most of that time his rule was admirable. Like several of his predecessors he founded a city. It was on the River Soar and was given his own name, Caer Leir. In English it became Leicester.

   Leir had no sons, but he had three daughters, Gonorilla, Regan, and Cordeilla. While all three were dear to him, the youngest, Cordeilla, was his favourite. At an advanced age he resolved to divide the kingdom among them, and marry them to husbands who could take a suitable share in government. Since an equal triple division was impracticable, he formed the notion of giving the largest portion to the daughter who loved him most. Questioned on that point, Gonorilla called the gods to witness that her father was dearer to her than her very soul. Regan swore that she loved him more than she loved anyone else on earth. Leir was taken in by their flattery, but hoped Cordeilla would somehow outbid them, so that he could award her the best share. However, she chose to test him just as he was testing her. She loved him, she said, with the love due from a daughter to her father, but no more. Worse, she told him that his value in others' eyes depended, in practice, on his possessions.

   Leir was furious and revised his plans. He married Gonorilla to Maglaurus, the duke of Albany, and Regan to Henwinus, the duke of Cornwall. Between them they were to have half the island, while he kept the remainder for himself. Cordeilla was cast off. Aganippus, however, the Frankish king, was willing to take her with neither land nor dowry, and she went to become his wife in Gaul.

   Though Leir was growing older and feebler, he went on living. At length his impatient sons-in-law seized the territory he still held. He could do nothing to stop them and was virtually deposed. Maglaurus and Gonorilla undertook to give him a home in their own large residence, with an entourage of a hundred and forty knights. The arrangement lasted for two years. Finally Gonorilla complained that it had become unworkable. The hundred and forty knights made excessive demands and quarrelled with her own servants. Despite her past protestations of boundless love, she told Leir that she would put up with only thirty henceforth and he must dismiss the rest. He walked out in a rage and went to Henwinus and Regan. After a few months Regan likewise insisted that most of his retinue must go. She would allow him only five. He returned to Gonorilla, but now she refused to accommodate more than one. After all, he had no possessions, no state to keep up. Why did he need attendants?

   With a hundred and thirty-nine of his knights gone, Leir tried to endure what he regarded as poverty, but found it unbearable. He swallowed his

47. 'King Lear
Weeping over the
Body of Cordelia',
by James Barry – an
eighteenth-century con-
ception of Shakespeare's
conclusion.

pride and set off with the one survivor for Gaul. Aboard the ship he was not
accorded royal treatment, and realised that Cordeilla had spoken the truth.
Without his possessions he was not particularly valued. He feared that she
also would reject him, in view of his conduct towards her, but she received
him with compassion and generosity, and supplied him with money, new
clothes, and a fresh retinue of forty. They returned together to Britain with
an army recruited by Aganippus, her husband, and routed the two sons-in-
law. Leir was king again. He reigned for three years more and died full of
days and honour.

Cordeilla became queen. She buried her father in a vault under the
riverbed of the Soar, downstream from his city Leicester. After five years of
peace her sisters' sons, Marganus and Cunedagius, began to stir up trouble
against her. Their fathers were dead and they had inherited the dukedoms.
Resenting female rule, they rose in revolt and took Cordeilla prisoner. In
her cell, despair drove her to suicide.

What relation was King Lear to Aeneas? It sounds like a nonsense question, but
the answer can be inferred from Geoffrey. One of these famous characters was
the great-great-great-great-great-great-great-great-great-great-grandson of
the other.

2   Has the king any antecedents? Welsh genealogies mention someone called Llyr, but little is said about him. Llyr may be the same as an Irish Lir, probably a sea-god, and there is a story concerning Lir and his children, but this is quite
3   different. Their stepmother turns them into swans and they spend nine hundred years in that shape. The spell breaks and they revert to humanity at a time when the Christian faith has reached Ireland and they can be baptised. No connection is apparent, and the likeness of name may be only a coincidence. Leir may well
4   have begun as a fictitious person supposed to account for the name of Leicester. Early spellings indicate that the first part of the word was once *Legra* and that this was the name of a tributary of the Soar, still surviving today in the village
5   of Leire. Cordeilla may have been suggested by a mythical maiden called Creiddylad, but, again, the idea has no support from any relevant tradition.
6   When Geoffrey gives Leir the history he does, he is probably adapting a folk-tale, and not necessarily a British one. Parallels occur overseas. The fame of the result is due to his literary successors. Higgins has this episode, and so does Holinshed's *Chronicle*, published in 1577. Spenser, in his verse paraphrase of Geoffrey, allots it six stanzas. Here, the youngest daughter acquires her familiar spelling, though not instantly. After Bladud the narrative goes on:

> Next him king Leyr in happie peace long raind,
>   But had no issue male him to succeed,
>   But three faire daughters, which were well vptraind,
>   In all that seemed fit for kingly seed:
>   Mongst whom his realme he equally decreed
>   To haue diuided. Tho when feeble age
>   Nigh to his vtmost date he saw proceed,
>   He cald his daughters; and with speeches sage
> Inquyrd, which of them most did loue her parentage.
>
> The eldest Gonorill gan to protest,
>   That she much more than her owne life him lou'd:
>   And Regan greater loue to him profest,
>   Then all the world, when euer it were proou'd;
>   But Cordeill said she lou'd him, as behoou'd:
>   Whose simple answere, wanting colours faire
>   To paint it forth, him to displeasaunce moou'd,
>   That in his crowne he counted her no haire,
> But twixt the other twaine his kingdome whole did shaire.
>
> So wedded th'one to Maglan king of Scots,
>   And th'other to the king of Cambria,
>   And twixt them shayrd his realme by equall lots:
>   But without dowre the wise Cordelia
>   Was sent to Aganip of Celtica.
>   Their aged Syre, thus eased of his crowne,
>   A priuate life led in Albania,
>   With Gonorill, long had in great renowne,
> That nought him grieu'd to bene from rule deposed downe.

But true it is, that when the oyle is spent,
  The light goes out, and weeke is throwne away;
  So when he had resigned his regiment,
  His daughter gan despise his drouping day,
  And wearie waxe of his continuall stay.
  Tho to his daughter Regan he repayrd,
  Who him at first well vsed every way;
  But when of his departure she despayred,
Her bountie she abated, and his cheare empayrd.

The wretched man gan then auise too late,
  That loue is not, where most it is profest,
  Too truely tryde in his extreamest state;
  At last resolu'd likewise to proue the rest,
  He to Cordelia him selfe addrest,
  Who with entire affection him receau'd,
  As for her Syre and king her seemed best;
  And after all an army strong she leu'd,
To war on those, which him had of his realme bereau'd.

So to his crowne she him restor'd againe,
  In which he dyde, made ripe for death by eld,
  And after willd, it should to her remaine:
  Who peaceably the same long time did weld:
  And all mens harts in dew obedience held:
  Till that her sisters children, woxen strong
  Through proud ambition, against her rebeld,
  And ouercommen kept in prison long,
Till wearie of that wretched life, her selfe she hong.

(II, x, 27–32)

It will be observed that Spenser's story is not quite Geoffrey's. In particular he makes Cordelia's sisters almost excusable. As he tells it, they simply grow tired of putting up an elderly relative who outstays his welcome. Their literary plunge into evil is due partly to a *Leir* play that preceded Shakespeare's. Tolstoy, who [7] had his knife into Shakespeare, preferred it. Like Spenser the anonymous author leaves out the trouble over Leir's attendants, but he invents deeper wickedness.

Shakespeare may have drawn inspiration from all these precursors and from Geoffrey himself. His own *King Lear*, of course, rises to heights of language, passion and imagination beyond the range of any of them. Among his added themes are the sub-plot of Gloucester and his sons, the king's madness, and the terrible conclusion. *King Lear* has a titanic quality which led Charles Lamb to the opinion that it cannot be acted. It can, though perhaps it could not in the theatre of Lamb's day. For many years it was judged too harrowing for audiences. In 1681 Nahum Tate (author of 'While shepherds watched their flocks by night', and afterwards laureate) concocted a softened version that replaced it on the stage.

Tate reworks the plot and cuts many speeches, but also adds new ones of his [8] own. His chief innovation is to portray Cordelia as in love with Edgar, Gloucester's legitimate son, who becomes more prominent. One object is to make the fairy-tale opening 'realistic': Cordelia offends her father on purpose, to avoid an unwanted marriage of state. She remains in Britain but keeps Edgar at

**48. 'Cordelia's Portion', from
a painting by Ford Madox
Brown of Lear handing over
his rejected daughter to the
King of France.**

arm's length to test his constancy till about half-way through, when he has saved
her from ruffians hired by his brother Edmund, with a view to raping her. Tate
eliminates the Fool and the invasion, but he moves the action towards its close
with a rebellion in which Lear and Cordelia are taken prisoner. When they are
about to be murdered, by Goneril's order, Edgar rushes in again as their rescuer
and scares off the assassins:

> Death! Hell! Ye Vultures hold your impious Hands,
> Or take a speedier Death than you wou'd give . . .

The evil-doers meet their doom, much as in the original, and the king is
restored, but he lets Cordelia take over the government, electing to end his days
in some peaceful retreat. One might applaud him for not trying yet again to
impose himself on a daughter, but the point is unlikely to have occurred to Tate.
Lear gives his blessing to the lovers, and Edgar, as in Shakespeare, has the last
word. Not the same last word:

> Divine Cordelia, all the Gods can witness
> How much thy Love to Empire I prefer!
> Thy bright Example shall convince the World
> (Whatever Storms of Fortune are decreed)
> That Truth and Vertue shall at last succeed.

Curiously enough, Nahum Tate, with his derided happy ending, is closer to the primary version. Geoffrey does restore the king. Even in Shakespeare – it is easy to overlook – the restoration happens, but only for a few seconds. Speaking as the residual holder of authority, Albany says:

> We will resign,
> During the life of this old majesty,
> To him our absolute power.

Lear, however, intent on the dead Cordelia, does not respond and dies himself a moment later. Tate preserves his life and royal dignity, and allows Cordelia to reign, being more like Geoffrey in both respects. True, Shakespeare gives the third daughter a tragic fate and so does Geoffrey, but with the older author this is quite separate, not part of her father's vicissitudes. Despite the nephews' dislike of being ruled by a woman, she has ruled for a full five years, with the acquiescence of most Britons. Her reign is another hint at a knowledge of Celtic queenship on Geoffrey's part, though, like Gwendolen, she would actually be pre-Celtic.

1. GM (1), 19–22, and (2), 81–7.
2. Bromwich, 427–9.
3. Rolleston, 139–42.
4. Ekwall, 294, art. 'Leicester';
   Westwood, 195–7.
5. Ashe (7), 22.
6. Bromwich, 429; Piggott (2), 278;
   Tatlock, 381–2; Westwood, 196.
7. *Leir*, ed. cit.
8. Spencer, 241–52.

18 *The End of Brutus's Line*

1   When Cordelia was gone, the two nephews who had deposed her divided the kingdom. That contrivance endured for only two years. Marganus tried to overturn it. Cunedagius, however, pursued and slew him at a place in Wales which is still called Margam after him, and then, for thirty-three creditable years, reigned as sole monarch. During that time Rome was founded by Romulus and Remus, and Isaiah prophesied in Jerusalem. Cunedagius was followed by his son Rivallo, and he by five very minor kings: his own son Gurgustius, then a relative named Sisillius, then a nephew of Gurgustius, then a son of Sisillius, and lastly Gorboduc.

2   By his wife Judon, Gorboduc had two sons, Ferrex and Porrex. When he was old they began quarrelling over the succession. Porrex, unscrupulous and ambitious, plotted to ambush his brother and assassinate him. Ferrex got wind of the scheme and escaped to Gaul. Returning with foreign support, he tried to re-establish himself in Britain, but this time Porrex did manage to kill him.

Porrex had reckoned without their mother. Ferrex had been Judon's favourite son, and his death unbalanced her mind. For Porrex she now felt nothing but hatred. When he was asleep, she burst into his room with her maidservants, and together they hacked him to pieces. By that time Gorboduc was a senile nonentity, and his own demise passed almost unnoticed. Neither Ferrex nor Porrex left an heir, so, in squalor and murder, the original British dynasty petered out.

Geoffrey borrowed the name Cunedagius from a Welsh genealogy, and Rivallo perhaps from a Breton one, belonging properly to periods long after this. Rome was founded in 753 BC, according to its own traditions, and Isaiah was active from about 747. Cunedagius's thirty-three-year kingship lies somewhere in the range 780 to 720, and Brutus's direct royal descendants fade from the scene in the seventh century BC or the early sixth. Not counting Ferrex and Porrex, since it is not stated that either reigned, there have been eighteen sovereigns altogether. So far as the average reign can be calculated, it works out as very like the historical English average for the eighteen from William the Conqueror – that is, about twenty-three years. Geoffrey's flights of dynastic fancy can be thoughtful, even, after their fashion, plausible. Also, to his credit, he is aware that any real monarchy, however noble its origins, would have had phases of decline and disaster. Such a phase starts with Gorboduc.

This sordid family mayhem was chosen by two Elizabethan poets, Thomas Sackville and Thomas Norton, as the subject of the first tragedy in English.

3   Their collaborative *Ferrex and Porrex*, better known re-titled as *Gorboduc*, was presented in 1561 and had a performance before the Queen. In its didactic intent the play resembles *A Mirror for Magistrates*, to which, it will be recalled, Sackville contributed. Modelled on Roman dramas by Seneca, it is extremely

49. Brutus, his wife
Imogen, and their
three sons.

static. The undeveloped blank verse remains rigid. Acts are prefaced with dumb
shows meant to underline major points, and brought to an end with choric
comments. Apart from these, nothing happens on stage but talk, with many
speeches too long and rhetorical for real dialogue. Violent action is reported,
not shown.

The authors make Gorboduc more like Leir. Though warned of trouble by
his secretary, Eubulus, he delegates regional powers to his two sons to train
them for government. Ferrex's domain extends to the Humber, Porrex has the
north. Once parted, they begin to harbour resentments and suspicions. Ferrex,

¶ The Tragidie of Ferrex
and Porrex,
set forth without addition or alte-
ration but altogether as the same was shewed
on stage before the Queenes Maiestie,
about nine yeares past, *vz.* the
xviij. day of Ianuarie. 1561.
by the gentlemen of the
Inner Temple.

Seen and allowed. &c.

Imprinted at London by
Iohn Daye, dwelling ouer
Aldersgate.

50. Title-page of a printed copy of *Ferrex and Porrex*, the first tragedy in English.

as heir-apparent, cannot see why Porrex has been given so much, and Porrex is aware of the ill-feeling that is building up. The plan of the play is symmetrical. Each prince has a sinister companion who insinuates that the other is plotting against him. Ferrex hesitates to take any action, and Porrex strikes first and assassinates him. Summoned before Gorboduc, Porrex professes repentance and pleads his belief that he was in danger. Gorboduc defers judgment and he goes out, but while the king is still talking with his counsellors, one of the queen's ladies enters and reports Judon's killing of her son. It is characteristic of this kind of drama that even in such a crisis, the lady takes time getting to the point:

> Oh where is ruth? or where is pity now?
> Whither is gentle heart and mercy fled?
> Are they exil'd out of our stony breasts,
> Never to make return? is all the world
> Drownèd in blood, and sunk in cruelty?
> If not in women mercy may be found,
> If not, alas, within the mother's breast,
> To her own child, to her own flesh and blood;
> If ruth be banish'd thence, if pity there
> May have no place, if there no gentle heart
> Do live and dwell, where should we seek it then?

Not unnaturally, Gorboduc says:

> Madam, alas, what means your woeful tale?

Even then she takes ten more lines to reach her essential message.

In the last act, we learn that the royal murders have stirred up a rebellion. It has collapsed, but the king and queen are both dead, and in the absence of a recognised heir a great noble is already making a bid for the crown. The line of Brutus is extinct and no provision has been made for the succession. Gorboduc's wise secretary concludes with a prophecy of prolonged civil strife.

Sackville and Norton picked out this ugly episode as illustrating Tudor ideas about order, legitimacy, and the fearful results of dissension in the State – topics destined to be explored on a far larger scale, and with far more dramatic power, in Shakespeare's history plays. Nothing like that could happen till English dramatists had learned all that Seneca could teach them and broken free from the constricting classical structure. Shakespeare himself was the greatest of those who did. Still, he remembered the pioneers. In *Twelfth Night* the Clown replies to a quip by Sir Toby:

> As the old hermit of Prague, that never saw pen and ink, very
> wittily said to a niece of King Gorboduc, 'That that is is' . . .

1. GM (1), 22–3, and (2), 86–8; Tatlock, 68.

2. GM (1), 23, and (2), 88.

3. Sackville, ed. cit.

19 *Molmutius and Marcia*

1 With Gorboduc, Ferrex and Porrex dead, and Judon insane, Britain slid into anarchy. At one stage there were five simultaneous pretenders, all mediocre, but all powerful enough to dominate portions of the island and harass each other. One of the portions was Cornwall. It had been a dukedom under the king of Britain, so long as Britain had a king, but in the course of the troubles it became temporarily independent. Its ruler, Cloten, had a courageous and handsome son, Dunvallo Molmutius, who was the first person of ability to arise from the chaos. When Cloten's death put him in authority he set out to enlarge his domain.

Loegria was held by a king named Pinner. Dunvallo defeated his army and he fell in battle. Rudaucus, King of Cambria, and Staterius, King of Albany, retorted by forming an alliance and marching into the country the Cornish now occupied. Dunvallo challenged them in a battle which, after several indecisive hours, he won by a stratagem. He assembled a picked force of six hundred men. They stripped armour and clothing off the corpses of enemies lying dead on the field, and used these to disguise themselves. Dunvallo led them unopposed to within striking distance of the two kings, and then pounced and slew them both, with many of their followers.

Victorious everywhere, he reunited Britain and had a new golden crown made, to signify that he had re-founded the kingdom. The major achievement of his forty-year reign was a code of laws called, from his second name, the Molmutine Laws. One of them established temples as places of sanctuary, a function eventually taken over by Christian churches. Another forbade the seizure of peasants' ploughs, on the principle that creditors should not be able to deprive debtors of their means of livelihood. The reign was marked by effective measures for the prevention of crime. The Molmutine Laws were written, naturally, in the British language. Long

2 afterwards the historian Gildas translated them into Latin, and later again, Alfred the Great adapted them in English for his own use.

This was not Alfred's only borrowing. A subsequent British king married

3 a gifted noblewoman, Marcia, who ruled after his death. She compiled a supplementary code, which in due course was also Latinised and called after her the *Lex Martiana*. This too Alfred translated, corrupting the name slightly through Anglo-Saxon ignorance: he made it the 'Mercian' Law.

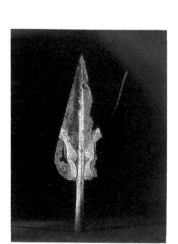

51. Weaponry of Molmutius's time: an iron spear-head embellished with bronze appliqué, from the river-bed of the Thames in London.

These characters owe something to law-givers of mythology and history. Rome had its Numa, Athens its Draco – from whose severity (almost every crime being capital) the word 'Draconian' comes – and the more flexible Solon. Sparta's constitution was said to have been dictated by Apollo through the Delphic Oracle.

Gildas was a real person, a British cleric in the sixth century AD, who wrote a partly historical tract on Britain's post-Roman misfortunes. Alfred the Great reigned over Wessex in the ninth century. But Gildas's translation of British laws, and Alfred's adoption of them for his kingdom, are patriotic inventions of Geoffrey's. Alfred did adopt some laws known as 'Mercian', but the Mercia in question was an English kingdom in the Midlands. Marcia is a fiction supplying a British derivation instead. She illustrates, once again, Geoffrey's possible awareness that a Celtic queen could reign herself and not merely as a consort.

Tudor historians believed in the Molmutine Laws. In *Cymbeline* Shakespeare picks up the name Cloten, though he bestows it on someone else, and he makes Cymbeline recall his distinguished predecessor:

> Mulmutius made our laws,
> Who was the first of Britain which did put
> His brows within a golden crown, and call'd
> Himself a king.

Cymbeline is inexact here, but, after all, Geoffrey's historical revelations still lie in the future for him. The king who re-founded the monarchy after the post-Porrex dissolution is seen as making a fresh start. The indications of date before and after the anarchy show that it must have lasted longer than a casual reader might think, far more than a lifetime, so that continuity would have been broken. Dunvallo Molmutius has to reign in the fifth century BC because his sons are datably in their prime in 390. The phase of change and the fresh start correspond quite well to a real change in Britain, the rise of a recognisable Celtic society. Could Geoffrey somehow have known of this, and reconciled it with Brutus by presenting it as a re-foundation and inventing a previous dynasty to bridge the gap? Roman legend did something like this to accommodate the long lapse of time between Aeneas and the foundation of Rome.

The relation of the new royal house to the old is not made clear. But all the contending kings, including Dunvallo's father, would doubtless have claimed legitimacy through some tie of blood with the progeny of Brutus, however remote. That is Spenser's interpretation (II,x,36), and it agrees with Brutus's status as the ultimate royal ancestor. *Gorboduc* is more specific: the first pretender is the duke of Albany, a descendant, presumably, of Gonorilla and thus of Leir.

1. GM (1), 23–4, and (2), 88–90.
2. GM (1), 26–7, and (2), 94; Tatlock, 279.
3. GM (1), 31, and (2), 101; Tatlock, 283.
4. Holinshed, 451.

20 *Belinus and Brennius*

1   Dunvallo Molmutius left two sons, Belinus and Brennius, both of whom laid claim to the throne. Their quarrel led to bloodshed and had to be settled by arbitration. Belinus became king, with Brennius subject to him, ruling as a regional overlord from the Humber to Britain's northern extremity. (The Picts had not yet arrived there.)

After five years of peace, Brennius was persuaded by evil counsellors to plan a breach of the treaty. He strengthened his position by going to Norway and marrying its king's daughter. Belinus realised what his brother was doing, and struck first by occupying Northumbria. Brennius sailed for home with his bride and a Norwegian army. On the way his fleet was attacked by the Danish king, who loved the princess and captured the ship that was carrying her. A shift in the wind drove the Dane to Northumbria, where, together with the princess, he fell into Belinus's hands. When Brennius disembarked, demanding his wife, Belinus's troops routed the Norwegians, Brennius fled to Gaul without her, and the Dane was allowed to take her home with him.

Belinus, now undisputed sovereign, reviewed and ratified the laws decreed by his father. He embarked on a programme of road-building. The first of his paved highways ran from Cornwall to Caithness, linking a series of inland cities. The second ran from St David's in Wales to Southampton. Two more crossed Britain diagonally. All were governed by a highway code for the safety of travellers, which Belinus appended to the Molmutine Laws. Any act of violence committed on them was sternly punished.

Meanwhile, the exiled Brennius was ingratiating himself in Gaul. Vengeful and turbulent as he was, he could exert charm, and his fine presence and skill at hunting and hawking endeared him to Segnius, the old duke of the Allobroges. He married again, Segnius's daughter this time, and succeeded to the dukedom himself. With an army of Allobroges, whose goodwill he had bought by sharing out the ducal treasure, he returned to Britain. A new clash with Belinus was imminent, but their mother Tonwenna was still living, and her passionate appeals persuaded Brennius to abandon thoughts of revenge. The brothers were reconciled.

After another spell of peace, they crossed the Channel with a combined British-Allobrogian force and subdued the Gauls. They pressed on into Italy. The Roman consuls bought them off and they withdrew northwards. Then the Romans changed their minds and prepared to attack them. Brennius marched to Rome and besieged it, Belinus arrived with reinforcements, and the Britons took and plundered the city.

Brennius stayed in Italy. Belinus went back to Britain and ruled tranquilly for the rest of his life. He restored towns that had fallen into disrepair, and founded a new one on the banks of the Usk in Gwent. This was the place that became, during the Roman occupation, the Legion City – Caerleon. Also, he improved New Troy with a magnificent gateway. On top of it was a

tower, at the foot was a water-gate giving access to the Thames. It was called after the king himself, Belinesgata. The name, as Billingsgate, survives to this day. Belinus's reign during his last years was just, pacific and prosperous. The Britons had never been so wealthy before. On his decease he was cremated, and a golden urn holding his ashes was set on top of the tower of Billingsgate.

52. Amphitheatre at Caerleon, where remains of large structures, actually Roman, suggested an ancient British city.

53. Bronze figure of a
Celtic warrior, found
in Italy and probably
made during the period
of Celtic invasions.

Geoffrey's story of the brothers' Roman campaign supplies one of his few good chronological fixes in the early period. He refers readers desiring more details to Roman history, and there they can be found, after a fashion. In a year which he would have taken as 390 BC (it may have been a little later) Rome did fall to a Celtic army, and was looted and set on fire. Moreover the army's leader was Brennus. The Celts in question, however, were Gauls who had settled in the Po valley and were making a temporary thrust southwards. Geoffrey turns their victory into an exploit by a British king, partly perhaps to set a precedent, which a greater British king will invoke later.

The Brennus who captured Rome was probably named after a god figuring in   2
other contexts as Bran, the Raven. Geoffrey takes Brennus over with a slightly altered spelling and a changed nationality, and supplies him with a brother. Belinus is a god himself, a Celtic one, humanised. Inscriptions testify to a cult of   3
Belinus or Belenos in northern Italy and southern Gaul, and Britain has traces of it. The druidic spring festival,' Beltain, may have some connection with him. Welsh legends introduce a Beli Mawr – Beli the Great – or 'Beli, son of Manogan', who is the same. He stands at the head of pedigrees of Welsh royal houses, as an ancestor-deity like the Woden from whom, in later times, most of the Saxon kings traced their descent. Beli is made out to be Bran's grandfather or uncle. He cannot be pinned down historically even when he appears in a human guise. Sometimes he belongs to an immemorial past, sometimes he is a kinsman of the Virgin Mary, sometimes he rules over Britain in the first century BC . . . or in the fourth century AD. The *History of the Britons* by 'Nennius' has 'Bellinus, son of Minocan' as king of Britain in Julius Caesar's time, getting the name closer to its divine original, as Geoffrey does.

Belinus's roads do not correspond to the Roman ones. That part of his career has not been concocted to account for them. In this respect he differs from another road-builder, Elen Luyddog, who comes on the legendary scene seven centuries later.

The Allobroges lived in southern Gaul and have a minor role in the history of republican Rome. But to judge from other passages, when Geoffrey says 'Allobroges' he means Burgundians. The Burgundians did not actually settle in   4
Gaul till long afterwards. However, they took over Allobrogian territory. The anachronism is on the same lines as Geoffrey's introduction of Norwegians, Franks, and other nationalities that do not belong. He feels free to refer to the inhabitants of an area by the name of any people who lived in that area, irrespective of when they did.

Place-names with 'Billing' in them are scattered widely. The etymology is   5
more likely to be Anglo-Saxon than British.

1. GM (1), 24–30, and (2), 90–100.
2. Ashe (7), 23–4; Bromwich, 284; Chadwick (2), 102, 131.
3. Bromwich, 281–3; Chadwick (2), 131–3, 196; Piggott (2), 279; Ross, 83, 472.
4. Tatlock, 100.
5. Ekwall, 43.

21 *The Royal Welsh*

Welshmen tell of a prince of ancient days named Pryderi. In tracing his career they tell of other famous men of his time, and women.

(1)

1   Pryderi's father was Pwyll, ruler of Dyfed in south-west Wales. Some years before his son's birth he was out hunting one day, when he encountered another hunt. A stag was brought down in his sight by a pack of luminous white hounds with red ears. He drove them away and took the stag himself.

54. Hounds pursuing a stag.

Then their owner appeared. He was Arawn, Lord of Annwfn, the Otherworld, and he was angry to see what Pwyll had done. Pwyll promised to make amends. Arawn decreed that they should change places for a year, and Pwyll, while in Annwfn, should slay an enemy of his. To effect this he magically changed Pwyll into his own likeness, and himself into Pwyll's.

Pwyll took up the lordship of Annwfn. When he slept with Arawn's wife he had no sexual relations with her, out of respect for the husband he was impersonating. In due course he slew Arawn's enemy. The two reverted to their normal appearance. But Arawn's wife accused him of neglect over the past year, and he had to tell her what had happened. He was much moved to hear of his substitute's honourable conduct, and Pwyll, for his part, learned that the disguised Arawn had governed Dyfed well. They became fast friends and Pwyll was given the title 'Head of Annwfn'.

One day he was at the royal seat of Arberth with his courtiers, and they climbed an enchanted mound. A lady rode by on a majestic white horse. Curious to know who she was, he sent a messenger to ask, but although she rode at a leisurely rate he could not overtake her. On two further days they saw her, and chased her with the swiftest horses they had, yet still she kept pacing gently ahead. At last Pwyll called out to her and she halted at once, saying she had come there expressly to see him. Her name was Rhiannon and she desired his help, because her father was giving her in marriage to a suitor she did not want. Pwyll, entranced by her beauty and bearing, offered to marry her himself.

On an appointed day he came to her father's court with a retinue. While everyone was drinking, the unwelcome suitor entered, a lord of great lands named Gwawl. Pwyll did not realise who he was, and Gwawl, by asking a boon without making its nature clear, tricked him into surrendering Rhiannon. She reproached Pwyll for his stupidity, but promised to save the situation. She gave him a small magical bag. He was to go to the wedding feast disguised as a beggar and ask Gwawl to fill the bag with food. It would grow larger and be impossible to fill. Pwyll should explain that it could only be filled if 'a true possessor of great dominion' got into it, stamped down the contents, and said 'Enough'.

The day came and all turned out as predicted. Gwawl, urged by Rhiannon, climbed into the bag. Pwyll tied up the mouth and summoned men he had kept in hiding, and they kicked and struck Gwawl. This was the origin of a game, Badger in the Bag. At last they released their victim, who emerged saying he was bruised and needed a bath, and would go his way. Thus Pwyll won Rhiannon.

Presently she bore a son. Her attendant women fell asleep, and when they woke, the boy had vanished. Fearing punishment, the women accused Rhiannon of killing him, and Pwyll's nobles were convinced. Pwyll was not, but admitted that *if* his wife was guilty she should do penance. Scornfully, she accepted the penance of sitting daily at the gate near a horse-block, telling her story to anyone who cared to hear it, and offering to carry guests to the court on her back.

Meanwhile Teyrnon of Gwent, a former vassal of Pwyll's, had seen a mysterious apparition and found a child on his doorstep. After fostering him for some time he heard of Rhiannon's penance and judged from the resemblance that the child was the one Pwyll had lost. Teyrnon took him to the court. Rhiannon cried out that she was 'delivered of her care', and the boy was named Pryderi (Care). Teyrnon went home rewarded, and Pryderi grew up handsome and accomplished. After Pwyll's death he married a noble lady called Cigfa, enlarged Dyfed, and ruled with credit.

(2)

About this time Bran, son of Llyr – Bran the Blessed as he was known – rose to be supreme king of Britain, the Island of the Mighty. One day he was at Harlech with his kinsfolk, among them a brother by the name of Efnisien, a strange, half-crazy person and a trouble-maker. Matholwch, King of Ireland, sailed in with a fleet of thirteen ships. He asked for the hand of Bran's sister Branwen, and proposed an alliance. This was agreed, and Bran, Branwen and Matholwch went to Aberffraw in Anglesey with their followers for the wedding. They sat down to feast in tents: Bran, a giant, had never been contained in a house.

Efnisien, however, was affronted at Bran's consenting to the marriage without consulting him. Next day he maimed the Irish horses. Matholwch, taking no leave, set off in a fury to return to Ireland. When Bran heard what had happened he sent messengers after the king, offering to replace the horses and to present him with a gold plate and a silver staff, in token of reparation. The Irish retraced their steps, but Matholwch remained cool. Bran increased his offer, giving the king a magical cauldron with the power of regeneration. If a man who had been slain was quickly placed in it, he would revive intact, except that he would not be able to speak. Matholwch accepted the gifts and asked where the cauldron had come from. Bran confessed that it was Irish in the first place and had belonged to another giant. Matholwch knew who he meant: he had once tried to execute this giant by shutting him with his wife in an iron-walled room and heating it, but they had burst out and gone to Britain.

Matholwch went home with his bride. At first she was treated with all honour. She bore a son, Gwern. But Irish resentment over the horses rumbled on, and the king's nobles threatened trouble unless he allowed vengeance to be taken on Branwen. He gave way, and she was forced to work in the kitchen, where she was roughly handled. The nobles imposed a ban on travel to and from Wales, so that Bran would not hear what was going on.

After a long time, Branwen managed to send him a message by tying it to a trained starling. He assembled an army (Pryderi was in it) and set out for Ireland, leaving a council of seven in charge in Britain, headed by his son Caradawg. The army sailed across the sea, but the giant Bran waded. In those days there was little deep water between the islands. It grew wide only afterwards when the ocean encroached. The Irish king's swineherds were the first to sight the Britons. They told him a mountain and a forest were approaching over the water. The mountain was Bran, the trees were the masts of his ships.

Judging resistance to be futile, Matholwch offered to abdicate and assign the kingship of Ireland to his young son Gwern, who, of course, was Bran's nephew. Bran hesitated. The Irish paid him a peculiar honour, or what appeared to be so, by building a house big enough to hold him. Branwen, alarmed at the prospect of war, persuaded him to accept and occupy half the house with his folk, while Matholwch and his warriors occupied the other half. The Irish planned a ruse, concealing more men in what purported to be sacks of flour. In this case Bran's unbalanced brother Efnisien was helpful. He discovered the plot and thwarted it. Bran, unaware of any intended treachery, agreed to Matholwch's peace proposals. Britons and Irish entered the house and Gwern was made king of Ireland. However, Efnisien's evil propensity suddenly took possession of him, and he thrust the boy into the fire. Branwen tried to save him, but her brother saw that it was hopeless and restrained her.

Fighting broke out. The Irish gained the upper hand, because they had recovered the cauldron and their dead kept reviving. Efnisien repented at last and smashed the cauldron, dying in the process. It was too late. The Irish were all slain, but only nine Britons were left – Branwen, seven warriors (among them Pryderi, and Manawydan, another brother of Bran), and Bran himself; and the king had been mortally wounded in the foot with a poisoned spear.

He told his companions to cut his head off and take it back with them to Britain. They should keep it at Harlech, where it would remain uncorrupted and they would live in happy enchantment for seven years, with three birds that belonged to Pryderi's mother Rhiannon singing to them. Then they

BRANWEN VERCH LLYR.

LLYMA YR EIL GEINC OR MABINOGI.

must take the head to a royal hall at Gwales in Penfro, and there they would remain eighty years. But eventually one of them would open a door on the side towards Cornwall, and then the spell would snap, and they should carry the head to London and bury it on the White Mount with its face towards the continent.

When they reached Britain, Branwen mourned at the loss which two kingdoms had suffered on her account. She died broken-hearted and they buried her by the river Alaw in Anglesey. On the road to Harlech they learned that Caswallawn, son of Beli, had made himself king of Britain. He had attacked Bran's regency council wearing a cloak of invisibility, so that

55. Nineteenth-century illustration of the Irish giant with his cauldron (the title means 'Branwen daughter of Llyr', designating the Second Branch of the Mabinogi).

56. Harlech Castle, on the site of Bran's stronghold.

only his sword was seen, and at the sight of the weapon in the air, felling his colleagues, Caradawg had died of shock.

Bran's companions went on to Harlech and made their home there as he had told them to do. The birds of Rhiannon sang to them across the water, and with the head and the unearthly music they remained in spellbound bliss for the seven years Bran had prophesied. Then they went on to Gwales and were there eighty years, and this was called the Assembly of the Wondrous Head. At last one of them did open the door on the side facing Cornwall, and all their grief came upon them, and they set off on the final journey and buried the head in London on the White Mount. There it protected Britain against afflictions from overseas.

(3)

When the task was done, Bran's brother Manawydan looked sadly around   3
him, and heaved a sigh. He had no home, no territory, nowhere to go.
Pryderi invited him to Dyfed and suggested he should marry the widowed
Rhiannon. Despite the eighty-seven years, Pryderi's mother was still living
and no older, and so was his wife Cigfa, and so was the usurper Caswallawn,
and indeed everything was much as before: an enigma not to be fathomed.
They went to Dyfed, where Manawydan and Rhiannon agreed well
together, and the marriage took place. Pryderi made his peace with
Caswallawn and did homage to him at Oxford. Seemingly secure, the
two couples, Pryderi with Cigfa and Manawydan with Rhiannon, lived
contentedly.

When they were at Arberth, they walked together one evening to the
mound where Pryderi's father had first seen Rhiannon. While they were
sitting on it there was a clap of thunder, and a fog swept across the land.
After it cleared no living thing was in sight, human or animal, except the
four themselves. They hurried back to the royal residence and searched. All
the rooms were empty.

For more than a year they roamed about Dyfed, finding no people or
flocks or herds, only wild beasts. They still had their pack of hounds, and
hunting and fishing gave them food. But at length Manawydan exclaimed,
'We cannot live thus!' He persuaded the others to move with him to
Lloegyr, England as it now is. There, life was going on. In Hereford,
Manawydan set up as a saddle-maker and trained Pryderi as his assistant.
They were so skilful that the other saddlers lost business, and conspired
against them with murderous intent. Pryderi wanted to kill these dis-
gruntled rivals, but Manawydan insisted that they should leave quietly. The
four moved on to another town, where Manawydan studied shields and
they tried shield-making, with the same result. Again Pryderi favoured a
counter-attack, but Manawydan said it would get them into trouble with
Caswallawn, and they should move on again without complaining. In a
third town Manawydan tried shoemaking, on the ground that shoemakers
were peaceful. Versatile as ever, he taught Pryderi the craft. They came to an
arrangement with a goldsmith, who made buckles for the shoes till Manawydan learned to make them himself. Therefore Manawydan is called one
of the three golden shoemakers of Britain. But when his excellence
threatened the other shoemakers they proved no more peaceable than the
previous craftsmen, and despite Pryderi's protests the four returned to
Dyfed and supported themselves as they had before.

One morning Pryderi and Manawydan were out hunting when a white
boar lured their hounds into a strange fortification they had never seen,
though they knew the area. The hounds failed to emerge, and Pryderi,
against Manawydan's advice, went in to look for them. Inside he found
neither boar nor pack. He did find a fountain, with a slab of marble beside it,
and on the slab a great golden bowl attached to chains, which rose into the
air and were suspended from nothing. Pryderi stepped on to the slab and laid
his hands on the bowl, and was promptly transfixed. His hands stuck to the
bowl and his feet stuck to the marble, and he lost the power of speech.

Manawydan waited for hours, and finally went back to the women and told his tale. Rhiannon commented: 'A bad comrade hast thou been, a good comrade hast thou lost.' Going to the place herself, she entered the fortification and found her son, bewitched. She laid hold of the bowl and was bewitched herself. At nightfall, thunder pealed and the building vanished, and Pryderi and Rhiannon with it. Manawydan and Cigfa were left alone. He assured her that he would respect her as Pryderi's wife and they considered what to do. Desolated, without even hounds to hunt with, they went to Lloegyr again and Manawydan set up again as a shoemaker, but again the resentment of other shoemakers drove them back to Dyfed and Arberth.

This time Manawydan tried farming. Swarms of mice kept eating his wheat crop. He caught a very large one and tied it up in a glove, and told Cigfa he would hang it. She thought this unworthy of him, but he went to the mound and prepared a miniature gallows. While he was busy, a clerk approached on his way back from Lloegyr – the first human that Manawydan had seen in Dyfed for seven years, apart from his own companions. The clerk, like Cigfa, told him the hanging was unseemly and offered him a pound to let the mouse go. He refused and the clerk passed on. Then a priest rode up and made the same request, offering three pounds. Again he refused and the priest departed.

Just as he was fixing a noose around the animal's neck, a bishop arrived with several attendants, and horses loaded with baggage. The bishop offered seven pounds, then twenty-four, then the horses and the goods they were carrying. Finally he asked what Manawydan did want as the price of sparing the mouse. Sensing that he was close to the heart of the mystery, Manawydan replied that he wanted Rhiannon and Pryderi back, and the spell lifted from Dyfed. The bishop promised this if the mouse were set free, and explained that it was his wife.

Now the truth came out. The bishop, or rather disguised enchanter, said his name was Llwyd and he had cast the spell on Dyfed to avenge the mistreatment of Gwawl, Rhiannon's rejected suitor, so long ago. To persecute Manawydan, as Pryderi's friend, he had turned his retainers into mice, and his wife and other women too when they asked to join in. Because she was pregnant Manawydan had caught her. Now, for her freedom, he would restore Pryderi and Rhiannon and lift the spell. Manawydan pressed a hard bargain, stipulating that Llwyd must never do the same again or take vengeance. All was granted and the vanished mother and son reappeared. They had been kept prisoner in the enchanter's court. Llwyd touched the mouse with a wand and they saw a fair young woman. Around them the land was inhabited again.

(4)

4   Pryderi reigned in prosperity over his restored realm. He met his death at last through an intrigue in North Wales. Math, King of Gwynedd, was a magician. This did not preserve him from a strange infirmity. His feet had to be held in a maiden's lap, and he could leave her only when war required his personal presence. The itinerant work of government was handled by two deputies, his nephews Gwydion and Gilfaethwy, the sons of Don. Gwydion too had magic powers, and was also an unrivalled story-teller, able to keep

audiences enthralled. His brother Gilfaethwy conceived a passion for Math's current foot-holder, Goewin. Since she was always with the king he had no idea what to do. To add to his problems, one of Math's magical gifts was that he could hear even whispers a long way off, and it was hard to keep anything secret from him.

Gwydion devised a scheme. Pryderi, as it happened, had lately acquired an incomparable herd of swine. They were a present from his father's friend Arawn, the lord of Annwfn. Gwydion gave Math a glowing account of these otherworldly beasts, and the king wondered if he could get them for himself. With his approval, Gwydion and Gilfaethwy set off southward with ten companions and entered Pryderi's court, posing as bards. Pryderi received them cordially and, in the evening, suggested that his courtiers would enjoy hearing a tale. Gwydion entertained the assembly till the atmosphere was friendly on all sides. Then he made his request. Pryderi was reluctant to part with the pigs before they had bred offspring he could keep. Gwydion, however, magically created some splendid but illusory horses and greyhounds, and an exchange was effected. The brothers left with the pigs.

By the time they got back to Gwynedd, the phantasmal horses and hounds had vanished, and Pryderi knew he had been tricked. He was already marching north with a military force. Since war was in prospect, Math's feet did not have to be held, and he left to lead his army. Gwydion's object was achieved. Goewin was alone in the royal bed, and Gilfaethwy raped her. Next day the brothers went to join Math. A battle was fought among the mountains. The southerners retreated and a truce was agreed, with the understanding that Pryderi would meet Gwydion in single combat, since it was he who had caused all the trouble. Partly by his strength, partly by his arts, Gwydion conquered and Pryderi was slain.

The men of Dyfed went sadly home, the men of Gwynedd returned rejoicing. With the war disposed of, Math was putting his feet in Goewin's lap again, when she confessed she was no longer a virgin and therefore could not serve as his foot-holder. She explained about the rape. Math gave such redress as he could by marrying her. Gwydion and Gilfaethwy had judged it prudent to go on an official tour, but Math cut off their supplies and forced them to come back. He told them there was no way they could make amends for the offence against Goewin and himself and, even worse, the death of Pryderi. However, he would punish them.

Striking them with his magic wand, he transformed them into a stag and a hind, and sent them away to couple. A year later they returned with their offspring, a male fawn. Math turned the fawn into a boy, as it properly was, and turned his nephews into a wild boar and a sow, reversing their previous sexes. A year later they reappeared with a male piglet, and this too the king gave human shape. Lastly he changed the pair into wolves, again with a sexual transposition, and did the same with the resulting cub. He was now satisfied. The guilty brothers had been put through a shameful ordeal, and the three boys would be true champions making up for Gilfaethwy's falsity. Math touched his nephews with his wand and they were human once more.

At this time Math was in need of a new foot-holder. Gwydion recommended a daughter of Don, Aranrhod. Math subjected her to a virginity test and, mysteriously, she gave birth to two sons. Both were separated from her. Gwydion took charge of the second and treated him as a son of his own,

57. The White Tower
in the Tower of
London, where Bran's
head was buried.

but left him nameless. After some years he brought him to Aranrhod. She resented the boy and inflicted three adverse destinies. He should not have a name till she gave him one, he should not bear arms till she equipped him, and he should not have a wife 'of the race that is now on the earth'.

Gwydion circumvented these dooms by magic. The boy was called Lleu, 'Fair' or 'Bright', and when he grew up Gwydion and Math created a non-human wife for him, Blodeuedd, meaning 'Flowers', these being their ingredients. Blodeuedd, however, took a lover, a chief named Gronw. The pair plotted to kill Lleu. He had a charmed life, and could be killed only under peculiar conditions. Blodeuedd learned what they were and tricked him into fulfilling them. Gronw threw a spear at him. He was struck and wounded but not slain, and changed into an eagle and flew away. With much trouble Gwydion traced him to an oak-tree, and brought him back to humanity and health. Gwydion turned Blodeuedd into an owl and told her she should henceforth be called Blodeuwedd (*blodeuwedd*, 'flower-face', is an old Welsh word for an owl). Lleu killed her lover.

Pwyll and the rest figure in four Welsh tales constituting the Four Branches of the Mabinogi, the first part of the collection known, through a misunderstanding, as the *Mabinogion*. The word *mabinogi* is related to *mab* meaning 'son' or 'youth', and may once have referred to a corpus of myth about Maponus, the Divine Youth who was worshipped as a British Apollo and became, in Welsh tradition, the hero Mabon. It was applied to the birth, youth and adventures of other heroes, and the nucleus of the Four Branches is a saga of Pryderi, though this has been heavily overlaid with other material. Pryderi may be a very distant prototype of the Arthurian knight Perceval.

In their present form the Four Branches are the work of a single author in the eleventh century. That is, they are slightlier earlier than Geoffrey of Monmouth, so that notions peculiarly his, such as calling ancient London 'New Troy', play no part. Much of the matter is far earlier still, and pre-Christian. The events are supposed to happen a long time ago, but are really dateless. Since the author begins with Pryderi's father, and ends with people who knew Pryderi himself, the period covered cannot be enormous. However, the period itself is all in an indeterminate once-upon-a-time.

The story of Bran and Branwen illustrates the datelessness. The narrow sea between Britain and Ireland would put it a very long way back. An appendix declares, unexpectedly, that the war almost depopulated Ireland and five survivors created its five provinces (Ulster, Connacht, Leinster, and East and West Munster, or, according to another account, Munster and Meath). This too has a whiff of antiquity, but not such extreme antiquity. The iron room episode implies the Iron Age, not Stone or Bronze. If Bran's father Llyr is the same as the Irish Lir, as he probably is, he belongs somewhere about 500 BC. But the usurper Caswallawn is Cassivellaunus, the British king who fought Julius Caesar in 54 BC; here he is mythified as a son of Beli and lifted out of any serious context. Aberffraw, the scene of Branwen's wedding, had a royal residence. Excavation, however, has indicated that this was a Roman fort, partially rebuilt for the kings of Gwynedd in the fifth or sixth century of the Christian era.

These linked tales are a literary creation using elements extending over a long stretch of time. Wherever we try to pin the action down there will be anachronisms. It is rooted, nevertheless, in Celtic antiquity, and pictured as taking place in a pre-Roman milieu. The main substance is Celtic myth, edited and re-thought by Celtic Christians, on whom their religion may have sat rather lightly, and who may even have been uncertain as to when it originated. Despite scattered allusions to God, to clergy, and to a form of baptism, there is no hint throughout Pryderi's lifetime that Britain has churches, that the weddings are Christian ceremonies, or indeed that the characters have the slightest inkling of Christianity. The religious allusions may quite well be meant to refer to the old religion; the author would not have known much about it.

One result of rehandling over the years is that changes and excisions have sometimes obscured the story. It is not clear how Pwyll's sojourn in Annwfn – the Celtic Otherworld, a sort of parallel universe, not a heaven or hell – is connected with the rest. Nor is it clear who stole Rhiannon's baby, or why it should have been deposited at Teyrnon's door. But in the latter case the loss of a 8 mythic factor is manifest. 'Teyrnon' is a Welsh form of the British *Tigernonos*, Great King. When we realize that 'Rhiannon' is *Rigantona*, Great Queen, the plot may be said to thicken.

9   Whoever Teyrnon is, or once was, Rhiannon is a British counterpart of the Gaulish goddess Epona. She is re-interpreted in human terms, yet not wholly deprived of superhuman attributes. Epona was worshipped not only among the Celts of Gaul but in Rome itself, as *Regina*, the Queen. She is portrayed with horses – her Roman devotees were cavalry soldiers – and the Uffington White Horse, and the similar figures on British coins, may have had some connection with her British equivalent. That equivalent, as Rhiannon, makes her entry on a wonderful horse and has equine associations later, such as her doom of giving rides to strangers. Epona is represented with birds as well as horses, and with a bag or cornucopia. Rhiannon has both. Her birds are mentioned in another *Mabinogion* tale, *Culhwch and Olwen*, where they are reputed to wake the dead and lull the living to sleep. The wafting of their song over the sea suggests that they live in an island-paradise, a recurrent theme of Celtic mythology.

Bran is the god who underlies Geoffrey's Brennius. Like Rhiannon, he is semi-humanised. Only 'semi' because of his huge size, though, like other giants, he expands and contracts. (Even Rabelais' Gargantua sits in an ordinary chair after a visit to the enchantress Morgan le Fay.) Bran's demotion from godhead, yet survival in kingship, is a further instance of Celtic Christian remoulding of 10   the pantheon, and his label 'blessed' – *bendigeit*, i.e. the Latin *benedictus* – looks like a specific Christian touch. Yet nothing in the tale explains it, and it may be adapted from a pagan epithet beginning *pen*, 'head'. The saga of Bran's head is derived from a Celtic cult of heads which is well attested by archaeology.

The themes of the marvellous vessel and the wound reappear in romances of the Grail. Bran may be the prototype of a character Bron who is sometimes the Grail's custodian in Britain. His name, as noted, means 'Raven'. The White 11   Mount where his head is buried is Tower Hill, and the motif of talismanic protection survives in the legend that the monarchy will endure as long as the Tower has ravens in it. The actual head is no longer there, because of a sequel in Arthur's time.

12   Bran's sister's name is properly 'Bronwen', 'white breast'. Its first vowel has been changed for the sake of the echo with 'Bran'. Anglesey has a cromlech called *Bedd Bronwen*, Bronwen's Grave. An eighteenth-century antiquary adds to the chronological confusion by saying that her father Llyr began to reign in the year 3105 from Creation, 899 BC. In 1813 an urn was dug up at Bronwen's Grave containing calcined bones of a young woman.

58. Epona, the horse-goddess, Rhiannon's original: a German portrayal.

Bran, in his divine origin, is the same as an Irish Bran who is likewise a theme of adventure and enchantment: both characters derive from the one Celtic deity. A similar background can be inferred for Bran's principal brother. Manawydan, son of Llyr, is equivalent to Manannan, son of Lir, an Irish character who began as a sea-god. There is a connection here with the Isle of Man, called Manaw in Welsh, Mana or Manu in Irish. The god underwent change in both versions of his humanisation. Manannan is a Druid, a weather-forecaster, or a craftsman. Manawydan has lost the marine and geographical links, but he too is a craftsman – in this tale, one of Britain's 'golden shoemakers' outdoing all competitors. The reason for his prowess in that particular line lies in a word-play; *Manawyd* meant an awl. 13

Don, the mother of Gwydion, Gilfaethwy and Aranrhod, is also originally divine and cognate with Ireland's mother-goddess Danann. Gwydion is interesting because of his narrative gift. When Pryderi calls for a tale, and Gwydion brilliantly responds, we are getting the only early glimpse of the kind of court story-teller (*cyfarwydd*) who transmitted such tales as these very ones. The story-tellers were not necessarily bards in the professional sense, but they were highly respected and literate entertainers, making creative use of traditional matter. 14 15

The nephews' return to humanity after expiating – so far as they can – the

59. A mythical monster, found in the Rhône Valley, illustrating the Celtic cult of the heads.

deeds leading to Pryderi's death, is properly the end. The sequel was originally separate. Owing to interference with source-material, it is tangled and hard to follow, drifting away from its authentic mythical moorings. These, however, undoubtedly exist. Lleu is a British counterpart of an Irish character, Lug, one of the principal Tuatha De Danann. Underlying both is a Celtic deity, Lugh or Lugus. He seems to have been a patron of craftsmanship. The Irish Lug is a master of many skills and Lleu is nicknamed 'deft-handed' – he is even presented in one episode as a 'golden shoemaker' like Manawydan.

16

17

1. *Mabinogion* (2), 3–24.
2. Ibid, 25–40.
3. Ibid, 41–54.
4. Ibid, 55–75.
5. FML, 388–91; Lacy, ed., art. '*Mabinogi*'; *Mabinogion* (2), xii.
6. Bromwich, 300–1.
7. White, 319–42.
8. *Mabinogion* (2), xv; Ross, 410–1.
9. Lacy, ed., art. '*Mabinogi*'; Rees, 45–6; Ross, 255, 286–90, 338–40.
10. Bromwich, 284–6; Chadwick (2), 102–5, 131–3; Newstead, 13–27; Ross, 155–6.
11. Westwood, 131–4.
12. Bromwich, 287; Westwood, 267–8.
13. Bromwich, 441–3; Rees, 49–50; Rhys, II, 619–20 fn 1.
14. Bromwich, 327; Ross, 290, 453.
15. Bromwich, lxxxiii–lxxxiv, 400-2.
16. Bromwich, 420–2; Rees, 33–5; Ross, 346, 457; Westwood, 293–5.
17. Bromwich, 176–7.

Magic and Secret Lore

22 Gwyn and the Fairy-Folk

The Britons who told of Bran and the rest were conscious of presences other than themselves. These beings inhabited the Otherworld or Underworld which Pryderi's father entered and the Britons' Welsh descendants called Annwfn; but they were not confined to it. Later generations were to know them as Fairy-Folk, and as such they passed into the popular lore of England and Scotland as well as Wales.

All of them are gone now, having withdrawn, perhaps, into their hidden realm. One of their last haunts on the human map was Craig-y-Ddinas in   1
Glamorgan. But they impinged on our world for many centuries, and much is on record about them. They were not the tiny, pretty, butterfly-winged creatures whom children have been invited to believe in. Their existence dated from . . . no one knew when . . . and they were not subject to the same mortality as ourselves. Though normally invisible, they could be seen when they chose to be.

The fairy race was not homogeneous. As classified by humans over the   2
years, it comprised Elves, Pixies, Goblins, and other species. There were wide variations in their looks, from spell-binding beauty to repulsive ugliness. There were wide variations in their size also. Some were like humans, if, on average, smaller. Some however were big; some were no larger than three-year-old children; and some were minute. The Portunes are said to have been only half an inch tall.

Fairies had a language. A medieval Welsh scholar thought it was the   3
language of Brutus's Trojans, from which later forms of British, and thence Welsh, had evolved. Many lived inside hollow hills, portals of entry to their

60. (above) Fairies dancing in a circle, a picture from an old English chapbook.

61. (right) Glastonbury Tor viewed end-on, the home of Gwyn ap Nudd, king of the fairies in Welsh folklore.

Otherworld. This had its own space and time. Humans could be lured into it. The Scottish poet Thomas the Rhymer dwelt underground with an Elf Queen for what he thought was only a few days, but was actually several years. The fairies' world was carefree, for them at least, and even today 'Fairyland' evokes pleasant images. Yet it was dangerous and better avoided. Eating their food could make a human their prisoner, and trouble could follow any attempt to take belongings of theirs outside. They were fond of dancing, especially in circles. At night a wanderer might catch a glimpse of their revels and probably have cause to regret it. 4

One human name for them, 'the good people', was a propitiatory compliment inspired by the uneasy knowledge that they were not good, or not reliably so. They could be mischievous, and far worse than mischievous. They were apt to steal away children for breeding purposes, and leave substitutes or changelings who were stunted, strange, disturbing. When angry they might use magical powers to inflict disease. 5

Fairy influence could be averted. Their special colour was green, and wearing green was an invitation. That is why it has been thought wise for brides to wear other colours. They could be kept friendly or neutral with ritual offerings of food and drink: a cake dropped in the furrow when ploughing, a libation poured on the ground at harvest. As charms against them, objects made of iron were potent. 6 7 8

Yet they could be benevolent. They might live unseen in a fireplace and help with housework, so long as the fireplace was kept clean for them. They could lend farmers wonderful cattle that yielded unending milk. If they took a liking to a child, they could bestow beauty, talent, good luck. Fairy women were known to marry mortal men and to bring them happiness. But most of the benefactions were subject to some taboo, and if this was broken, however trivially, with whatever absence of intent, all was lost. 9

The fairies had kings and queens. The oldest name given to their ruler is Gwyn ap Nudd. Gwyn was an immortal and overlord of Annwfn. (In the *Mabinogion* Arawn has that title, but he may be only Gwyn under another name; it is noteworthy that both have an uncanny pack of white hounds with red ears.) When Christianity was making its way, the sterner clerics denounced all fairies as demons, and Gwyn acquired an ambiguous reputation. He was viewed by some as divinely appointed to keep them under control. God had given him power over the demons of Annwfn lest the world should be destroyed. Some, on the other hand, saw him as more fully identified with the 'demons'. 10 11

One entrance to Annwfn was Glastonbury Tor. An early Welsh saint, Collen, lived in a hermitage on its slope. He heard two men outside speaking of Gwyn, who, they said, was king of the fairies and lord of the Underworld, and had a home on that very hill. Collen urged them not to show the fairies so much respect, since they were diabolic. They replied that he had offended Gwyn and would have to answer for it. Soon afterwards, a fairy messenger arrived and invited him to climb higher and meet the king. He declined, but on the ensuing days the messenger returned, with threats. Finally Collen consented and climbed farther up, taking some holy water with him. The summit led mysteriously into a castle. Gwyn sat on a golden chair surrounded by retainers and musicians and beautiful damsels. He offered Collen food, but the saint knew better than to accept. Then Gwyn 12

said: 'Have you ever seen men better dressed than these, in their red and blue liveries?' Collen replied: 'Their dress is good of its kind, but the red is the red of fire and the blue is the blue of cold.' Having delivered this verdict on the court's hellish nature, he scattered the holy water around him. Gwyn, his courtiers and his castle all vanished, and the saint found himself outside, alone on the Tor.

Crucial to the interpretation of fairies is their aversion to iron. Celtic fairy lore probably had its origin in Iron-Age awareness that there had been *others* who did not have the metal and feared the weapons made from it. Fairies remained, so to speak, previous, and uncanny because the past had an alien air. Their hollow hills were often the barrows of the dead, not 'our' dead, but the dead of an older, different era. In some unseen form those dead still lived. The fairies may have begun specifically as a pre-iron layer of population, who lingered in out-of-the-way places and were seldom seen, yet disquietingly known to exist: not the long-since departed 'giants' who raised the megaliths, but perhaps the intermediate, ill-defined Bronze-Age people who would not all have been Celticised. If so, however, the world of the fairies became a composite, drawing in other folklore – ghost stories relating to the barrows, stories of nature-spirits, myths of the old gods.

13

Gwyn, whose name means 'white', was a product of the last process. He may not have been divine in his own right, but his father Nudd was the god Nodons. Nodons was still a popular deity as late as the 360s AD, when a new temple was built for him at Lydney in the Forest of Dean. He had a variety of aspects. He was a god of water and of dogs, a fisherman and a huntsman. For those who resorted to his shrine he was chiefly important as a healer, and as a finder of lost objects, like St Anthony. Pilgrims slept in cubicles, hoping that he would cure them or enlighten them, and left trinkets and coins and votive images.

14

The account of Gwyn's Tor abode is in a sixteenth-century Welsh text. It shows no influence from Glastonbury's literary legends and undoubtedly preserves much older tradition. The possible Tor maze has been mentioned, and the early Christian settlers may have felt the hill to be eerie. They built their first known church on a spot where another hill cuts off the view of it, and their successors surmounted it with another church dedicated to St Michael, angelic conqueror of the infernal powers. The first Michael church collapsed in an earthquake in 1275. Since buildings in England are scarcely prone to collapsing in earthquakes, it might be inferred that the infernal powers were not entirely suppressed.

Among Celtic Britons, official Christianity was perhaps more successful against the fairies than against the gods, with their capacity for survival in disguise. Nevertheless, an ambivalent fairy lore went on, not only with the Welsh but in due course with the English. In the Middle Ages, while the clergy of a stabler Romanised Christianity hardened towards paganism and magic in their human flock, there was not much clerical concern over the fairies. Church bells and crucifixes could more or less tame them. They had been put in their place and were no longer influential, except when humans were foolish enough to get involved with them. Chaucer's Wife of Bath notes this opinion and makes fun of it at the beginning of her Tale.

Puck and his colleagues in *A Midsummer Night's Dream* are still mischievous, and scornful of mortals, but the idea of outright malignancy is absent. At this

62. (opposite) Fairy glen, Wales.

stage it even becomes thinkable – though for Shakespeare, setting his comedy in ancient Athens, the issue does not arise – that some of the fairies have accepted Christianity. They are understood, however, to have stayed Catholic after the Reformation. They never catch up; they still belong to a senior world, and are fading from this one. Richard Corbet (1582–1635), in his poem 'Farewell, rewards and fairies', laments their passing and, though a Protestant himself, blames Protestantism:

> Witness those rings and roundelays
>   Of theirs, which yet remain,
> Were footed in Queen Mary's days
>   On many a grassy plain;
> But since of late Elizabeth
>   And later James came in,
> They never danced on any heath
>   As when the time hath been.
>
> By which we note the fairies
>   Were of the old profession;
> Their songs were Ave-Maries,
>   Their dances were procession.
> But now, alas, they all are dead;
>   Or gone beyond the seas;
> Or farther for religion fled,
>   Or else they take their ease.

Corbet may be right. The fairies are said to have abandoned their stronghold, Craig-y-Ddinas, because of the local Methodists. [15]

The decline leading to such characters as Tinker-Bell begins with another Shakespeare allusion, the Mab passage in *Romeo and Juliet*, and is set firmly on course in Michael Drayton's poem *Nymphidia*.

1. Bord, 237–8.
2. FML, 116–21.
3. Giraldus Cambrensis, 133–6; Westwood, 296.
4. FML, 419; Hole, 128–31; Westwood, 350–2, 367–9.
5. FML, 117; Hole, 131–2; Westwood, 388–9.
6. FML, 58; Hole, 132; Westwood, 369.
7. FML, 68; Hole, 41.
8. FML, 120; Westwood, 397.
9. FML, 398; Hole, 135–6; Rhys, I, 2–12.
10. Carley, 160–1; Graves (2), 88; *Mabinogion* (2), 3; Rhys, I, 143; Rolleston, 353.
11. *Mabinogion* (2), 119.
12. Carley, 98–9.
13. FML, 120; Hole, 125–7; Rhys, II, 659–70, 683–4; Westwood, 417.
14. Carley, 161; Chadwick (2), 197; Ross, 230–3, 258, 262 n. 46.
15. Westwood, 295.

23 *The God over the Water*

In the eyes of most Greeks and Romans, Britain was the end of the inhabited world and hardly seemed, even, quite to belong to it. The Britons themselves knew better: there was more beyond. Westward from Britain five days' sail, they said, there was a land with adjacent islands where the summer night was less than an hour long. Past it was a further expanse of sea, about five hundred miles wide, where navigation could be impeded by ice and debris. Past that again was a continental land-mass with a great bay and three more islands. On one of those islands – very beautiful, with a pleasant climate – there dwelt a banished god. Formerly powerful, he had been deposed by a junior god, but treated with respect. By his successor's wish he lay sleeping in a deep cave resting on rock that looked like gold. Around him were spirits who had been his companions in the days of his power. They learned and interpreted his dreams.

Every thirty years, when the planet Saturn was in Taurus, parties of pilgrims crossed the ocean and visited the bay and its islands, where they acquired esoteric lore concerning the stars and other matters. So at least it was asserted by some.

About 330 BC the Greek explorer Pytheas was introduced to an arctic land called Thule (Iceland?), apparently by British informants. The Britons' awareness of land beyond themselves was more than fantasy. Some classical authors recognised this, and transferred the limit of the world to Ultima Thule. To most people in the Mediterranean area, the remoteness and difference of Britain itself were such that Roman troops directed by the emperor Claudius to invade the island broke out in a mutiny and had to be calmed down. The Britons' account of the sleeping god in his retreat, when handled, as it was, by a Greek writer, embodied the geographic consciousness of 'land beyond Britain' at a time when Britain had become more familiar, and retained and transferred the sense of strangeness.

The Greek who gave it a literary form, soon after the Roman conquest, was Plutarch. He thus preserved one of the few myths of the British Celts to be recorded by an outside observer when their pre-Roman culture survived. The problem is to decide how much is authentic, how much is fancy and embellishment. He got his data directly or indirectly from an imperial official, Demetrius, who was in Britain in 82 AD. Some at least of what he reports was undoubtedly gathered on the spot. But he wraps it up in mystification, citing an intermediate informant, Sylla. The assertion that people regularly made the crossing sounds like a flight of Sylla's imagination, or Plutarch's, rather than anything really British.

Plutarch follows an annoying habit of classical authors, who seldom name foreign deities, but refer to them by the names of classical ones imagined to be equivalent. He speaks of the banished god as Cronus, and of his supplanter as

Cronus's son Zeus. The reason is that in Greek myth Zeus did supplant Cronus, and Cronus, according to one version, was exiled to a western region beyond the ocean. Plutarch adds to the obfuscation by calling the place with the short night Ogygia, a name borrowed from Homer, and even alleging that the human inhabitants of the distant continent are descended from companions of Hercules, who travelled farther west in the course of his tenth labour than is usually supposed.

4   Yet in spite of all this Greek-style remodelling, the geography points to non-Greek information. No classical geographer has anything remotely like it, and it is curiously good – better than some classical descriptions of known regions. If a ship starts from Britain's northern end, at Cape Wrath, a voyage more or less due west takes it to a land with adjacent islets, southern Greenland. Sailing time is more than five days, yet even this error has an odd plausibility, because early geographers who mention Greenland underestimate the distance in the same way. Southern Greenland, below the Arctic Circle, does have a very brief summer night. Five hundred miles or so beyond Greenland, over the icy Davis Strait, is the coast of a real trans-Atlantic continent. Plutarch's bay could be the Gulf of St Lawrence, which has enough islands for his description, and if hardly the mild climate, there is evidence for deterioration since he wrote. He states, most surprisingly, that the mouth of the bay is in about the same latitude as the north end of the Caspian Sea, a statement which can be proved to fit the Gulf by tracing the forty-seventh parallel.

Whatever the explanation of all this – knowledge based on forgotten voyages (as perhaps with Thule also), or remarkable guesswork – Plutarch's report has links backwards and forwards. Behind it is the account of Atlantis given by Plato, who likewise mentions a quasi-American continent, reached from Atlantis by way of islands. Behind it also is a passage in Seneca's tragedy *Medea* which is said to have stirred the imagination of Columbus:

> The time shall come at length when Ocean will unloose the bonds he imposes, when the vast Earth will lie open, when the sea-goddess will disclose new worlds, and Thule will not be the last of lands.

After Plutarch come several Irish voyage-romances confirming the Celtic provenance of his theme. One voyage, ending in permanent residence across the ocean, is ascribed to Bran – in this case, the Irish humanisation of the god. It has

5   been conjectured that the deity on Plutarch's island actually was Bran.

The Cronus of the Greeks, whom Romans equated with their own Saturn, was the chief of the Titans who ruled the universe before Zeus's Olympians. Mythographers blackened them in retrospect as a violent, barbaric crew, but could never suppress an ancient conviction that Cronus's reign was a golden age and that his western retreat was an Elysium where the golden age was still going on. There is no telling whether the god whom Plutarch identified with him had such an aspect, though, if he was indeed Bran, his 'blessedness' might be a hint. Certainly, as will appear, he was to play a part in the making of a new myth raising the issue.

1. Plutarch (1), chapter 26, and (2), chapter 18.
2. Ashe (9), 126–8.
3. Ashe (7), 24.
4. Ashe (9), 176–83, 213–6.
5. Graves (1), par. 6.2, and (2), 65.

24 *The Druids*

Britain, it is said, was the fountain-head of doctrine for a mighty religious 1
order, which flourished in Gaul and Ireland as well. This was the order of
Druids, an élite body with wide-ranging functions. Druids were priests and 2
magicians, seers and poets, judges and doctors. They advised rulers and
could exert control over them, even stopping inter-tribal battles.

Their order was not a separate priesthood but a kind of caste. Druids had
wives and children. Women as well as men could belong, though not with
equal status. The dominant male element was recruited from society's 3
highest ranks. Membership conferred exemption from service in war, but
was not an easy option. The recruit underwent a novitiate of twenty years,
spent in sacred caves and wild forest sanctuaries, learning immense amounts
of oral lore, for the Druids committed little or nothing to writing. Much of
this lore took the form of verse – charms, riddles, incantations, mythical
narratives. Much of it was concerned with cosmology. The druidic world
was a flux, kept in motion by the strife of a fire-principle and a water-
principle. It could be interpreted, to some extent, by astrology. There was a
complex hierarchy of gods, and only the Druids, through contact and
communion, knew fully who they were and how to come to terms with
them. For human beings, the Druids taught, death was not the end: souls 4
transmigrated to new bodies.

Druids officiated at rituals of many kinds, magical and religious, with no
sharp distinction. Ritual indeed pervaded most of their activities. Thus, they
practised herbal healing, but the herb was less important than the pro-
cedure. One variety had to be gathered – plucked, not cut – at an auspicious 5
hour by a practitioner dressed in white, with bare feet. Another had to be
gathered left-handed and fasting. Druids' counsel was apt to be given by
inspired divination. They dealt with the gods through various forms of
sacrifice. One famous ceremony involved mistletoe. When it grew on an oak 6
tree, a rare occurrence, worshippers gathered on the sixth day of the moon,
and a Druid in a white robe cut a sprig off the parasite with a golden sickle.
He then sacrificed two white bulls and the assembly feasted. Reputedly, all
this had a sinister side. To propitiate their gods, the Druids sacrificed human 7
beings as well as animals. This custom incurred the enmity of the Romans,
who gradually abolished it as their power spread. The Druids opposed
them, in Gaul and later in Britain, but Rome was too strong, the outer
world was at last breaking in.

As remarked, many have supposed that Stonehenge is a Druid temple.
That is why one of its stones, which lies flat, is called the altar stone, having
presumably been used for the human sacrifices. But some deny this feature
of Druidism as a libel spread by the Romans from political motives, or a
decadent practice unknown to the order in its purity. It has been maintained, in fact, that the Druids were outstanding in wisdom and knowledge,
that they were custodians of a well-governed society, that they instructed

63. The Gundestrup Cauldron, found in Denmark, perhaps a gift from a Celtic chief to a Danish one; it shows druidic figures with human sacrifice (at the back, left).

8 nations outside the Celtic world; even that Druidism had the same antecedents as Christianity, and prepared the way for it in Britain with foreshadowings of its Saviour and Trinity.

The Druids' bardic aspect is recalled in the Welsh Eisteddfod, its 'Archdruid' in the chair, its ritual and regalia. Modern Druid groups seek to reconstitute the order's true wisdom, and hold ceremonies at sites deemed to be druidic, including a dawn gathering at Stonehenge marking the summer solstice.

In spite of a large literature on the Druids, not much is known about them. There are no extant documents in which they speak for themselves. Though a Celtic phenomenon, they seem to have been rooted in a deeper antiquity. Some
9 of the clues are curious. An Irish legend tells of a Druid named Mog Ruith dressing up in a bird costume, apparently worn over an inner garment of bull's hide. Having assembled some further druidic equipment he rises into the air.
10 This is one of a number of hints pointing to Asian shamanism as a remote source, Druidism being a western outgrowth, carried to a higher degree of sophistication. The Druid's ancestor was perhaps the medicine-man, dancing and drumming in ritual gear, conversing with spirits, wielding influence through oracular utterances and a rapport with the powers of nature. While the
11 etymology is disputed, 'Druid' may mean 'oak-knower' and refer to a secret lore of trees.

In the last centuries BC the Druids certainly existed as an inter-tribal order, more prominent in Gaul than in Britain. Though their power has been exaggerated, they had most of the functions traditionally ascribed to them – magical, priestly, poetic, judicial, mediumistic – and their training involved a long course of study. But study of what? One of the few things which can be said with confidence is that some of the subject-matter was astronomical, and had to do with the calendar. Druids harmonised the solar and lunar years by means of a nineteen-year cycle which was known also in Greece, as the cycle of Meton. Its druidic version is attested by that passage of Hecataeus construed wrongly as referring to Stonehenge, and by an inscribed plate called the Coligny Calendar, found near Bourg-en-Bresse in the French department of Ain. Hecataeus, by the way, says that in Britain you can observe the moon much closer and see mountains on it. Perhaps, who knows? the Druids invented telescopes.

It is Julius Caesar who records that Druidism was systematised among the Britons, and that its advanced colleges were on the island. The historian Tacitus confirms that the order included women, or, at least, that they figured in its magical workings. He describes what the Romans saw on the far side of the Menai Strait when they prepared to invade Anglesey, where the Druids were strong:

> Drawn up on the seashore was a dense mass of armed warriors. Among them, bearing flaming torches, ran women with funereal robes and dishevelled hair like Furies, and all around stood Druids, raising their hands to heaven and calling down dreadful curses.

The Druids' theology is almost a closed book. It is not certain that they presided over the cults of the gods in general, of Bran and Belinus for example, or that the myths concerning them were all comprised in druidic lore. It may have been so, it may not. Druidism's principal known features are two, one being a part of its practice, the other a part of its belief.

Druids sacrificed animals, as in the mistletoe ceremony. The charge that they sacrificed humans too appears to be well-founded. This was one reason for Roman hostility to them, as barbarians deserving suppression. Their rituals were performed in wooden shrines and in sanctuaries among the forests, with grotesque carved images of gods. Victims were put to death by several methods. They were stabbed, or shot at with arrows, or plunged head-downwards into tubs full of water, or shut in huge wicker cages in human shape, which were set alight. A point which may be significant is that there is almost no evidence for Celtic archery in hunting or war: it may be thought to follow that the bows and arrows of sacrifice were ritual weapons.

As to post-mortem survival, it was unquestionably a major tenet. Yet reincarnation as a doctrine of mainstream Druidism is very dubious. A few Irish allusions concern deities and other exceptional beings who live earthly lives. With the human species in general, the truth seems to be that the Druids had an emphatic teaching on immortality, which attracted notice from classical authors because they were not familiar with anything quite like it, yet, for that very reason, was misunderstood. Some Greeks and Romans believed in life after death as a privilege for initiates of the Eleusinian Mysteries and kindred cults, but few had much notion of it for people at large, who were consigned to near-nullity as shades. In philosophic thought, the only positive idea on the subject had come from Pythagoras, who saw survival in terms of reincarnation. Therefore, some writers on Celtic matters inferred, reincarnation was what the Druids taught.

But this was probably a mistake, and not all those who took an interest in Druidism fell into it. The Celtic after-life was another one quite like this, in some Otherworld region, on an island or inside a hill. Conviction was so firm that a Celt could borrow money on an IOU payable in that future existence. Lucan, the Roman epic poet, expounds the topic in the first century AD with unusual insight:

12

13

14

15

> You, ye Druids . . . you who dwell in deep woods in seques-
> tered groves: your teaching is that the shades of the dead do
> not make their way to the silent abode of Erebus or the
> lightless realm of Dis below, but that the same soul animates
> the limbs in another sphere. If you sing of certainties, death is
> the centre of continuous life. Truly the peoples on whom the
> Pole Star shines are happy in their error, for they are not
> harassed by the greatest of terrors, the fear of death. This
> gives the warrior his eagerness to rush upon the steel, a spirit
> ready to face death, and an indifference to a life which will
> return.

The enhanced image of Druids as philosopher-statesmen, and masters of ancient wisdom, took shape in the wishful thinking of Alexandrian Greeks. They wanted to believe in an unspoilt far-away people who had not declined from the golden age. Blending semi-mythical Hyperboreans with romanticised Celts, they evoked a sort of northern Utopia enlightened by the Druids, and, inevitably, improved them in doing so. They were helped by the assumed ideological kinship with Pythagoras. It was surely plain that Pythagoras must have taught the Druids. The imaginative process did not halt there. Alexandria produced Clement, a Father of the Church, who argued that the truth was the other way round: the Druids taught Pythagoras. The idea did not fade away as a mere eccentricity. It was still very much alive when Milton wrote *Areopagitica*, in which he extended it:

> Writers of good antiquity and ablest judgement have been
> perswaded that ev'n the school of Pythagoras, and the Persian
> wisdom took beginning from the old Philosophy of this
> Iland.

During the eighteenth century, societies were formed professing to recover the 'old philosophy'. It was largely because of these that Stonehenge was drawn in. Antiquaries had been wondering about it for years. Inigo Jones thought it was Roman, because he knew no record of anyone else who could have built it. Since it was glaringly un-Roman in style, others guessed at Ancient Britons, Phoenicians, and Danes. The Danes were too late, and there was no reason to think that Phoenicians had come so far, or, if they did, had settled. As for Ancient Britons, it was not easy to define them. Geoffrey's giants and Trojans were out of favour, as was his Merlin story.

John Aubrey, however, spotted the evidence for eligible pre-Romans in Britain: namely, the Druids. Once published, in 1695, his conception of a druidic Stonehenge began to take hold. The person who chiefly established it was Stukeley. Though acquainted with Aubrey's work, he first studied the monument with an open mind, but he found his way into a neo-Druid circle, and, in 1740, published a book of his own that fitted Stonehenge into the Druids' scheme of things. There it remained, well into the twentieth century, when its much earlier date at last became clear. The utmost that can still be claimed is that its real builders may have practised a religion ancestral to Druidism. But such a link is conjectural, and so is the plea that while the Druids did not *build* Stonehenge, they may have *used* it.

Stukeley also gave the first major impulse to the theory that the Druids were proto-Christians, associates of Abraham in the patriarchal faith, and believers in a divine Trinity. The number three was conspicuous in Celtic thinking – it

64. Romanticised scene of the advent of Christianity in Britain, with the Druid still performing his oak-tree ceremony, but presumably on the brink of eclipse.

survived, notably, in Welsh summaries of bardic tradition known as triads – but the theological leap was unjustified. Speculation nevertheless grew more flamboyant. Edward Davies in *Celtic Researches* (1804) constructed a new model of prehistory. Just after the Flood, the families of the world were united. The Druids propagated a pre-Deluge curriculum which included writing and other arts. They also tried to keep society peaceful. Violence broke it up, and the Druids, in their British headquarters, deteriorated. But some of their wisdom survived, and not only among the Celts. It created the religions and philosophies of the Greeks and Hindus. Others of the Davies school took the risky step of adding the Hebrews, or, at any rate, claiming that scriptural and druidic teachings were identical if you went back far enough.

20

William Blake carried these notions to their apogee and used them in his poetic mythology. For Blake, 'All things Begin & End in Albion's Ancient Druid Rocky Shore'. Before the Flood, before the entire biblical history, Albion's sages taught the whole earth, and all the world was of one language and one religion. Atlantis joined Europe to America. 'Adam was a Druid, and Noah; also Abraham was called to succeed the Druidical age.' The primordial sages betrayed their trust, and degenerated into the Druids of history, setting up monstrous temples – Stonehenge, for instance – and practising human sacrifice. Disasters such as the Flood swept over the world, and Atlantis vanished beneath the sea, so that the nations were divided. Yet all was not lost, the original glory can be reinstated, the golden age can return.

A reconstruction of Druidism by another poet, with more claim to a scholarly basis, is in Robert Graves's *Claudius the God*.

21   Cultural neo-Druidism in Wales, at the Eisteddfod, is something else again. The Welsh bardic tradition, which did derive tenuously from the Druids, survived through the Middle Ages and after. An Eisteddfod was a session at which musicians and poets competed. In 1792 some Welsh bards in London assembled on Primrose Hill, and set up a ring of stones surrounding an altar called the Gorsedd, with a sword on it. They were following the precepts of an imaginative stonemason, Edward Williams, who had assumed the *nom de plume* Iolo Morganwg and forged a mass of 'old Welsh literature' that has sown confusion ever since. His ceremony was built into a Carmarthen Eisteddfod in 1819, and has continued, with more pseudo-druidic elements, in the National Eisteddfod of more recent times.

22   In 1781 an Ancient Order of Druids was founded in London. Splits ensued, with one group becoming a friendly society, others keeping up a mystical stance. The Albion Lodge initiated Winston Churchill in 1908. Today, besides holding the annual Stonehenge ritual, self-styled Druids perform at Glastonbury and elsewhere. Stukeley and Blake are said to have been practising

23   members, even leaders. Attempts to devise a convincing Druid costume have a long history and are almost wholly fanciful. Apart from the vague allusions to robes, the only description is the brief Irish one of Mog Ruith's attire, and that suggests a shamanic outfit which neo-Druids might be reluctant to imitate.

1. Piggott (1), 96.
2. Ibid, 91–4, 97–8.
3. Piggott (1), 94–6, 100; Ross, 62, 79, 81; Rutherford, 66, 71–2.
4. Ross, 81, 450.
5. Piggott (1), 99; Rutherford, 80.
6. Piggott (1), 98–9; Ross, 82.
7. Piggott (1), 99.
8. Morgan, 9–29; Piggott (1), 81, 135.
9. Ross, 333.
10. Piggott (1), 159–64; Ross, 83, 87; Rutherford, 59–63, 129.
11. Piggott (1), 89.
12. Ibid, 105.
13. Kightly, 35; Ross, 462–3.
14. FML, 101; Piggott (1), 98.
15. Piggott (1), 102–4.
16. Piggott (1), 75–83; Rutherford, 13, 44.
17. Piggott (1), 81.
18. Chippindale, 57–69; Piggott (1), 125–8, 131–42.
19. Chippindale, 70–86.
20. Ashe (2), 154–5; Todd, 29–60.
21. Piggott (1), 142–6.
22. FML, 19; Piggott (1), 155–7; Rutherford, 16–18.
23. Piggott (1), 144–6.

Excursus II

Beyond Britain

Fairy lore, mythic geography and Druidism all open up vistas. While the vistas are different, insight can be achieved with all three by going outside in space, backwards in time.

Fairy-folk are an amalgam, as is proved by the variety of types. That is also true in Ireland, where they are more notorious. The Irish record is clearer, and confirms the role of traditions about an earlier people. The Irish fairies were the *sida*, later *sidhe*, pronounced 'shee'. The word *sid* meant an enchanted mound-dwelling, and the *sida* had homes in tumuli such as New Grange. *Sid* as a proper noun denoted the Otherworld, the Irish version of Annwfn. This was associated also with the Tuatha De Danann, or Danaans, the glorious people who were Erin's last occupants before the 'Milesian' ancestors of the present Gaels. When the latter arrived they took over the surface of the island, and the Tuatha De Danann 'went into hills and fairy regions', mingling with the *sida*, whom they dominated. Christianity could not extinguish them, but it kept them on what it considered a proper level, with a consequent blended fairy-folk comprising several varieties and a Danaan aristocracy.

The king of the Tuatha De Danann was Nuadu. He is the Irish equivalent of Nudd, Gwyn's father, and, like him, is an embodiment of the Celtic god whom the Britons called Nodons. When the Tuatha De Danann fought their forerunners the Fir Bolg, Nuadu lost a hand in battle. It was replaced by a silver one, so that he became Nuadu Airgetlam, Nuadu of the Silver Hand. Later he had to contend with the sinister Fomorians as they inflicted various disasters. Their chief was Balor, who had an evil eye. To defeat them Nuadu temporarily resigned power to Lug, a hero of rare versatility and resource. Lug overwhelmed the Fomorians with magic. Balor, however, had slain Nuadu in the battle. It was after this that the Milesians occupied

Ireland, and the Tuatha De Danann faded into the Otherworld and the realm of faerie.

While all this supports the belief that pre-Celts went into fairy lore in Britain too, they seem to have been more fully assimilated. Nothing survives about invasions, conflicts, or mergers. Legend supplies only vestigial equivalents of the Tuatha De Danann, such as Math's relations. The fairies slip through its net. They are quite distinct from the giants, and there is no sign of a connection with some stray branch of the Trojans. Even if the Welshman was right about their speaking the Trojan language, they must have picked it up from Brutus's settlers.

65. Decorated stone at the entrance of the New Grange passage tomb, a home of Irish fairy-folk.

With the Britons' far-off god in his western Elysium, it is Ireland again that sheds light, and impressively. But that topic is best deferred till a more famous legend can be taken into account.

As for the Druids, two things can be said about them in a broader perspective. First, they neither imported nor invented a whole new ideological package. Features of Druidism were present among the earlier populations – sacrifice, ritual weaponry, religious awe of fire and water, interest in the calendar, reverence for the number three. But while Druidism was a development rather than a complete novelty, at least one foreign ingredient played a part, at whatever stage it entered the process. This was the shamanic element, and because it laid the foundation of the druidic élite, and in some degree shaped this, it might be thought the most important. The shaman is an Asian rather than a European figure, and Stuart Piggott has shown a likelihood, not only from broad probabilities but from parallelisms in detail, that the shamanism infused into the Druid scheme drifted west from Siberia. This master-thread of druidic ancestry is thousands of miles long, and thousands of years long.   6

Ironically there is a real connection, if a backdoor one, with the Greek matters invoked by Druid fantasists. Pythagoras was linked with the 'northern wisdom' by way of a sage called Abaris, a Hyperborean who visited Greece. The key to this notion lies in the cult of Apollo. Pythagoras was a devotee of this god – according to legend, a son – and Apollo had a special relationship with the Hyperboreans, spending three months of every year in their company. The ones he stayed with were mythical sky-dwellers, but it was accepted that Hyperboreans existed at ground level in a geographic home.   7

Hence, it appears, a common source with Druidism. Apollo-worship developed in Greece and was acclimatised there, but the god in his original form came from outside. W. K. C. Guthrie, followed by E. R. Dodds, argued persuasively for an ancestry in Siberian shamanism. Despite Apollo's acquired patronage of civilised arts such as music and mathematics, his cult never shed shamanistic features, including prophetic ecstasy, astral travelling, and magical healing. That explains his link with the semi-mythic Hyperboreans in their distant northland. Among them, or whatever real people inspired the semi-myth, were his original shamans.   8

Evidence locating them more exactly comes from an expedition in the seventh century BC by a priest of Apollo, Aristeas, who went to look for them. He was aware that their name meant, strictly, not 'dwellers at the back of the north wind' but 'dwellers beyond Boreas'. In its primary sense Boreas was the strong cold wind which, in Greece, does blow from the north, but in some other countries may blow from the north-east or east. Aristeas's story survives only in fragments. However, he describes a traceable journey to the region of Lake Balkhash and gives reports from farther on, saying, notably, that Boreas lives in a cave and the cold wind issues from it. This is folklore still current in the Dzungarian Gate, where the fierce winds are said to issue from a cave. Aristeas puts the Hyperboreans, naturally, beyond the cave. Their country is more or less in the Altai Mountains. This works very well, because Altaic shamanism is an especially potent and influential variety. Dodds remarks that if Apollo's friend Abaris was a real person, he was probably an Asian shaman; and his best-known possession, a magical arrow, echoes known practices of the Altaic region specifically. Piggott's clues to the remote wellsprings of Druidism belong to very much the same part of Asia.   9

After Aristeas, more Greeks wrote of the Hyperboreans. Losing sight of the pioneer explorer, and the Altaic home he had identified, they shifted them westwards and confused them with other peoples. They had no serious grounds for doing so, yet this gradual extension over an immense area matched the apparent drift of Altaic influence. Hyperboreans were located in Scythia, and on the upper Danube, and in the Alps. They turned up in the Celtic west and showed signs of becoming Celtic. When   10

Hecataeus at last put them in Britain, he made it plain that, in his view, they were Druids or at least had Druids among them, because of the nineteen-year astronomical cycle. The semi-equation of Hyperboreans and Druids follows on in the writings of later Greeks.

Britain and Greece, therefore, both point back to the same Altaic 'holy land', the original Hyperborean region, so far as there ever was such a thing. It was a centre of diffusion from which shamanic practices and beliefs travelled over the continental mass, and went into the making of religious systems: Druidism in Gaul and the British Isles, and the Apollo cult in Greece, the latter with Pythagoras as a distinguished product. Several Asian legends look towards the same territory, reinforcing, however puzzlingly, the impression of its importance. Outstanding among them is a lamaistic belief in a northern abode of spiritual wisdom, Shambhala. Here, a visitor to Mongolia, Stephen Jenkins, has added a strange footnote. He quotes the lamas as speaking of a kind of second Shambhala in Celtic Britain. This may reflect a real tradition of influence westwards, and, if so, is interesting if hard to interpret. Or it may be another modern myth, inspired by notions about the Druids which somehow found their way to Mongolia. The original Shambhala at least is an authentic conception, and the best clues to its whereabouts, or supposed whereabouts, suggest the Altai.

Thus far established scholarship. Possibilities, however, extend farther still. On the basis of certain recurrent themes, it looks as if influences from this Asian centre may also have been transmitted to senior civilisations – to Vedic India, to Sumeria, to Babylonia. North-Central Asian ideology may have gone into the formation of a seed-bed system, which established itself anciently over an area on the confines of the Middle East, and effected the transmission. The evidence is apparent, the process is less so. But it would make better sense in the light of the possibility aired by Renfrew, and still admissible in essentials, however right his critics may be, that there was an Indo-European spread over much of Asia earlier than assumed hitherto, providing a medium. The cultural factors raise questions, yet also show how such a hypothesis could resolve them.

If anything of the kind happened, Druidism was a late offshoot from an Asian phenomenon on a grandiose scale. It was an offshoot that went its own way, and took on a regional Celtic character, with few obvious traces of the shared ancestry. Yet at least where India is concerned, the difference is looking less, in the light of comparative studies by Anne Ross; and the septenary maze-spiral, which occurs in the British Isles and in Greece and in India too, may furnish a clue to the diffusion.

1. Rees, 38–9; Rhys, II, 685; Rolleston, 69, 136–7.
2. Rees, 32–3.
3. Rees, 33–8; Rolleston, 113–8.
4. Rees, 51.
5. Keys.
6. Piggott (1), 108, 160–4.
7. Ibid, 82.
8. Dodds, 139–50, 161–2 n. 36; Guthrie, 74–80, 86 n., 193–6, 204.
9. Ashe (1), 204–6; Bolton, passim.
10. Ashe (1), 206–8.
11. Ashe (1), 242–4; Jenkins, 39–40, 158.
12. Keys.

The Roman Era

25 Lud

King Belinus had established a strong royal authority. For a long while the succession in Britain was generally smooth, with fewer clashes between would-be rulers. But while some of those who did rule were good, few were notable. The old monarchy had one last sovereign of stature, and with him it reached its term, though no one knew that during his lifetime.

Lud, son of Heli, was a zealous builder and town-planner. He strength-   1
ened the ramparts of New Troy, incorporating towers at strategic points. Also he issued edicts regulating building within the walls, so as to make the city the finest on earth. He had a special love for it and spent most of his time there, holding banquets and celebrations. Consequently it was re-named Lud's City, Caer Lud, later corrupted into Caer Lundein, from which 'London' is derived. Lud had two brothers, Cassivellaunus and Nennius. The latter objected to the change, insisting that the Britons should not betray the memory of their Trojan descent. He was overruled.

When Lud died he was buried beside a city gateway called after him, Ludgate. His sons, Androgeus and Tenuantius, were not yet of age, so Lud was succeeded by his brother Cassivellaunus, who tried to forestall potential disputes by making Androgeus Duke of Kent and Tenuantius Duke of Cornwall. Danger, however, was brewing in another quarter. Cassivellaunus and Tenuantius were both to be counted on the list of kings, but they were not to hold that office in the unimpeded way of their predecessors.

The Welsh call London's godfather Lludd and his brothers Caswallawn   2
and Nyniaw, and add a third brother, Llefelys, who was very wise and much loved by the king. They acknowledge the importance of Lludd's work on the capital, but tell a more picturesque story about his reign, in which, they say, Britain was afflicted by three plagues. One was an invasion by sinister folk with magic powers, the Coranieid, who could hear every word borne

66. Ludgate as reconstructed after the collapse of the original in the Great Fire; this final version was pulled down in 1760.

on the wind, and could thus eavesdrop at a distance and learn any opponent's plans. The second was a terrible shriek heard every May-eve, which drove people mad, and no one could tell where it came from. The third was a constant disappearance of food from the royal stores, with no thieves ever being caught.

Llefelys had been living abroad. Lludd went to consult him, and they met on a ship in the Channel. Llefelys sent for an artificer and had him make a bronze speaking-tube, so that they could confer through this without the wind carrying the sound to the Coranieid. At the first attempt they were thwarted by a demon inside the tube, who scrambled the words, but Llefelys washed him out with wine. Then he told Lludd what to do about the first plague: the king must mash certain insects in water to make a spray. This would be poisonous to the Coranieid but harmless to the Britons.

Next, as to the shriek: it was uttered by a British dragon fighting a foreign one. Lludd must find the exact centre of Britain and have a pit dug there, and lower a tub of mead into it with a silken cover. When the dragons next grew tired of fighting they would turn into piglets, fall on the cover, and be deposited in the mead. They would drink themselves into a stupor, and then Lludd should wrap the cover around them and bury them in a safe place.

Lastly, as to the vanishing of royal provisions: the culprit was a giant who lulled the guards to sleep by enchantment while he robbed the stores. Lludd should keep watch himself with a bath of cold water ready, so that when he became drowsy he could get in and shock himself into wakefulness.

Lludd returned to Britain and acted on his brother's advice. First he wiped out the Coranieid with the infusion of insects. Then, by measuring his kingdom, he found that the centre was at Oxford, trapped the dragons, and hid them in a stone coffer on a hill in Snowdonia – an action that was to have a sequel, like the burying of Bran's head. Finally, thanks to his cold bath, he was awake when the giant entered the store-room. They fought, and the giant was beaten, and promised to make good all the loss.

In the *Mabinogion* tale, *Lludd and Llefelys*, the brothers are sons of Beli, i.e. Belinus. Geoffrey changed the initial letter of 'Beli' because he had already put Belinus much earlier.

Lud or Lludd is another humanised deity, already made a king of Britain in Henry of Huntingdon's work, before Geoffrey. Ultimately he is the god Nodons. Nodons's renown extended to Ireland, where, as noted, he became Nuadu of the Silver Hand, king of the Tuatha De Danann. In Wales he became Nudd, father of Gwyn, the lord of Annwfn with the fairy palace in Glastonbury Tor; and he also became Lludd. Lludd was sometimes said to have a silver hand like his Irish counterpart. Welsh story-tellers lost sight of the fact that Nudd and Lludd were the same. They told how the immortal Gwyn, son of Nudd, loved Creiddylad, a daughter of Lludd, and was destined to fight a rival for her each May Day till the end of the world.

The tale of Lludd and Llefelys somewhat resembles that of Nuadu enlisting Lug's aid against the Fomorians. Both could derive from some myth of the original god. The Coranieid (variously spelt) may be a kind of fairy-folk from some other country. In Breton, a name for the fairies is *Korriganed*. However, one of the triads encapsulating Welsh bardic tradition states that the Coranieid came from Arabia.

6   'London' is first recorded in Latin as *Londinium*, and found afterwards in a number of forms before it becomes standardised. It is British, and may truly be derived from a personal name, though this would have been something like *Londinos*. The name might also have been a tribal one. It would have meant 'the

7   wild' or 'the bold'. The derivation of 'Ludgate' is uncertain. During the Middle Ages a gate actually stood there, decorated with images of Lud and other kings. Under Edward VI the heads were struck off, under Mary new ones were stuck on. The gate was reconstructed in 1586 but destroyed in the Great Fire. An image of Elizabeth I survived, and is now on the front of St Dunstan's Church in Fleet Street.

    Cassivellaunus, who fought Julius Caesar, brings us at last into history. So, in a puzzling way, does Tenuantius. His name in this form results from a long

8   process of orthographic mangling. Historically he is Tasciovanus, who reigned during the last two decades BC over the Catuvellauni, north of the Thames. What is odd is that Tasciovanus is known to us only from his coins, not from any document, yet his name, corrupted but recognisable, turns up in Welsh genealogies centuries later. Geoffrey makes him, as 'Tenuantius', the father of Cunobelinus, Shakespeare's Cymbeline; and so he was. He looks like evidence for a lost source such as Geoffrey claims to have used. Shakespeare makes a passing allusion in *Cymbeline* to someone being ennobled by him.

1. GM (1), 15, 34–5, and (2), 74, 196.
2. *Mabinogion* (2), 89–94.
3. Bromwich, 428; Chadwick (2), 197.
4. Bromwich, 424–7; Rees, 46.*
5. Bromwich, 84, 86.
6. Ekwall, 303, art. 'London'.
7. *Brewer*, art. 'Ludgate'.
8. Ashe (7), 31; Piggott (2), 280; 'Nennius' (2), 106, 107.

26 *Caesar, Cymbeline and Others*

While Cassivellaunus was king, Julius Caesar conquered Gaul and arrived 1
on the Channel coast. He gazed across to Britain and asked about its
inhabitants. Informed that they were of Trojan stock like the Romans
themselves, he said they should be induced to acknowledge Roman
supremacy and pay tribute, but if possible without violence, as they were
kinsfolk. He dispatched a letter to Cassivellaunus inviting his submission.
Cassivellaunus replied in defiant terms: the two Trojan-descended nations
could and should live in friendship, but if the Romans attempted to
dominate, the Britons would resist.

Caesar took up the challenge, sailed over with an army into the Thames
estuary, and effected a landing. Cassivellaunus held a council of war,
bringing together his nephews Androgeus and Tenuantius and several
subordinate rulers. They attacked Caesar's camp and prevented the Romans
from breaking out. The king's brother, Nennius, fought heroically, meeting Caesar in hand-to-hand combat and capturing his sword. Mortally
wounded, he died soon after and was buried by the north gate of London
with the sword beside him. The invasion had been repulsed, and Caesar
returned to the continent, where the Gauls, fired by news of the British
victory, were becoming so restless that he had to make concessions to pacify
them.

Two years later he tried again. Cassivellaunus planted sharp stakes in the
river-bed below London. When the enemy ships sailed up the estuary, many
were holed and sunk, and the legionaries who got ashore were too few to
achieve anything. Again Caesar withdrew to Gaul. But during victory
celebrations a quarrel arose between Cassivellaunus and Androgeus over a
fatal blow foully struck in a wrestling match. The culprit was a nephew of
Androgeus, who protected him from punishment. A civil war began and
Androgeus decided on an act of betrayal. He wrote to Caesar asking for
help. The Romans landed a third time, at Richborough. With a British force
led by the traitor, they attacked Cassivellaunus near Canterbury and
besieged him on a hill. Androgeus, satisfied with his revenge, was now
willing to mediate. The British king agreed to pay Rome an annual tribute.
Caesar left in a conciliatory atmosphere and Androgeus accompanied him
to Rome.

Cassivellaunus died and was buried at York, and Tenuantius became
king. He paid the tribute and was succeeded after a quiet reign by his son
Cymbeline (Cunobelinus), who had spent his youth in the household of
Augustus. Cymbeline was a much more distinguished sovereign. Great 2
Kimble in Buckinghamshire is said to be named after him, and a nearby
earthwork is Cymbeline's Castle. He was so firmly entrenched, and on such
excellent terms with Rome, that he could have held back the tribute with
impunity, but he elected to continue it. Late in life he resigned power to his
elder son Guiderius, and Guiderius did stop payment. Roman goodwill

67. Roman soldiers being transported by ship, a type of operation that caused problems for Caesar.

towards the father did not extend to the son. The Emperor Claudius invaded Britain and Guiderius fell in battle. His successor was his brother Arviragus, who defeated the Roman general Hamo at a seaport, afterwards called Hampton, or Southampton, in memory of this event.

Claudius meanwhile was gaining the upper hand near Winchester, but he feared Arviragus, and preferred to negotiate from strength rather than risk more fighting. A treaty was concluded by which Britain became an imperial dependency, but retained self-rule under its own kings. Arviragus married Claudius's daughter Genuissa. The ceremony took place on the bank of the Severn, and Claudius and Arviragus founded Gloucester there in commemoration.

Arviragus had second thoughts and refused any further homage to Rome. Claudius sent Vespasian with an armed force. At Richborough Arviragus refused him permission to land. Instead of abandoning the mission he took his fleet down the Channel and landed at Totnes, where the Trojans had come ashore so long ago. He besieged Exeter. Arviragus arrived and an indecisive battle was fought. His Roman wife Genuissa intervened, peace was restored, and Britain reverted to the treaty relationship, which was to keep it in the imperial system for more than three centuries. The king reigned peacefully for the rest of his days and was widely renowned abroad. One notable act of his was the dedication of a temple at Gloucester in honour of Claudius, and there he was buried.

His son was Marius, a just ruler, who maintained friendship with Rome and paid the tribute without demur. At this time the Picts landed in northern Britain, as already told, and Marius managed to contain them in Caithness, though they remained independent and increasingly strong.

In the last century BC much of Britain was dominated by 'Belgic' tribes. There were Celts of this strain on both sides of the Channel. Thanks to influence from the continent, and an influx of new people, society in Britain was registering advances. The Belgae made pottery on the wheel, exploited mineral resources, farmed the heavy soil of the valleys, and minted gold coins. Cassivellaunus, who became the Caswallawn of the *Mabinogion*, was king of the Catuvellauni, living between the Thames and Cambridgeshire. He commanded great respect beyond. On his eastern border he threatened to master the Trinovantes, the tribe that generated Geoffrey's name 'Trinovantum' for London. When it became clear that Julius Caesar had designs on Britain, Cassivellaunus was accepted widely as the architect of resistance.

Caesar's first British foray was in 55 BC. It was a sideshow of his war to subdue the Celts of Gaul. The Belgic chiefs in the north had support from their kinsfolk across the Channel. The main aim of Caesar's expedition was to overawe and discourage the Britons concerned. Geoffrey's account is right in treating his success as extremely limited, though the details are much improved. His ships, beached near Deal, were badly damaged by a high tide, and legionaries who probed inland were ambushed by Britons in chariots. The islanders' chariot-fighting was notorious. In the following year Caesar made a second, better planned, attempt. Cassivellaunus, leading a force drawn from several tribal groupings, harassed the Romans in the Canterbury area. This time Caesar had cavalry, and by keeping his horsemen and infantry close together, acting in concert, he found an answer to the chariots. He crossed the Thames near the site of London. The Trinovantes, afraid of Cassivellaunus's ambitions, put themselves under Roman protection, and other Britons came over as well. With their aid Caesar located Cassivellaunus's stronghold at Wheathampstead and broke into it. The British king agreed to pay Rome an annual tribute (here Geoffrey is right) and to respect Trinovantian independence. Satisfied for the moment, Caesar returned to Gaul. He probably contemplated conquering Britain later, or part of it, but he never pursued the project, nor did Augustus.

Cassivellaunus was succeeded by that Tasciovanus who became Tenuantius in legend. Tasciovanus's son was Cunobelinus – Cymbeline – who reigned for more than thirty years, extending the kingdom. His name means 'hound of Belinus', that is, the god's faithful follower. Great Kimble is not actually called after him, though 'Kimble', a name derived from the Anglo-Saxon, does mean 'royal hill'. Regarding the treaty with Caesar as having lapsed, he conquered the Trinovantes and made their capital Camulodunum (afterwards Colchester) the centre of his own rule. In the portion of the island nearest the continent, his pre-eminence was such that the Roman historian Suetonius calls him in retrospect 'the king of the Britons'. Foreign trade increased. Exports included wheat, cattle, pearls, hides, slaves, hunting dogs, and several metals. Imports were mostly luxuries for the nobles, such as wine, amber, glass, ornaments, jewellery. For the necessities of life Britain was self-sufficient. In Shakespeare's play, the king's stepson rejects a Roman demand for arrears of the tribute in words that would have been apt:

68. A coin of Cuno-
belinus (Cymbeline).

> Britain is
> A world by itself, and we will nothing pay
> For wearing our own noses.

The invasion that brought most of Britain into the Empire was launched in 43 AD. Claudius was responsible, but his motives were more complex than Geoffrey makes out. Cunobelinus had just died, and his sons, Togodumnus and Caratacus, were fomenting anti-Roman activities. There was a pressing need to re-establish the Empire's prestige, recently lowered by Claudius's predecessor Caligula, who had prepared a British expedition and then lost his nerve. On the economic side, Britain's resources were alluring; its rich wheatfields would have particular value as a source of bread for the legions. Also, the Druids were implacably hostile to Rome, and the suppression of their insular colleges would remove a seed-bed of Celtic sedition. Some years later, when the Romans invaded Anglesey and the Druids opposed them, the attack ended in an authorised massacre, annihilating the last organised druidic body in Britain.

Claudius's army, numbering about 40,000, was ordered to assemble on the Channel coast at Boulogne. It was at this juncture that some of the troops mutinied, with spokesmen clamouring that the sea was the boundary of their world and the enterprise was ill-omened. Britain was 'other', and although it obviously had human inhabitants, the people of the mainland should not become involved with them or attempt to draw them into an unreal union. At last the tumult subsided and the invasion went ahead. Cunobelinus's sons put up a brave fight, but again many Britons were willing to make peace and seek Roman protection. Claudius himself was not in Britain for long; Vespasian carried on the campaign after his return to Rome. The conquest took many years and indeed was never completed, because the country beyond the Clyde-Forth line, though subjected to occasional marches and battles, remained outside Roman Britain.

6   Arviragus existed, but it is not known how he fits in. The Roman satirist Juvenal indicates that a British leader so named was causing concern during the reign of Domitian (81–96). He depicts a soothsayer telling that emperor: 'Either you will capture a certain king, or else Arviragus will tumble from the
7   British chariot-pole' – i.e., be defeated or deposed. Geoffrey quotes the passage, and may have brought in Arviragus where he does because he misunderstood it as making him contemporary with Nero (54–68). Nothing associates Arviragus with Gloucester, or with a temple honouring Claudius, though it is a fact that Claudius was worshipped in Britain after his death, this being the first instance of the official emperor-cult which the whole Roman world was to practise later. The improbable Hamo is another etymological figment.
8   Southampton is 'the south town in a *hamm*', meaning a low-lying piece of ground by a river.

Geoffrey, nevertheless, is now beginning to make serious use of real persons and events. He can hardly do otherwise, in view of the existence of Roman histories. But he weaves the strands together in a new story, which is not reality, but might be taken for it by a reader who knew no better . . . and in the Middle Ages, many readers did not. This is what he does in the rest of his book, comprising well over two-thirds of it. Once he is out of unrecorded antiquity, he seldom or never contrives major episodes from absolutely nothing. He cannot be trusted for facts, yet he habitually *uses* history or what he would like to think is history, however firmly a genuine historian might dismiss it as legend.
9   The hint for his patriotic tale of Caesar's defeats comes from 'Nennius'

69. Tombstone of Longinus at Colchester, mutilated by Britons rebelling against the Roman conquest.

70. A Roman legionary, wearing a cuirass.

(the alleged compiler of the *Historia Brittonum*, not the alleged brother of Cassivellaunus). It is here, incidentally, that the Welshman introduces Belinus. Geoffrey, who has put Belinus centuries earlier, does not ignore this. He assumes that there was another man of the same name, and duly finds him in Henry of Huntingdon, who mentions such a man and makes him a British 10 commander. Geoffrey does likewise. The Marius episode looks like pure fiction, 11 yet even this has a basis of a sort in an actual monument.

Despite the well-devised speech quoted on page 138, Shakespeare's *Cymbeline* is a romance, considerably farther from fact than Geoffrey. Besides the king, Shakespeare introduces Guiderius and Arviragus, but even more fancifully. Robert Graves in *Claudius the God* gives a lively account of the British war, which, like Geoffrey's, is not history but makes use of history, with the advantage of vastly greater knowledge and scholarship.

1. GM (1), 35–46, and (2), 107–24.
2. FML, 264; Westwood, 108–9.
3. Ashe (7), 27–34.
4. Ross, 425.
5. Ekwall, 276, art. 'Kimble'; Westwood, 108.
6. Juvenal, IV, 126–7.
7. GM (1), 45, and (2), 123; Tatlock, 120.
8. Ekwall, 431, art. 'Southampton'.
9. 'Nennius' (1), chapters 19–20.
10. Henry of Huntingdon (1), I, 12, and (2), 13.
11. Tatlock, 20.

27 *Caractacus and Boadicea*

Before Britain's absorption into the Empire, there were others who fought
back. Cunobelinus's son Caratacus – his name is often spelt 'Caractacus' – not
only opposed the Roman advance, but declined to join other southern
Britons in submitting to Claudius. He kept up an audacious guerrilla war
from bases in the Welsh hills, succumbing only when he risked a pitched
battle, at Caer Caradoc in Shropshire, near Knighton, or perhaps at
Hereford Beacon near Malvern. Betrayed into enemy hands, he was taken to
Rome with his family. His fame preceded him, everyone wanted to see him,
and, when put on public view, he won universal respect with a dignified
speech. Claudius could have punished him as a rebel, but granted him a full
pardon, together with his wife and brothers. As he strolled about the city,
gazing at its huge buildings, he remarked: 'When you have all this, why do
you covet our poor huts?'

71. Coin of Caratacus.

The other great anti-Roman champion was Boudicca, commonly remembered as Boadicea. She was queen of the Iceni in Norfolk. Her
husband, Prasutagus, had tried to retain some independence by staying on
good terms with Rome as a client king. But when he died, the Romans took
charge and plundered the royal possessions. They regarded these as including the queen and her daughters. Boudicca was flogged and her daughters
raped. She appealed to her people to take revenge. After delivering a warlike
speech she sought an omen by releasing a hare. It ran in an auspicious
direction and the Britons cheered. She thanked the goddess Adraste,
bestower of victory, and launched a revolt.

The Trinovantes, her neighbours to the south, joined in. The Romans
had been converting their capital, Camulodunum, into a town on their own
lines, Colchester. Their retired soldiers were to form the dominant population. As it happened, they were nervous because of omens they had noticed
themselves, such as the collapse of a statue of Victory. A combined force of
Iceni and Trinovantes under Boudicca's leadership destroyed the place, and
marched on to destroy the new cities of London and Verulamium (St
Albans). Wild revels, massacres, and human sacrifice marked each success.
At last the Romans recovered and defeated Boudicca's army. She took
poison.

72. Coin of Claudius.

No one knows the heroic queen's grave. Stonehenge itself was once
claimed as her monument. Some say that she lies under a mound in
Parliament Hill Fields in Hampstead; others, that she is under Platform 10
at King's Cross Station. Her ghost, however, haunts the earthwork of
Amesbury Banks in Epping Forest, and in 1950 she was seen driving her
chariot out of the mist near Cammeringham in Lincolnshire.

Where Geoffrey tried to deal with the Roman conquest, his fiction grew less persuasive. Here, at last it, was too blatantly at odds with fact. The only Britons of that period who have shown durability are these two, and he ignores them both.

The son of Cunobelinus is immortal in the repertoire of W. S. Gilbert's Major-General (*The Pirates of Penzance*):

> Then I can write a washing bill in Babylonic cuneiform,
> And tell you every detail of Caractacus's uniform.

Edward Elgar composed a cantata about him. Boudicca, her name spelt in various ways, has several literary settings. One is an ode by Cowper from which two lines of prophecy, uttered by a Druid, were taken as a motto for her statue on the Thames Embankment:

> Regions Caesar never knew
> Thy posterity shall sway.

Her revolt is the theme of a longer poem by Tennyson, experimenting with a Latin metre which has an odd barbaric gallop. In this too she takes heart from druidic utterances:

> 'While I roved about the forest, long and bitterly meditating,
> There I heard them in the darkness, at the mystical ceremony,
> Loosely robed in flying raiment, sang the terrible prophetesses,
> "Fear not, isle of blowing woodland, isle of silvery parapets!
> Tho' the Roman eagle shadow thee, tho' the gathering enemy narrow
>   thee,
> Thou shalt wax and he shall dwindle, thou shalt be the mighty one
>   yet!
> Thine the liberty, thine the glory, thine the deeds to be
>   celebrated . . ."'

73. **Brigantia, the 'High One', war-goddess and bestower of victory – a northern British counterpart of Adraste, invoked by Boudicca.**

To turn to history, Caratacus's main support came from two tribes in Wales, the Silures in the south-east and the Ordovices in the north. He took advantage of a change of Roman governor to counter-attack. The Romans checked him, but without winning decisively, and the process of his reduction was slow. In 51 AD he was finally beaten. The battlefield is unknown; neither of the traditional sites is likely. His wife, children and brothers fell into Roman hands. He escaped himself, and made his way north from Wales to the Brigantes, but their queen, Cartimandua, was pro-Roman and handed him over. His courageous bearing in Rome, and his comment on the city's magnificence, are historical. He died in 54 AD.

Boudicca's campaign was not an act of resistance to conquest, but a reaction after the event. Her career illustrates the equality of Celtic queens, and their ability to take charge and command armies. Her name, perhaps an assumed one, means 'Victory', and her attachment to the war-goddess Adraste may hint at a religious quality in her leadership. She is described as tall, fierce-looking, and harsh-voiced, with a mass of red hair down to her waist.

Her personal grievances are obvious, and so are her public ones, since the Romans made it plain that they were annexing her territory and not letting her continue as queen. She could enlist the Trinovantes – no longer subject to the

74. Boudicca's omen of the hare, which fled in a direction portending victory.

75. Head of a statue of Claudius, severed by Britons in the revolt, and found near Saxmundham in Suffolk.

Catuvellauni — because of the Romans' treatment of Camulodunum in the course of its transformation into Colchester. Army veterans seized land by evicting Britons in possession, and the authorities extorted money and labour for a building programme such as no Briton could have foreseen. Particularly resented was a temple devoted to worship of the emperor. This did not mean the current ruler himself, Nero, but the late Claudius, who had been officially deified by the Senate. More generally the cult paid homage to the spirit of Rome which the god-emperor embodied. But however construed, what it meant in practice was a large building with a great deal of expensive marble, and wealthy Britons were expected to prove their loyalty by paying for this.

Boudicca, therefore, exploited the indignation of the whole of East Anglia, a populous area. Late in the year 60 AD, probably, a horde of Britons under her leadership destroyed Colchester. The Roman forces in Britain were divided, and she captured London and Verulamium, burning both to the ground and massacring thousands, not only Romans but British collaborators. Rome's historians take her triumphs no farther, but there are archaeological hints of outbreaks beyond.

The governor, Suetonius Paullinus, was away in Anglesey stamping out Druids. During 61 he managed to assemble ten thousand men, and stationed them in a well-chosen spot, partly enclosed by hills and woods that nullified the Britons' advantage in numbers. Its location is doubtful. One suggestion puts it near Towcester, in Northamptonshire; another near Mancetter between Nuneaton and Atherstone. The queen attacked, but Roman discipline prevailed and the Britons were routed. Her suicide may well be historical, and there is certainly no clue to her grave. The King's Cross theory is due to Lewis Spence, who conjectured that she fought her last battle on the future site of the station.

Paullinus carried out ruthless reprisals. However, his treasury officer Classicianus was a Gaul with ideas about enlightened Romanisation. Under his influence the regime grew milder, and the Britons, those of the upper classes at least, were largely reconciled and assimilated.

76. Boudicca 'loftily charioted', in Tennyson's phrase – her statue on the Embankment in London.

It is worth reiterating that Geoffrey has not a word about either leader. Spenser inserts Boudicca in his paraphrase, but, lacking guidance, puts her a century too late. Geoffrey's omission is at first sight amazing. Even the incoherent Gildas, whom he read, knows about Boudicca. The logic of his silence is best understood in the light of previous tradition. Among the Britons, and their Welsh descendants, the Roman domination was retrospectively altered. Gildas, in the sixth century, has a low opinion of his own nation and is quite clear that the Britons were conquered. Indeed, he goes too far in stressing their negativity and the conquerors' triumph. He does not concede that they were Romanised or learned imperial ways, even though he uses Latin himself, an imperial legacy. But then a change sets in. 'Nennius', in ninth-century Wales, still treats the Romans as aliens who had little influence, so that Britons remained Britons, but he is less definite about the conquest itself. While noting emperors who took an interest in the island, he almost seems to regard them as interlopers. In the end, he says, the Britons rejected Roman authority altogether, and the connection ended. [8]

What Geoffrey is doing is carrying the notion further. In his *History*, not only do the Britons remain Britons, but there is no real conquest at all. Britain becomes a tribute-paying protectorate, part of the imperial system, but not a province. His line of British kings simply goes on, and while he acknowledges some emperors who wielded power in the island, he ingeniously makes out that they were Britons themselves, or demi-Britons, or Britons-by-marriage, and includes them in his king-list.

That is why he cannot do anything with the resistance leaders. To trace their careers, ending, however heroically, in well-attested defeat and repression, would have been to admit the conquest. After such a breakdown, such a collapse, it would have been too hard to portray the monarchy as continuing. Therefore he leaves them out, ignoring Cunobelinus's real sons, and turning Arviragus into an heir who can do what needs to be done for the story's sake. His notion of British kings surviving with the Empire's agreement is not entirely baseless. In the early phase, a few regional client rulers actually were allowed to carry on. Boudicca's husband managed it, and so, for a while, did the northern queen Cartimandua. This turned out to be an interim measure only, and the clients' domains were all annexed, but Geoffrey is giving fictional development to something that did, temporarily, happen.

Nor is his patriotic fantasy without a sort of backhanded insight. The old schoolbook image of the conquest, still by no means defunct, was like Gildas's. Britain became a land of colonial 'natives' oppressed by foreign overlords from Italy, neither preserving much character of their own nor acquiring much from the overlords. These negations are at most half-truths. While the Britons lost political power, Romanisation in the upper strata did not create a society of mere quislings and serfs. In the third century all free men subject to the Empire were granted equal citizenship. From then on the imperial world was cosmopolitan. Even emperors came from different parts of it, and major initiatives were taken in the provinces, including Britain. The ancestral Celtic culture was never erased. When Britain ceased to be part of the Empire it began to revive, and the ex-Roman land maintained itself for several decades with an imperial heritage yet an individuality too.

1. Kightly, 9–29.
2. FML, 313; Kightly, 26–7.
3. Kightly, 31–54.
4. FML, 219; Kightly, 49–52; Piggott (1), 125.
5. FML, 241; Kightly, 52.
6. Kightly, 32, 39–40; Ross, 454.
7. Gildas, chapter 6; Henry of Huntingdon (1), I, 20, and (2), 19. Cp Lloyd, I, 89–90.
8. 'Nennius' (1), chapter 28.

28 *The Coming of Christianity*

Some say that Jesus himself visited Britain during the hidden years before 1
his public ministry. He was in Somerset, perhaps for an appreciable time.
The Druids were prepared for him because they had a god Esus or Yesu. On 2
the future site of Glastonbury Abbey, he put up a small building which was
his home for a while. He walked over the Mendip Hills to the north where
Priddy now is. He may also have been in Cornwall, where the Jesus Well
near the mouth of the Camel is said to commemorate him, and there are
scraps of folklore about his visit in other places, such as St-Just-in-Roseland.

If he did come to Britain it was probably as a youth, in the company of
Joseph of Arimathea, the rich man who, after the crucifixion, obtained his
body from Pilate and laid it in the tomb. Glastonbury Abbey had nothing to 3
say of any visit by Jesus, but its account of its beginnings makes much of
Joseph. In 63 AD, the story goes, he was in Gaul on a mission with the
apostle Philip. Philip sent him over to Britain at the head of a party of
twelve. They sailed up the Bristol Channel and proceeded by boat along
inland waterways to the Glastonbury hill-cluster, known in those days as
Ynys-witrin, the Glass Island. Disembarking at the foot of one of the hills,
they were *weary all*, so it is called Wearyall to this day. Joseph drove his staff
into the ground and it grew into a tree, the Holy Thorn, blossoming at 4
Christmas. Arviragus, the British king who was reigning then, was not
interested in their preaching, but out of goodwill he made them a grant of
land. There they built Britain's first church, in obedience to a command
from the angel Gabriel. They lived on the spot and died there, and it
reverted, for the moment, to wilderness. Joseph is reputed (though not in
the monks' account) to have brought the vessel of the Last Supper, the Grail
as it was called. It had supernatural properties, passed into the care of an
elusive custodian, and became the goal of a mystical quest several centuries
later.

Further stories of early Christians are centred on St Paul. He is said to 5
have made a brief journey among the Britons in person, and that is why
London's cathedral is dedicated to him. In *Romans* 16:10, he sends good
wishes to 'Aristobulus's household' but not to its head, and the reason is
that Aristobulus was away on a British mission. Attention focuses more
minutely on a married couple living in Rome, Pudens and Claudia. Paul 6
passes on greetings from them, together with Linus, in *II Timothy* 4:21.
These two are identified with Aulus Pudens and Claudia Rufina, known in a
different context, because the poet Martial addresses epigrams to them.
Pudens he salutes as a friend and a valued reader of his verses; Claudia is a
Briton, the child of blue-painted parents, yet in Rome she has acquired
every civilised grace. Claudia, therefore, is the only Briton in the Bible.

It does not appear that she ever went back to her native land. Linus, who
succeeded St Peter as head of the Christian body in Rome, was reputedly a
relation of hers, perhaps a brother. She had a daughter, St Pudentiana, to

whom a church in the city was dedicated. A few Welsh authors, echoed by
7 fewer English ones, state that Claudia's father was none other than Caratacus and that she was taken to Rome in 51 with the rest of his family. Some
state further that Caratacus's own father went too, was converted by St
Paul, and returned to Britain in his old age to spread the word. His name
was Bran. This is the only real Bran, all else is heathen fable.

77. Joseph of
Arimathea and his
companions receiving
divine inspiration, as
they kneel before the
table on which they
kept the Grail, their
wonder-working
memento of Christ.

8   None of these initiatives can have had much impact. It is written,
however, that at some date between 174 and 189 a Roman mission was
dispatched by Pope Eleutherius, at the request of the British king Lucius,
Marius's grandson. He received baptism together with many of his subjects,
and set up bishoprics in the major cities. Britain's Christianity is properly
9 dated from this event. The principal papal envoys were Faganus and
Duvianus. They led a party west into Somerset and found Joseph's derelict
church, with crosses and other signs of the former occupancy. Twelve of
their companions settled in the place as hermits, meeting for worship in the
church, which thus became the nucleus of a Glastonbury community
existing without a break from that time onwards. It was to grow into the
great medieval Abbey. Lucius, having endowed his establishment with
goods and lands taken from pagan temples, died in Arviragus's city of
Gloucester and was buried there.

10   Gildas, writing in the sixth century, attests a belief that Christianity reached
Britain during the first. The sentence is long and convoluted, and can be

construed in more senses than one, but on the likeliest reading it claims that the Christian advent occurred during Boudicca's revolt or its immediate aftermath, that is, in the 60s AD. Gildas is supposed to have spent some time in the Glastonbury community, and while that may be legend, a passage further on in   11
his tract does seem to imply acquaintance with it. He may be thinking of some early version of its claim about its origins. The Joseph version that takes shape afterwards, by giving the date 63 (not a natural one to hit on in view of his implied age), is in line with that possibility.

As to the actual date of Glastonbury's first Christian presence, it remains a   12
mystery. There may have been individual residents, or scattered hermits, before there was anything like a monastery. The monastic legends, however, grew around a material fact. While Joseph himself could hardly have built a church as such – buildings for Christian worship were unknown till much later – the church which he was alleged to have built did exist. Fire destroyed it in 1184;   13
the Lady Chapel today marks its site. Before that it had stood within the precinct from time immemorial, so long that there was no authentic record of its foundation. It was a simple structure of wattle-work, twigs bound with clay, plus reinforcements of timber and lead. Understandably it was known as the Old Church, and if Gildas's seeming Glastonbury allusion means what it appears to mean, it was already on the site in the sixth century. Its dedication, unparalleled in Britain till long after, was to the Virgin Mary, a fact that may hint at pre-Christian Glastonbury having been a goddess sanctuary (as the Tor maze, if real, may also do). Such substitutions occurred early at Ephesus and elsewhere.

Saxon charters mention the Old Church without accounting for it. Presently we find a legend of its having been built by no human hands: it was miraculously   14
planted by God himself. The historian William of Malmesbury, writing towards   15
1130, testifies to the unique reverence it inspired, and speaks tantalisingly of a sacred mystery concealed in its floor design. As to its origin he notes, without commitment, a current idea that it was built in the first century by disciples of Christ. He puts no names to them. It was not till the thirteenth century, in an enlarged copy of William's book, that the monks specified Joseph as the   16
disciples' leader. By then he had become a hero of romance, the bearer of the Grail . . . which, however, the monks did not mention. This is all rather confusing. Moreover, there are traces of a tradition locating hermits close to the Tor, and Joseph himself is sometimes said to have settled there, not on the   17
Abbey ground at all. How, why and when the unlikely Arimathean was first connected with Britain, either as Grail-bringer or as founder of Glastonbury, no one knows.

Despite the lack of evidence that this happened early, the legend has touches of plausibility and may reflect a long-standing belief, even, as suggested, a belief known to Gildas: not necessarily about Joseph in person, but about someone or something. At the beginning of the Christian era the Glastonbury hill-cluster   18
was almost an island in times of high tide and flooding. Vessels could reach it from the Bristol Channel. Two nearby lake-villages, centres of the La Tène culture, had long had overseas trade connections. Voyagers from distant countries could thus have known the area and made their way to it. Again, the notion of a British king being able to make land grants in 63 would, until recently, have been rejected, because the Romans were assumed to have conquered south-west Britain by then and stamped out its independence. Yet excavation of the Cadbury hill-fort a few miles off has demonstrated a Roman assault in the 60s or even later. Boudicca's rising may have had a western

offshoot. A British chief may have been holding out, like Hereward the Wake, in a miniature realm among the hills, islands, lakes and marshes of central Somerset. Arviragus? In Geoffrey he is impossibly a king of all Britain. Yet it is curious that the one authentic allusion to him, Juvenal's, shows Romans recalling him as a Briton who made trouble for them.

78. Glastonbury: the Lady Chapel, built on the site of the Old Church which reputedly dated from Joseph's time.

On the face of it, the monks who composed the story of Joseph could scarcely have known any of this, because the data on the lake-villages and Cadbury have emerged only from archaeology. They would not have contrived their tale as manifestly plausible. Apparently it was not. Perhaps they did draw on knowledge that has escaped documentation.

19   Those who believe in Joseph literally have stressed the scriptural reference to his wealth. He might, they argue, have been a merchant. He might have become acquainted with Britain through the tin trade. Granted that the mission of Philip is baseless, Joseph might still have chosen the island for his final retreat – a refuge, let us say, from persecution, well out of reach of the persecutors. The

trouble is that the tin came from Cornwall, and a trader would have had no obvious motive to sail up the Bristol Channel.

The legend concerning Jesus is linked with the tin theory. Its advocates assert that Joseph was related to the Holy Family and took Mary's son with him on one or more of his voyages. The problem here is to decide how old the legend actually is, and how it started. It cannot have been known at Glastonbury during the Abbey's lifetime, because the monks would have exploited such a splendid distinction, and they never so much as hint at it. Probably the idea arose from a too literal reading of the story about the Old Church being of divine foundation, though there is an evident difficulty here, because if Jesus built it, Joseph did not. Enthusiasts have had to argue that the reference is to a small house 20 which Jesus did build and which became a chapel. Another medieval legend that may have been influential speaks of Christ appearing in a vision to say that he dedicated the Old Church to his mother . . . not necessarily, however, during his earthly career.

William Blake is generally thought to refer to the visit:

> And did those feet in ancient time
>   Walk upon England's mountains green?
> And was the holy Lamb of God
>   On England's pleasant pastures seen?

But this is uncertain in view of Blake's highly individual use of symbolic language. The Priddy variant is dismissed by sceptics as Victorian. The village schoolmistress wrote a play for the children in which she imagined Jesus coming to Priddy, and this harmless fancy, like other fancies, became an 'ancient Somerset tradition'. The Druids did have a god called Esus, though in Gaul 21 rather than Britain, but so far as he was identified with anyone else, it was with Mars or Mercury. Since the main fact known about him is that he was worshipped with human sacrifice, he seems an unpromising character to bring in.

As for the Glastonbury Thorn, the parent tree grew on the slope of Wearyall 22 Hill, or correctly, Wirral. A Puritan cut it down in 1643, but many descendants are flourishing, including a fine specimen in front of St John's Church in the High Street. The famous white blossoms do make their appearance round about Christmas, and a sample from St John's is dispatched to the reigning sovereign. Allusions to the Thorn are found in the reign of Henry VIII, not certainly before, and even then it is not associated with Joseph. His miraculous staff is post-Reformation. The tree is a kind of hawthorn, *Crataegus oxyacantha praecox*, and is not quite like any other English tree, but does resemble varieties in Syria and Palestine, whatever one cares to make of that.

British missions by Paul and Aristobulus are mentioned only in writings of slight authority, hundreds of years later. The legends about Caratacus's family are Welsh antiquarian speculation, later still. Caratacus's father, it will be 23 recalled, was Cunobelinus. Bran was substituted through a false equation of Caratacus with Caradawg, the son whom Bran leaves in charge at home during his Irish war (though the date for this, in so far as there is one, does not fit). Bran's Christianisation may have been inspired by his epithet 'blessed', and perhaps also by romances of the Grail, in which Joseph has a companion Bron who becomes its custodian in Britain. This Bron may have been derived from the Bran of mythology, but nothing connects him with Caratacus, or with history of any kind.

Pudens and Claudia, looked at apart from their fanciful involvement, are at 24

least interesting. Paul's letter does not show that they were husband and wife. Still, if there is no evidence for their being the couple in Martial's epigrams, there is no downright disproof. While their daughter may be fictitious, her church is not. Catholic archbishops of Westminster have sometimes been styled 'Cardinal of St Pudentiana'. But even if Paul's Claudia was indeed Martial's cultured Briton, she can hardly have had much to do with the Christianity of a homeland she left.

King Lucius appears in Bede and Geoffrey of Monmouth, whereas the earlier missions do not. He is mentioned, with his request to the Pope, in a sixth-century Roman record. Conceivably he was a British chief, or an office-holder of royal blood under the Roman government, but he cannot have been more, and no Briton could have had the power or influence to set off a mass conversion or create a new religious organisation. The key to the story may lie in a simple blunder. About the time of Eleutherius's pontificate a king of the eastern state of Edessa, named Lucius, did become a Christian, and his stronghold figures in documents as 'Britium Edessenorum', raising the possibility that someone misunderstood *Britium* as 'Britain'. [25]

In the upshot, Christians may have reached Britain in apostolic times, and Gildas and the legends suggest a vague belief that a few did. But they fail to supply trustworthy names or details. Two Fathers of the Church, Tertullian and Origen, imply Christian penetration of the British Isles by the year 200. In the last major persecutions Britain had three known martyrs, Alban, Julius and Aaron, but that is a tiny number beside the thousands who suffered in other countries. British bishops attended the Council of Arles in 314, and Britain became nominally Christian with the rest of the Empire in the fourth century, yet its identifiable churches remain few and small. British Christianity produced outstanding individuals such as St Patrick. However, although paganism faded out, it was a long time before the new faith was effective as the majority religion, and then only in the west, because the heathen Saxons were moving in.

79. (opposite) Wearyall Hill, Glastonbury, where the parent Holy Thorn grew and there is now another, planted in 1951.

1. Dobson, passim; Lewis, 51–9, 162–3.
2. Dobson, 35–6.
3. Lewis, 28–34; Scott, 43–7 (*De Antiquitate*, chapter 1).
4. Lewis, 32–4; Vickery, 6.
5. Lewis, 26, 122–4; Morgan, 100–28.
6. Holinshed, 40–1.
7. Lewis, 26–8.
8. Bede, I, 4; 'Nennius' (1), chapter 22; GM (1), 46–7, and (2), 124–5; Lewis, 35–44. Dates given by early authors do not correspond to Eleutherius's pontificate.
9. Scott, 47–51 (*De Antiquitate*, chapter 2).
10. Gildas, chapter 8.
11. Gildas, chapter 28; Ashe (1), 142–3.
12. Carley, 1–5.
13. Ditmas (1), 4, 5–6, 8.
14. Ashe (1), 23; Carley, 184; John of Glastonbury, 279 n. 73; Scott, 47 (*De Antiquitate*, chapter 1).
15. Scott, 168–9 (reconstruction of William's original text).
16. Carley, 87–94; Ditmas (1), 12–13; Lacy, ed., arts. 'Glastonbury', 'Joseph of Arimathea'.
17. Ashe (1), 29–33; Carley, 4–5.
18. Ditmas (1), 4–5.
19. Dobson, 13, 19–20; Lewis, 52, 167–8.
20. Dobson, 23–4.
21. Ross, 60, 317–8, 350.
22. Carley, 181–4; Vickery, passim.
23. Bromwich, 285, 298–9, and in Loomis, ed., 51.
24. Butler, art. 'Claudia', August 7th.
25. Butler, art. 'Lucius', December 5th.

29 *Old King Cole*

1   In the days of the emperor Diocletian, who persecuted the Christians, Asclepiodotus was King of Britain. He maintained his autonomy against the Empire. But Coel, Duke of Colchester, overthrew him and became king himself. Rome sent the senator Constantius to negotiate. Coel agreed to pay the tribute, but no more, and Constantius accepted this settlement. Only a month afterwards Coel died. Constantius was still in Britain. He assumed the crown himself and married Coel's lovely daughter Helena, whose late father, having no other heir, had trained her for government.

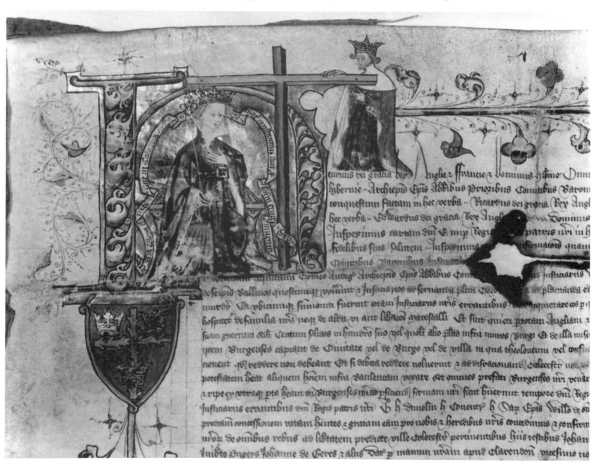

80. Colchester's civic charter of 1413, portraying Helena, and describing her as the mother of Constantine and the finder of the True Cross.

Some say that Constantius besieged Colchester for three years and that it
was Coel's handing over of Helena to him that persuaded him to raise the
siege. Some also claim that Colchester was not merely named or renamed
after him, but founded by him. In any event he is better remembered by a
rhyme:

> Old King Cole was a merry old soul
> 　And a merry old soul was he;
> He called for his pipe and he called for his bowl
> 　And he called for his fiddlers three.

Like many other eminent men, Coel is said to have been buried in the monastic
graveyard at Glastonbury.

While Constantius ruled Britain, his wife Helena bore him a son, Constantine, destined to great fame.

Constantius (nicknamed Chlorus, 'Paleface') was a real person, one of a group
who shared out the government of the Empire when this was reconstructed by
Diocletian in the late third century. At that time Roman Britain was in the hands
of a certain Allectus, who was carrying on a rebellion begun by Carausius, an
enterprising admiral. Carausius had been popular and successful; Allectus, who
had seized control by murdering him, was not. Constantius reconquered the
country and remained in it for some time, reconciling its people, improving its
administration, and strengthening its defences against marauding pirates and
Picts. An Asclepiodotus was involved in all this, but on the Roman side.
Geoffrey of Monmouth's portrayal of him as a British king is a flight of fancy,
invented to confuse the facts surrounding what was actually an imperial
triumph.

Constantius did marry a woman called Helena. Her father is a different
matter. Old King Cole was created by a false etymology of 'Colchester', the later
name of Cymbeline's Camulodunum. Transformed by the Romans, it became
'the Roman station on the Colne', this being the true derivation. The name of
the river was British, originally 'Colun', with a variant 'Clun' in Shropshire (also
responsible for place-names, assembled in a poem by A. E. Housman). There is
no reason to think that the Colun was named after a person, or that a person was
named after the Colun. The fictitious lord of Colchester – whose alleged
foundation of it augments his incredibility – might have remained in limbo if it
had not been for a need to establish Constantius's wife, the mother of the great
Constantine, as a British princess, and hence to give *her* a British parent.
Geoffrey adopted the idea from Henry of Huntingdon a few years before him.

'Coel', however, Geoffrey's spelling, is taken from someone who quite likely
existed, a fifth-century northern magnate. In later years many nobles in the
north, and not only there, claimed descent from him. Geoffrey probably noticed
the name in a Welsh genealogy and made out – or even genuinely supposed –
that Coel was the same person as Colchester's reputed lord.

Legends of King Cole, with further variations in spelling, have been noted as
far away as Ayrshire, where he used to be cited to account for other place-names,
such as Coilsfield. One known source of inspiration is the chronicle of Hector
Boece, written in the 1520s. Boece puts him in an impossible antiquity, but is
more likely to be using traditions about the northern Coel than relocating the

81. King Cole fighting an enemy chief, Alspradoc.

7

Colchester character. Some early versions of the rhyme, dating from the eighteenth century, are Scottish. Robert Burns knew several. The Coles in fact are fused. Until quite recent years, visitors to Colchester were shown King Coyle's Castle (a Roman gateway) and, in the High Street, King Coyle's Pump.

1. GM (1), 49–51, and (2), 130–2; Henry of Huntingdon (1), I, 37, and (2), 28.
2. Kightly, 63–4.
3. John of Glastonbury, 31 (chapter 14), 276 n. 43.
4. Ekwall, 116, art. 'Colchester', 117, art. 'Colne'; Tatlock, 34.
5. Bromwich, 238–9, 266; Kightly, 88–91; Morris, 54, 213.
6. Kightly, 83–7; Westwood, 355–7.
7. Kightly, 64.

30 *St Helen and the True Cross*

Constantius reigned over Britain for eleven years. After his death, at York, his son Constantine succeeded him. When Constantine grew up he proved a strong and just ruler. Rome meanwhile had fallen into the power of a tyrant, Maxentius. Refugees from his oppressions came to Britain and appealed to Constantine for help. He led an army to the continent, defeated Maxentius, and became emperor of all the Roman dominions.

Maxentius had been active in the persecution of Christians. During the war Constantine saw a vision of a cross in the sky and heard the words 'In this sign shalt thou conquer'. After his victory, convinced that the God of the Christians was the true one and had aided him, he favoured the Church throughout the Empire. His mother Helena, to whom he gave the honorary title of empress, was a much more devoted convert than he was himself.

1

82. Constantius's marriage with Helena, and the birth of their son Constantine.

Posterity knows her as St Helen, and in the story of her religious works, that is how she is properly referred to.

2   When Constantine ordered the building of a church in Jerusalem, he expressed a wish to find the original cross of Christ, if that should still be possible. Helen, encouraged by a dream, went to Jerusalem in 326 to investigate. Suspecting that the Jews had a secret tradition about the cross's hiding-place, she questioned their elders. One, named Judas, did know the truth. He also knew a prophecy that if the holy object were brought to light, the Christians would increase and the Jews would decrease. Nevertheless, his grandfather had told him that if anyone directly asked, he should divulge the tradition. Hence he was in two minds. He consulted the other elders when Helen was not present, and they too hesitated. But when she met them again, and threatened them with punishment if they kept silent, they told her that Judas was the one to ask.

She did. Even now he held back, and some say that she imprisoned him in a cell where he stayed for a week. At last he capitulated and found the way to the place, an old rock-cistern on the east side of the hill of Calvary, once used as a dumping ground for rubbish and never cleaned out. Helen set an excavation party to work. They unearthed three crosses, and the panel of wood set over Christ's head with the title 'King of the Jews'. To settle which was the right cross, the bishop of Jerusalem brought a sick woman to the spot, or according to another account a dead man. One of the three effected a miracle. Afterwards, supernaturally guided, St Helen also found the nails with which Christ was crucified.

Important as Constantius's wife was, she was not a Briton, though the family background invented for her son Constantine made her British in legend before

3   Geoffrey. Genuine misunderstanding may have played a part, since legend adopted and confused other persons bearing the same names, and some undoubtedly were British. The original Helena was born at Drepanum in Bithynia, now part of Turkey. She is spoken of as a *stabularia*, generally taken to mean that she owned, or worked in, a low-class tavern. Constantius, who was of Balkan origin, had not only married but divorced her before he went to take charge of Britain, and there is no evidence that she was even there. Their son, however, born about 280 at what is now Niš in Yugoslavia, joined Constantius in Britain on a second visit and, when he died, was proclaimed emperor at York in 306. After governing Britain for several years, marked especially by road-building in Wales and the north, Constantine marched against Maxentius – also a real figure of history – and eventually did become sole emperor and favour the Church. His celestial portent is a thing improved in the telling. He may have seen a halo phenomenon caused by ice crystals in the sunbeams.

4   When his power was secure he brought his mother out of retirement, renamed her birthplace Helenopolis, and gave her the title 'Most Honourable and Religious Empress'. His own beliefs were equivocal, his conduct was little influenced (to put it mildly) by Christian morality, and he was baptised only at the end of his life. But St Helen, as it becomes proper to call her, was a sincere Christian. Her journey to the Holy Land was a personal pilgrimage rather than a search for a relic. In the course of it she helped to direct a programme of church-building which her son had undertaken. The True Cross, or what passed

for the True Cross, undoubtedly was brought to light about this time, but the discovery may simply have happened while she was in the neighbourhood, supervising the building of a church on Calvary. The nails of the crucifixion were also produced as legend affirms, though, again, nothing is known with certainty as to Helen's role. Constantine attached one of them to his horse's bridle.

Helen died about 330, Constantine in 337. The first known allusions to the discovery of the cross are made shortly afterwards by St Cyril of Jerusalem. In a letter to one of Constantine's sons he says it was found in the city during the great emperor's reign. He speaks also, in a lecture delivered on the spot about 346, of the distribution of fragments throughout the Empire. St Helen herself begins to be named some decades later. Once she is introduced, her role is accepted without dispute. The legendary account starts its career in a Latin tractate *On the Finding of the Cross of the Lord*, which was popular (and stigmatised by the Church as untrustworthy) in the sixth century, and may be older. Some form of it was current in Wales at least as early as the tenth.

The rapid spread of 'fragments', as noted by St Cyril, is notorious. Plainly the cross was not left long intact. Part of it was kept in Jerusalem in a silver-gilt reliquary and displayed for public veneration every Good Friday. Another part was sent to Rome, where Constantine enshrined it in a palace where his mother

83. Miraculous identification of the Cross.

5   had lived. Smaller pieces were scattered more and more widely. A tenth-century reference to King Arthur has been read as meaning that he carried one of them into battle. When sceptics wondered whether so many could all be genuine, the superstitious asserted that the miraculous wood grew again as fast as it was reduced. In modern times the same scepticism has inspired the gibe that there are enough relics of the True Cross to build a ship. Measurement, however, has shown that the gibe is mistaken and the fable of miraculous growth was unnecessary. If all the alleged pieces were collected and stuck together, they would fall far short of making a cross big enough for a crucifixion. As far as actual volume goes, they could all be genuine. If some might have to be rejected as being of a wrong kind of wood, their elimination would only underline the small aggregate bulk of the ones retained.

    Germans used to claim that St Helen was born at Trier (Trèves) and that another relic of Christ which its cathedral has, the Holy Coat, was presented by her. But in her time the basilica which is the nucleus of the cathedral had not yet been built. She is celebrated in an Anglo-Saxon poem by Cynewulf, and in

6   Evelyn Waugh's one historical novel. Medieval Colchester, insisting on its own claim to the saint, alleged that one of its chapels was founded by her, and incorporated the cross in its coat of arms and Helen herself in its civic charter and corporation seal.

1. GM (1), 51, and (2), 132–3.
2. Ebbutt, 53–62; Kightly, 59–60. Cp Bede, V, 16.
3. Bromwich, 341; Kightly, 81–2; Westwood, 291–2.
4. Butler, arts. 'Macarius', March 10th, 'The "Invention" of the Holy Cross', May 3rd, and 'Helen', August 18th; Kightly, 60.
5. Alcock (1), 52.
6. Kightly, 63–4.

31 *Maximus*

While Constantine was still supreme in the Roman world, Octavius, ruler of 1 the Gewissei in south-east Wales, made himself king of Britain. He defeated attempts to depose him and outlived the emperor. Towards the end of a long and happy reign, when he was old and verging on senility, he decided to make arrangements for the succession. He had no sons and only one daughter. Some of his advisers favoured a proposal to offer her in marriage to a Roman senator, Maximus, who was of partly British blood, being descended from the family of Constantius's famous wife. He, they urged, would be eligible to rule Britain. Others wanted to give the crown to Octavius's nephew Conan Meriadoc, who was ambitious, and more than willing to cooperate.

The chief advocate of the Maximus plan sent an envoy to sound him out. As it happened, the senator was in dispute with the emperors Gratian and Valentinian, claiming that they should share power with him. The envoy astutely argued that if Maximus married the old king's daughter and accepted the crown, Britain's resources would make him strong enough to return to Rome and become sole emperor, just as Constantine had, starting from the island. Maximus took the point and set out for Britain, recruiting a host of followers on the way. He landed at Southampton. Octavius, whom nobody had told what was going on, thought the landing was an invasion and ordered Conan to oppose it. After some tense parleying the king grasped the situation, consented to Maximus's marriage with his daughter, and resigned the crown to him. Conan was furious, but failed in an attempt to dethrone the new sovereign.

84. A gold coin of Maximus, minted in London and showing him as emperor.

After five years of peace and prosperity, which filled the treasury, Maximus made his move against the emperors. Assembling the soldiery of Britain, he crossed the Channel and headed first for Armorica, in the north-west of Gaul, which he conquered with great ruthlessness. To appease Conan he handed over this territory to him, promising to stock it with settlers and turn it into a second Britain. Conan remained there with part of the British army, consolidating his hold, while Maximus conquered the rest of Gaul, killed Gratian, and chased Valentinian out of Rome. However, he was presently killed himself by supporters of the legitimate power, together with many of the Britons who had marched to Rome in his company. Survivors went to join their compatriots in Conan's Armorica. It was thus well on the way to becoming the Lesser Britain or Brittany, as it still is.

Concerning Maximus and his British bride the Welsh tell a more roman- 2 tic tale. Macsen, as they call him, was emperor before ever he went to Britain, the handsomest and wisest ever to hold the office. One hot day, when out hunting with thirty-two vassal kings, he lay down to sleep and dreamed that he was making a long northern journey. He glided effortlessly over a high mountain, and across a plain to the sea, where he boarded a ship with planks of alternate gold and silver. It wafted him to the fairest island in the world, which he traversed, coming at length to a strait with another island on the far side.

Close to the shore stood a castle. He walked in through its gateway and entered a hall with a roof of gold, and walls gleaming with gems. Two youths dressed in black silk were sitting on a couch playing at gwyddbwyll, a game of skill, with pieces made of gold on a silver board. Near by sat a majestic old man carving pieces for the game, and facing him, on a spacious golden chair, was a richly dressed maiden whose beauty shone like the sun. As Macsen approached she rose to greet him, and they sat down together.

At which point the emperor woke. But he was convinced that the maiden was real, and her image haunted him. He sent out messengers to look for her. After much fruitless inquiry, he managed to recall more of his dream, enough to supply guidance for a new search party. They passed the mountain and the plain, sailed over to the Island of Britain, and crossed it till they came to Snowdonia and Caernarvon. There in truth the castle stood, and they found the old man, the two youths, and the maiden in her chair. The old man's name was Eudaf, the youths were his sons Cynan and Gadeon, the maiden was his daughter Elen.

Elen accepted Macsen's marriage proposal, but said she would not leave Britain to marry him, he must come to her. He did, and stayed in Britain, neglecting Rome. He removed Beli, son of Manogan, the overlord of the country, and appointed Elen's father instead. Also he converted three towns into personal strongholds for her, Caernarvon itself, Caerleon and Carmarthen. She built new roads linking them, and because she employed such a multitude of workmen, she was known as Elen Luyddog, Helen-of-the-Hosts.

After seven years a message from Rome notified Macsen that because of his long absence, a new emperor had been proclaimed and he must never return. He collected an army and marched back to the imperial city, taking Elen with him. All the Empire as far as Rome submitted, but Rome itself held out. A long siege was unsuccessful. Finally a new army of Britons arrived, led by Elen's brothers Cynan and Gadeon, and they were worth more in battle than twice the number of Romans. Cynan devised a plan. First he gauged the height of the rampart and had new scaling-ladders made that exactly fitted. Then he took advantage of the fact that whereas the Romans stopped fighting at noon to eat, the Britons ate earlier, and drank till they were in high spirits. During a noon lull, in high spirits, the Britons unexpectedly scaled the wall and captured the city. So Macsen received his capital from his British brothers-in-law.

In reward he authorised Cynan and Gadeon to take a province for themselves. They conquered Armorica. Gadeon returned to Britain, Cynan remained in the country as its lord with a large part of the British army. During the conquest the Britons slew all the Armorican men, but kept the women for themselves. Not wanting their language to be corrupted in half-alien households, they cut out the women's tongues, so that in the first Breton generation, one sex talked and the other did not. And the language never became foreign, and Breton and Welsh, descendants of a common original speech, remain alike.

Octavius, whose daughter marries Maximus, is equivalent to Eudaf in the *Mabinogion* tale of Macsen's dream, while Conan is Cynan with his name spelt Breton-style instead of Welsh, though Geoffrey gives them a different relationship – his marriage-of-state theme rules out an obvious male heir. He makes Octavius king of Britain from as far back as Constantine's time to bridge a gap of forty-odd years. The daughter supplies a dynastic link with the husband she brings in, who is the next character of substance. Actually, Geoffrey calls him Maximianus, through confusion with an earlier emperor who, like Constantius, was a colleague of Diocletian; but history leaves no doubt who he means. He relates this man to the house of Coel in a cousinly way which is difficult chronologically. However, he contradicts himself here, and the general notion of a collateral kinship to Constantine is all that matters.

The kinship is probably fictitious, but Maximus is tangible and important. He   3
was Spanish by birth, and served as a soldier in Britain in 368. He remained there, and, in the 380s, held a high command, but harboured a grievance because he thought his promotion had been too slow. The Roman world was ruled by a trio of co-emperors; Theodosius (the eldest of the three) in the east, Valentinian II in Italy, Gratian in the remainder of the west. Geoffrey introduces the second and third of these but not the first, an omission that causes trouble in getting Maximus off the stage. Theodosius was the capable son of a capable army officer, and also a Spaniard; Valentinian was a boy, under the thumb of his attractive mother Justina; Gratian was an incompetent who pleased the clergy by a display of piety, but antagonised almost everyone else. By contrast Maximus was popular, and in 383 the army in Britain proclaimed him emperor.

He followed Constantine's course, taking many of the troops over to Gaul, with a reinforcement of British volunteers. Gratian was defeated and killed,   4
Theodosius gave the pretender a provisional recognition. Maximus ruled Gratian's portion of the Empire ably and without evident corruption, making Trier his capital. He kept the friendship of most major ecclesiastics, among them the celebrated St Martin, Bishop of Tours. However, in the religious field he set a grim precedent. When the doctrines of Priscillian, yet another Spaniard, unsettled the Church, Maximus executed some of the heretics and thus became the first Christian persecutor. Martin courageously opposed his action, and it was also condemned by St Ambrose, Bishop of Milan, one of the principal western prelates.

To meet the cost of maintaining his forces, without which he could expect to be ousted sooner or later, Maximus needed to follow Constantine further and occupy the richer parts of the Empire. He tried to win control of Italy by diplomacy, but found that he had to deal with Ambrose, who acted for Valentinian and Justina; and while the bishop had his differences with them, he was not disposed to give way. Maximus withdrew more troops from Britain, crossed the Alps, drove the boy and his mother into flight, and entered Rome in January 388. But Theodosius at last moved against him, and in July he was captured and beheaded. His death was against the wishes of the eastern emperor, who was magnanimous in victory. Theodosius vetoed mass reprisals, and provided for the pretender's young daughters, who became imperial wards.

Maximus has a special interest as marking a watershed. He is an outstanding figure in Roman history, yet, as the 'Dream' story shows, legend makes him an

85. Caernarvon Castle at sunset; here, or rather in an earlier stronghold near by, Maximus found the bride he had seen in his dream.

5

honorary Briton. The same might be said of Constantine, but with Maximus the process goes further. He is called a 'gwledig' or prince, a Welsh term; Britain becomes his adoptive country, which he leaves only to deal with opposition; and he is claimed as an ancestor of Welsh dynasties. Crucial here perhaps is his wife. Non-British history glances at her listening reverently when Maximus had conversations with Martin, waiting on the bishop at meals, even, to his distress, cooking for him herself. While history thus takes note of her respect for the saint, it is silent as to her nationality and name. Welsh tradition, in making her British and calling her Elen (Geoffrey leaves her anonymous), might seem to be merely duplicating Constantine's pious mother. But in this case there is no contrary evidence. Whatever her name, she may really have been British. In **383** Maximus had already been living in the island for fifteen years. He had a son

86. Roman soldiers engaged in building operations.

87. Sarn Helen, Helen's Causeway, one of the Welsh roads said to have been made under the direction of Maximus's British wife.

Victor who, towards the end of his adventure, was old enough to be employed as an envoy. Yet if he married a Briton soon after his arrival, it is not impossible. Or, of course, 'Elen' may have been a second wife.

6   In the hands of story-tellers, at any rate, she is an interesting composite heroine. Her sobriquet Elen Luyddog, Helen-of-the-Hosts, is due to her absorbing the mythic lore of a tutelary spirit presiding over the roads – those famous roads where the legions marched. And this patroness was to some extent a mythification of the original Helena, whose son developed the highway system in Wales, and who is called 'Helen Luicdauc' in a Welsh genealogy long

7   prior to the Macsen romance. A Roman road south of Ffestiniog is Sarn Helen, Helen's Causeway, and Wales has other roads named after her. A second genealogical item lists both 'Elen' and Maximus – but in different generations. When the author of *The Dream of Macsen* presents the lady, road-building and all, as Maximus's wife, he is blending roles and characters, though he does not quite grasp the point of 'Luyddog'.

The notion that Maximus was emperor before coming to Britain, and that he came because he was drawn by the maiden and her enchanting island, is of course fantasy. But her relationship to Cynan, otherwise Conan, and Conan's foundation of Brittany under Maximus's aegis, take the story on to problematical ground. British settlement in the Armorican corner of Gaul, changing it into the Lesser Britain or Brittany, is a fact of history. That is why the Breton language is akin to Welsh: they have a common ancestry in the British of Late Roman times. Moreover, a belief that the change began with a plantation of Maximus's soldiers is much older than Geoffrey or the *Mabinogion*. It is in the

8   ninth-century *Historia Brittonum* of 'Nennius'. Nevertheless, there is no hard evidence for British colonisation so early. It may be significant that in *The Dream of Macsen*, while the conquest of Armorica does begin in Maximus's time, Brittany is not definitely established as such till many years later.

As for the ugly legend about the women's tongues, so painfully out of key with the rest of the romance, it is drawn from older tradition and was invented to explain a Welsh name for Brittany, Llydaw. This was wrongly supposed to be derived from *lled* and *taw* and to mean 'half-silent'. The same legend appears in

9   the preface to a text written in Brittany itself, the *Legend of St Goeznovius*, which is earlier. There, by the way, the foundation of Brittany is ascribed – with geographical details suggesting real knowledge – to Conan alone, and Maximus is not mentioned.

Beli's brief and surprising reappearance, as ruler of an independent fourth-century Britain, emphasises his unhistorical character.

1. GM (1), 51–6, 58, and (2), 133–41, 143–4.
2. *Mabinogion* (2), 79–88.
3. Ashe (7), 60–6; Bromwich, 451–4; Morris, 20, 26–7, 419.
4. Alcock (1), 96; Gildas, chapters 13–14; Lloyd, I, 93.
5. Bromwich, 453–4, 518.
6. Bromwich, 341–3; Chadwick (2), 93–4, 108–9; Kightly, 63; 'Nennius' (2), 103; Westwood, 291.
7. Lloyd, I, xlvii, 68 n. 57; Westwood, 289–91.
8. Bromwich, 316–8; 'Nennius' (1), chapter 27.
9. Chambers, 93, 242; Fleuriot, 277.

32 *St Ursula and the Eleven Thousand Virgins*

Ursula was a British princess. A pagan prince asked for her hand in marriage. Preferring to remain single, and certainly not wanting a heathen husband, she asked for three years' postponement. Ursula had ten ladies-in-waiting. She and her ladies each gathered a thousand companions, and all eleven thousand of the company (or to be precise, eleven thousand and eleven) were virgins. 1

They put to sea in eleven ships and, after some voyaging about, were driven by strong winds into the mouth of the Rhine. Up the river the fleet sailed, to Cologne and thence to Basle. There Ursula and her companions disembarked. They crossed the Alps and went on to Rome to visit the tombs of the apostles. Their pilgrimage completed, they returned by the same route. At Cologne, however, the heathen Huns had moved in. The Huns' chief wanted to marry Ursula, but she had put off her first heathen suitor and now she refused the second. Exasperated by the faith which placed such obstacles in their way, the Huns massacred all the eleven thousand. Then angels appeared, somewhat belatedly, and dispersed them. Cologne's citizens buried the martyrs, and a Christian named Clematius, who had come from the east, built a church in their honour.

Some tell the story differently, linking it with the British settlement in Armorica and the beginnings of Brittany. Conan, having taken possession of the land, wanted to people it with a new British stock. He sent a request for wives for his soldiers to Dionotus, the duke of Cornwall, who had been left to rule Britain while Maximus campaigned against the emperors. Ursula was Dionotus's daughter and Conan desired her for himself. The duke consented, assembled a fleet in the Thames, and put Ursula aboard with eleven thousand maidens of noble birth and sixty thousand from the ranks of the commoners. Those who were reluctant to leave their homeland, or who wished to remain celibate, were overruled. 2

On the way to Armorica a storm scattered the fleet. Many of the maidens were drowned in shipwrecks. Others were cast ashore on islands with barbarous inhabitants, or among Huns and Picts, who were enemies of Maximus and therefore of his henchman Conan, and showed no mercy. They were sold as slaves, or were killed outright, or died resisting their captors' lust. None of the intended wives reached Armorica. The Breton nation had to be based on mixed marriages, but it kept its language and character, and their survival was assured by massive migrations from Britain in later years.

88. Disaster strikes
Ursula's company
when many of the
virgins are ship-
wrecked.

The legend of Ursula and her host began at Cologne, where an old inscription   3
on a stone – afterwards installed in a church dedicated to her – declared that
Clematius, a man of senatorial rank coming from the east, saw a vision of some
virgins who had been martyred there. At his own expense, he restored a ruined
chapel built in their honour. The damage to it may have been caused by Frankish
raiders in 353, and the inscription was cut, probably, at some time during the
next few decades, to mark Clematius's restoration. It named no names, and it
gave no details and no definite number.

Over the next centuries that lack was abundantly supplied. According to a
sermon preached at Cologne about four hundred years later, on the day of the
martyrs' commemoration, they perished in Diocletian's persecution, the person
directly responsible being his colleague Maximianus. Their leader was called
Pinnosa; there were a great many of them (though the inscription clearly
implied that there were only a few); and they were probably Britons returning
from a pilgrimage to the Holy Land. About the same time we find a reference to
'thousands of virgins of Christ' suffering on the Rhine on October 21st in an
unspecified year.

By the tenth century, eleven names had been given, including Ursula's. Quite
early in that century the total was fixed at eleven thousand. Perhaps someone
combined the 'eleven' who had been listed with the 'thousands' vaguely known
to tradition. Or perhaps the abbreviation XI.M.V – *undecim martyres virgines*,
eleven virgin martyrs – was misconstrued as *undecim millia virginum*, eleven
thousand virgins. Whatever the reason, the entire story now took shape. The
massacre was impossibly redated to 451, when the Huns under Attila were in
western Europe.

At Cologne alleged support came from the discovery of bones, culminating in
a mass find in 1153 when an old burial ground was excavated. But the virginity
of dismembered skeletons could scarcely be proved, and worse, the remains
included bones of men and young children. Under pressure to resolve the
difficulties, two visionary nuns named Elizabeth and Helentrudis improved the
story further. Men and children, it was revealed to them, had been slaughtered
together with St Ursula's company. Meanwhile clerical forgers, who had
encouraged and publicised the visions, were busy producing bogus relics and
faked inscriptions, among them epitaphs of Pope Cyriacus, King Picmenius of
England, and King Papunius of Ireland, all imaginary. Further revelations were
claimed for a third visionary, Canon Herman Joseph, who was active in
promoting the cult. The burial site was dubbed the *Ager Ursulinus*, Ursula's
field. Another query raised by the legend, why the Huns left their victims'
virginity intact, was not answered.

The alternative account is Geoffrey's, though, for some reason, the best   4
copies of his work leave the principal maiden as nameless as Maximus's bride.
There may be no more behind his version than his confusion between Maximus
and Maximianus, the latter being the emperor originally charged with the
martyrdoms. A hazy recollection that the maidens suffered 'in the time of
Maximianus' could have led Geoffrey to shift the story into the context of
Conan's activities. He had to explain how Armorica became Brittany, with a
British population, if all Conan's settlers were soldiers – persons of one sex only.

First he says (like the author of *The Dream of Macsen*) that they killed the   5
Armorican men but spared the women, presumably taking over the latter

themselves. Then it occurs to him that intermarriage would have produced a nation of mixed blood, and he says Maximus ordered a cross-Channel transfer of many Britons of both sexes. Then he seems to forget this, and plunges into his adaptation of the Ursula legend. But since, on his own showing, Dionotus's shipment of wives never got there, it appears that the Bretons must be a mixed people after all, descended, as first implied, from Conan's soldiers and indigenous women. That is what Welsh and Breton traditions do suggest, adding the gruesome detail about the women's tongues to explain the purity of the language. Actually, while there is evidence for a trickle of British settlement beginning in the 450s, the change of Armorica into Brittany was effected chiefly by large emigrations in the sixth century, the previous inhabitants being submerged and absorbed.

From the historical point of view, the Ursula legend's most intriguing feature is that German devotees of the martyrs should have been convinced that they were British. Conceivably they were: that is, the few real ones. In the tenth century St Dunstan, the great abbot of Glastonbury, chose St Ursula's day – October 21st – for his consecration as a bishop, and he is sometimes cited as an authority for the story. Several of the named members of Ursula's party were venerated at Glastonbury itself and elsewhere in the west of England.

1. Butler, art. 'Ursula', October 21st.
2. GM (1), 57, and (2), 141–3.
3. Butler, art. 'Ursula'; Tatlock, 236–40.
4. Bromwich, 333–4.
5. GM (1), 56–7, and (2), 140–3.
6. Cp John of Glastonbury, 19 (chapter 5), 167 (chapter 89).

Transition

33 Vortigern

Maximus's downfall left Britain in a desperate plight. He had taken most of 1
the troops overseas, and few returned. A lieutenant of his, Gracianus,
assumed control in the island, but his tyranny enraged the Britons and he
was assassinated. With no strong authority, Britain lay open to barbarian
onslaughts – by Irish in the west, some of whom seized territory and did not
go home; by Picts from Caledonia; and by other marauders from across the
North Sea.

Rome still honoured her protectorate and sent rescue expeditions, but as 2
soon as Roman pressure relaxed the barbarians reappeared. The Britons,
deprived of permanent forces, were ill-trained and ill-equipped for their
own defence. Weary of the trouble and cost of propping them up, Rome
withdrew. Even after that they tried one further appeal for aid, but it was
rejected. Britain sank into leaderless chaos and the assaults continued.

Guithelinus, the bishop of London, stepped in. Aware that the new 3
Breton realm was stable and flourishing, he crossed the sea and invited its
king Aldroenus, a successor of Conan, to take charge of the parent country.
Aldroenus declined, having a poor opinion of the insular Britons, but put
forward his brother Constantine, who was willing to shoulder the alarming
burden. He sailed over to Totnes with a picked force of two thousand men,
and recruited Britons to enlarge it. Under Constantine's command this
fresh army dispersed the barbarians. An assembly held at Silchester gladly
made him king. He had three sons: Constans, who entered a monastery;
Aurelius Ambrosius; and Uther.

Constantine reigned in peace for ten years. But the Picts became dangerous again in a new way, through influence instead of warfare. They had a
secret ally at court in the person of an unscrupulous noble, Vortigern, 4
overlord of the Gewissei. He was called Vortigern the Thin. Born in a family

associated with Gloucester, he had made an advantageous marriage with a daughter of Maximus, Sevira. Perhaps with his connivance – nobody was ever quite sure – a Pict asked for a private audience with Constantine, and stabbed him to death. Whether or not Vortigern inspired this deed, he was well prepared to exploit it. In the midst of public wrangling about the succession he slipped away to the dead king's eldest son, Constans, and persuaded him to leave his monastery and assume the crown. Despite much resentment at the breach of monastic vows, Constans complied. As intended he was a puppet in Vortigern's hands.

The schemer appointed friends of his own to key posts, got control of the treasury, and imported a hundred Picts as a royal guard, ostensibly for Constans, actually for his own use. Duly bribed and prompted, the Picts began clamouring for the coronation of Vortigern, and murdered Constans in his bedroom. Vortigern was delighted, having, it was suspected, instigated the crime himself, but he made a show of grief and had the assassins beheaded. Whatever the extent of his guilt, he succeeded in making himself king. The guardians of the younger princes, Aurelius and Uther, hurried them away to Brittany out of his reach.

Vortigern now reigned undisputed over the kingdom created from the post-Roman wreck. But the spreading rumours of his true character were

89. King Constantine's assassination, an improved medieval version.

making enemies for him, and his execution of the Pictish assassins, who had carried out his own wishes, was resented by their northern compatriots as a betrayal. Knowing that the exiled princes would soon be old enough to return, and lead the opposition, he was never able to feel secure.

At some time during this phase of change, a British leader laid the foundations of dynasties in Wales. His name was Cunedda and his home land was Manau Guotodin, beside the Firth of Forth. Though the Romans had never fully controlled the region north of Hadrian's Wall, its tribes had lived in treaty relations with them, and assisted in defence and administration. Cunedda, the head of a powerful family that had long supported Roman Britain, moved to Wales with his household and followers, and crushed the Irish who had been occupying parts of the country. He had eight sons with him. The main line of his descendants ruled in Gwynedd, while the names of some of his sons survived in areas held by their own descendants. Ceretic, for instance, gave his name to Ceredigion, now Cardigan. 5

In its exposed position, Britain was harassed by barbarians long before the Empire relinquished it. A concerted attack in 367 amounted almost to a full-scale invasion. It was an expedition to restore order that brought Maximus to Britain. Then and at other times, the Irish (still commonly called Scots; the migration that launched a separate 'Scotland' had not yet happened) were raiding from the west and even planting colonies. Picts from beyond the Firth of Forth made recurrent trouble in northern areas. Legend recognises these, and also assailants from across the North Sea, though it does not specify the most fateful of the latter, the Saxons, till surprisingly late. They were notorious for piracy as far back as Constantius's time. A long stretch of Britain's coastline was called the Saxon Shore and defended with forts. From ancestral homelands, mainly in Schleswig-Holstein, the Saxons had spread through the corner of Germany into Frisia, now Holland, and taken to the sea for plunder. They were heathen, savage, and deeply dreaded. Pressure of population drove them to seek new lands in Gaul and Britain, with momentous results . . . but not quite yet. 6

About eight years after Maximus's fall, the imperial general Stilicho did undertake a rescue of the weakened island. He put together a new defensive force, though not all of it stayed there. In 406 a vast surge of barbarians into Gaul – Vandals, Alans, Suevi – left Britain almost cut off from Rome. The feeble western emperor, Honorius, was unable to cope. There were British attempts to set up an interim emperor. Geoffrey's Gracianus is suggested by one of these ephemeral figures, and he takes a hint for his Constantine from another, a real Constantine who was proclaimed in 407 and may have been a Briton. This pretender had a son Constans, and Constans did leave a monastery, though with the motive of supporting his father. 7 8

Constantine took the attenuated army to Gaul, where he spent years trying to bring the barbarians to heel and assert his own sovereignty. In 410 Britain had to endure violent Saxon raiding, which Constantine could do nothing to check. The Britons, represented by civic and regional councils, rejected his authority. Their theoretical ruler, Honorius, could likewise do nothing, and told them to take measures for their own safety, which meant allowing them to create and arm a militia and, in effect, recognising their independence, though it was a long 9

90. An early representation of Roman coastal forts, built along the 'Saxon Shore' for defence against raiders from the sea.

time before the loss of Britain was accepted as final. Constantine and the ex-monk never got back. They were killed soon afterwards.

Little is known of the immediate sequel. Britain still kept a sort of unity for perhaps a half-century, but assorted heirs of the imperial system – administrators, commanders, tribal leaders – seem to have gradually assumed regional powers. If Cunedda existed (the modern form of his name is Kenneth), he was an early instance. According to genealogists his father, grandfather and great-grandfather all had Roman names, and his grandfather was 'red-robed', an epithet hinting at an official post. The alleged Cuneddan take-over of Wales, through which the Irish were subdued and, in the end, expelled, could have been part of a political re-structuring either before or after 410. So could the apparent rise in the north of the magnate Coel, the man who came to be fused anachronistically with Old King Cole. Cunedda is reputed to have married Coel's daughter.

All this would fit in with the probabilities about Vortigern, whose existence is 11 fairly certain. In the fifth-century context, 'Vortigern' would have been a title or designation rather than a personal name. It meant 'over-chief' or 'over-king', and the Briton so styled would have been a high king such as the fellow-Celts of Ireland had, nominally supreme above several regional rulers. His marriage to a daughter of Maximus is asserted in an inscription near Llangollen. Presumably 12 she was one of the daughters who were children in 388, and became imperial wards. Her name is given as Sevira, perhaps more correctly Severa. A marriage of Sevira to a British noble might have been part of a treaty devolving power on him. Notes appended to the *Historia Brittonum* of 'Nennius' make the reign of Vortigern – that is, the paramountcy of the Briton who adopted that style – begin in 425. If he had indeed played any part in the destruction of Constantine and Constans, he cannot have profited as quickly as Geoffrey's story makes out.

In the matter of Sevira, Geoffrey gives the inscription a curious backhanded support, all the more intriguing because it is inexplicit and doubtless unconscious. He calls Vortigern the ruler of the Gewissei, meaning the people of 13 Gwent, and his only other character with that status is the fourth-century Octavius. The underlying notion may be the transmission of a territorial right from Octavius to his daughter, whom Maximus married, and thence to a daughter of hers whom Vortigern married, thereby acquiring the same lordship as Octavius.

King Constantine's second son, Aurelius Ambrosius, also has an original. He is based very loosely on another fifth-century Briton, Ambrosius Aurelianus, a 14 member of a distinguished Romanised family, bearing a Roman name like Cunedda's forebears. He could – just – have been a son of the pretender Constantine, but there is no reason to believe that he was. Of him, more will be said.

91. Figurehead of a Saxon ship; the 'three ships' are constant in early accounts of the Saxon advent.

1. Bede, I, 11–12; GM (1), 58, and (2), 144; Gildas, chapter 14; 'Nennius' (1), chapter 27. Cp Bromwich, 452.
2. GM (1), 58–60, and (2), 144–8; Gildas, chapters 15–20; 'Nennius' (1), chapter 30.
3. GM (1), 60–2, and (2), 149–51.
4. GM (1), 62–4, and (2), 151–5; 'Nennius' (1), chapters 31, 48–9, 66.
5. 'Nennius' (1), chapter 62.
6. Alcock (1), 95; Campbell, 13; Hodgkin, I, 12–14, 19.
7. Alcock (1), 98; Morris, 21–2.
8. Alcock (1), 98–9; Bede, I, 11; Campbell, 16; Morris, 22, 29–30.
9. Lapidge and Dumville, eds., 5–6, 25.
10. Alcock (1), 125–8; Blair, 41; Lloyd, I, 116; Morris, 66–8.
11. Alcock (1), 102–5; Bromwich, 392–6; Chadwick (2), 26–33; Morris, 55–6.
12. Alcock (1), 98; Bromwich, 394; Chadwick (2), 18–19, 254–61; Westwood, 291.
13. Chadwick (2), 108–9.
14. Gildas, chapter 25.

34 *The Coming of the Saxons*

1   In the fourth year of Vortigern's uneasy reign, while he was visiting Canterbury, messengers reported that three longships manned by foreigners had beached on the Kentish coast. These newcomers were Saxons, ancestors of the English, who thus got their first footing on the soil of Britain. At the head were the brothers Hengist and Horsa. Conducted to Vortigern, Hengist explained that he and his followers had been compelled to leave their homes on the continent, because of a custom of enforced emigration when the people multiplied too fast for subsistence. He expressed a willingness to enter Vortigern's service. The British king saw that these men were tall and warlike, and, though unhappy about their heathenism, he undertook to keep them provided for if they would enrol as auxiliary troops. The Picts had withdrawn their previous support for him, and were causing trouble again in the north.

Hengist agreed to this arrangement, and the Saxons fought well. Vortigern allotted them land, some in Thanet, some in Lincolnshire. Realising that the king had his weaknesses and apprehensions, and could be manipulated, Hengist decided to strengthen his own position and suggested recruiting more Saxons. Vortigern approved. As soon as they were in Britain, Hengist held a banquet at which his beautiful daughter Renwein was present. She handed Vortigern a goblet of wine with the salutation 'Was hail!' He consulted his interpreter and gave the correct reply, 'Drinc hail!' Her father saw that the king was infatuated and offered him Renwein's hand (his first wife being dead) in return for more territory. Vortigern presented him with the whole of Kent, not even informing its regional ruler Gwyrangon. More and more Saxons now poured in with wives and families of their own, and Vortigern fell increasingly under Hengist's control.

2   At that time the Gallic bishops Germanus and Lupus came to Britain to regulate the Church, which was divided by the Pelagian heresy. News reached them of a combined raid by Saxons and Picts; for there were Saxons in the island who did not hold themselves bound by the new agreements. Under Germanus's direction, a British force waited in ambush above a valley till the raiders entered it, then, at a signal from him, shouted 'Hallelujah!' three times, whereupon they all fled in terror. Though

3   Germanus helped the Britons against their enemies, he was on bad terms with their king, and denounced the sensuality Hengist had exploited, accusing Vortigern of committing incest with his daughter.

4   Whatever the truth about that, Vortigern's Saxon marriage infuriated his sons by the late Sevira. The eldest, Vortimer, broke with his father and consented to be proclaimed as a rival sovereign. He campaigned boldly against the Saxons in Kent, driving them back to the sea. But his stepmother Renwein poisoned him, and Hengist recovered all the lost ground with a larger following than ever. He invited Vortigern and his nobles to a conference at Amesbury, pretending to have proposals for a new treaty. The

92. Hengist's defeat
and death at the hands
of Aurelius Ambrosius.

Saxons attended the conference with daggers hidden in their boots and massacred most of the Britons. Three or four hundred were killed, and buried in a mass grave on Salisbury Plain. Hengist threatened the king with death and extorted still more territory. In practice he now had a free hand. The Saxons occupied London, York, Lincoln and Winchester, and roved about the country plundering and destroying.

In desperation Vortigern had recourse to magicians, who advised him to build himself a stronghold in Wales. He assembled workmen on a hill in Snowdonia, with supplies of timber and stones, but the building materials kept sinking into the earth. His magicians told him that he must find a boy without a father and make him a human sacrifice, sprinkling his blood on the foundations. Messengers discovered a boy whose mother denied having intercourse with any man; the child had been begotten by a spirit, an incubus. When he was brought to Vortigern he turned out to be a seer. He revealed what the royal wizards had not known, that the subsidence was due to an underground pool with two giant serpents or dragons in it, a red and a white. These were the monsters concealed by Lludd long before. As soon as they were out in the open, they fought, and at first the white had the advantage, but then the red recovered and drove it back.

The boy explained that the red one symbolised the Britons, the white one the Saxons. Sooner or later the Britons would overcome their disasters, but Vortigern himself had no future. The king asked the boy his name, and he said he was Ambrosius, or, as the Welsh afterwards called him, Emrys Gwledig. Vortigern, shaken and afraid, gave up the sacrifice idea and handed over the hill to Ambrosius, making him sovereign in western Britain. The hill is known as Dinas Emrys, Ambrosius's Fort, to this day.

93. Vortigern and the red and white dragons in the pool.

6   Down below in the valley, Nant Gwynant, a son of Maximus named Owen (that is, Eugenius) once encountered a giant. They fought with arrows and missiles of steel till both were dead.

7   As to the end of Vortigern himself, the Welsh tell different stories, but agree that he moved hopelessly from place to place, detested by his subjects, and perished without honour. Nothing could erase his guilt. Because of him, the richest portion of the Island of Britain had begun falling into alien hands. It had begun to turn into England.

8   Whatever else may be legendary, the Saxons – meaning, as noted, a medley of Saxons, Angles, Jutes, and others – planted themselves in ex-Roman Britain during the fifth century. Over ensuing centuries they multiplied and expanded. Most of the former imperial domain became England, Angle-land, and the Anglo-Saxon language eventually evolved into English. However, the process was gradual and its opening phase was confused and erratic.

9   The Briton Gildas, writing in the sixth century, speaks of the arrival of a body of Saxons in three ships or *cyulae* (the first recorded word in their language; its modern form is 'keel'). The tradition of their three ships is thus very old. So is the belief that they were enlisted by a British ruler, the man usually called Vortigern, as auxiliaries to fight the Picts, with a large and ruinous influx following. Gildas attests this also, though he has them come by invitation rather than accident, and spreads the blame over a royal council of which no more is said.

10   Until recently, an error in early accounts led historians to put their advent far too late, 449 being a year often mentioned. The error was due to a misplacing of

a British appeal for aid to the imperial commander Aëtius, about 446, which was wrongly supposed to have preceded the Saxon advent when actually it followed it and may well have been prompted by its catastrophic results. The *Historia Brittonum*, which gives 425 for the rise of Vortigern, assigns the   11 landing of his pioneer band of Saxons to his fourth year, 428, with a respectable Roman-style dating by the names of the consuls. It is Geoffrey of Monmouth who, consistently, makes his main treaty with Hengist contemporary with the British visit of Germanus and Lupus, a documented event that happened in 429. According to one modern theory, the true reason for Germanus's anathematisa-   12 tion of Vortigern was that the king was a kind of Celtic Nationalist and favoured the Pelagian heresy, a doctrine of British origin, which Germanus had come to Britain to combat. The semi-historical Hallelujah Victory attests a Saxon presence in Britain at this time, and is in keeping with the view that the country now harboured both controlled Saxons and hostile or independent ones. Welsh   13 conjecture identifies the site as Maesgarmon, Germanus's Field, near Mold in Clwyd, but that location seems unlikely.

The entire legendary story is a simplification of a far more piecemeal, disjointed settlement, with many others responsible besides Vortigern. It is based on traditions handed down to the Welsh from their British ancestors, and dramatises a violently anti-Saxon view. Early Saxon accounts of the same events are brief, quasi-historical, and not even wholly independent of British ones; there is no comparable legend from the other side. As a matter of history, a few Saxons were apparently living in Britain before the break with Rome, some perhaps being squatters, some perhaps already auxiliaries. Whatever Vortigern did himself, the momentum of migration vastly increased during his reign, and the Britons' Welsh descendants made him the scapegoat for all the conse- quences. The detail about a ruler of Kent, over whose head he effected his deal with Hengist, supports the view of him as something like an Irish high king. It   14 remains doubtful whether the Kentish settlement was actually the first on a serious scale. Angles and Saxons were also in Lincolnshire, Cambridgeshire, East Anglia and the Thames valley long before the middle of the fifth century.

94. Dinas Emrys in North Wales, where the dragons hidden by Lludd reappeared and portended Britain's future.

The approved settlers are best interpreted as *foederati* in the Late Roman sense, barbarians allotted a foothold and supplies in return for keeping order and repelling other barbarians, in this case chiefly the Picts, led perhaps by Drust, son of Erp, who fought a hundred battles. Vortigern, and whatever other Britons enrolled them, were following imperial precedents without imperial resources. When the *foederati* were reinforced by many more settlers, and their increasing demands were not met, they mutinied. Instead of fighting the Picts they made common cause with them, falling into line with the Saxons Germanus had opposed, and raided lowland Britain at will. Their depredations, presented in legend as the sequel of the treacherous conference, occurred somewhat later than the date implied for this. Britain's time of trouble seems to have started in the 440s and continued, on and off, for a decade or more. There is little evidence for Saxon seizure or destruction of Roman towns, but the towns were mostly abandoned or nearly so, with a shift of British population into rural areas and Iron Age hill-forts. The emigration to Armorica, connected in legend with Maximus, appears in fact to have begun as a flight of refugees, though the main colonisation that formed Brittany as such was later still and much more deliberate.

Vortigern's abortive stronghold is mentioned first in the *Historia Brittonum*. Human sacrifice for the magical support of walls was a pre-Christian practice, archaeologically attested at Cadbury Castle in Somerset. In this version the young prophet Ambrosius is identified with Ambrosius Aurelianus, who afterwards rose to fame as a British leader and, in Wales, is known as Emrys Gwledig. 'Gwledig' – a style applied to Cunedda also – originally meant a 'land-holder' or regional overlord, probably on a military basis, though it came to have a vaguer sense, as when it was bestowed retroactively on Maximus as a British courtesy title.

Dinas Emrys is a hill-fort near Beddgelert, with a triple line of earthwork defences. Inside are traces of Roman buildings, and even of a pool, an artificial one. Furthermore, some fairly opulent person, a Christian, lived on the enclosed hilltop during part of the fifth century. An awareness of this occupancy, many years later, may have inspired the localisation of the tale and the name of the hill. As for the two serpents, they grow into dragons as the story improves. This is the ultimate source of the red dragon of Wales.

Owen's battle with the giant is not on record early, but has a curious interest because of its family aspect. If Owen was a son of Maximus, and Vortigern married a daughter of Maximus, they were brothers-in-law. Owen's presence in this neighbourhood may be a relic of some lost dynastic saga.

1. Bede, I, 15; GM (1), 65–8, and (2), 155–61; 'Nennius' (1), chapters 31, 36–8, 66.
2. Bede, I, 17–20.
3. 'Nennius' (1), chapters 39, 47.
4. GM (1), 68–71, and (2), 161–6; 'Nennius' (1), chapters 43–6.
5. GM (1), 71–3, and (2), 166–9; 'Nennius' (1), chapters 40–2.
6. Bromwich, 478–9; Rhys, II, 564.
7. 'Nennius' (1), chapters 47–8.
8. Blair, 9–11; Campbell, 30; Hodgkin, I, 1–17; Oman, 209.
9. Gildas, chapter 23.
10. Alcock (1), 108–9; Campbell, 31; Morris, 39–40.
11. 'Nennius' (1), chapter 66.
12. Alcock (1), 100; Chadwick (2), 33.
13. Alcock (1), 102; Morris, 554; n.63.1.
14. Cp Westwood, 89–91.
15. Lapidge and Dumville, eds., 20–1; Morris, 75–86.
16. Bromwich, 345–6.
17. Alcock (1), 179, 208, 214–5; Ashe (5), 92–5; Tatlock, 38; Westwood, 277–8.

35 *Merlin*

Reputedly, the Welshman who first told of the boy-prophet made a mistake   1
about his identity. He was not the Ambrosius called Emrys Gwledig but
someone else who bore the same name, and he is better known to posterity
by his other name, Merlin.

   Merlin was born in the town afterwards called Carmarthen. His birth did
come about through the coupling of his mother with a being that was not   2
human. But – so the tale goes – this was no spectral incubus but a devil,
acting in execution of a plot concocted in hell, to create a man with
supernatural powers who would combat the Christian faith. The mother's
piety thwarted this purpose, but her son, though lacking the malignity his
begetter tried to instil, inherited prophetic and magical gifts.

   His full name was Merlin Ambrosius; hence the aforementioned confusion. When he was brought before Vortigern and revealed the red and
white dragons, he slipped into a trance and spoke many more prophecies
than the Welsh recall. He foreshadowed the coming of a mighty British
ruler, symbolised as the Boar of Cornwall, and he passed on to a long series
of cryptic utterances about the later vicissitudes of Britain. Finally he told
Vortigern that the rightful princes, Aurelius Ambrosius and Uther, were
returning from overseas and would soon dethrone him. They landed at

95. Vortigern is burnt
to death in his castle
of Genoreu – Little
Doward above
Ganarew, near
Monmouth.

Totnes (Totnes again!). Vortigern moved to the castle of Genoreu, and there Aurelius besieged him and he was burnt to death.

3   Merlin remained for a while on the Snowdonian site, which received the name Dinas Emrys from his own second name. Before leaving he filled a golden cauldron with treasure, hid it in a cave, and blocked the entrance with a great stone and a heap of earth. Its destined discoverer is a youth with yellow hair and blue eyes. When he is near the spot a bell will ring, and when he reaches the cave-mouth the barriers will fall. Other treasure-seekers will have been frightened away by storms and apparitions.

4   Aurelius, as king, captured Hengist and put him to death for his atrocities. The Saxons were driven back and confined by another treaty to a limited area. (Pro-Saxon English will not admit this, or anything like it. Some of them have rejected the whole tale of fifth-century Britain, not only in detail but in substance. They have depicted the Britons as a pusillanimous people who fell into chaos and helplessness when the legions left, and the Saxons as virile conquerors who swept over the land, wiped out most of the Britons, and drove the survivors into Wales. So they have alleged. But the chronicles of their own Saxon ancestors convict them of falsehood.)

After Aurelius had seen to the repair of the worst damage, he decided to set up a worthy monument over the mass grave, on Salisbury Plain, of the nobles Hengist had massacred. He sent for Merlin – now out of boyhood; perhaps he matured unusually fast – who told him of the huge circle of standing stones in Ireland, the Giants' Ring. Merlin suggested uprooting it and re-erecting it over the nobles' grave. He accompanied Uther to Ireland with a host of Britons, and employed his secret arts to dismantle the circle. The stones were loaded on to ships and ferried to Britain, and Merlin reconstituted the circle over the grave. That is how Stonehenge came to be there.

Uther kept Merlin close to him as an adviser. One day when the prince was marching against a resurgent Saxon force, a portent appeared in the sky, a brilliant star with a train of light that expanded into the shape of a dragon. Two rays issued from the dragon's mouth, one towards Gaul, one towards the Irish Sea. Merlin declared that Aurelius was dead, as indeed he was, poisoned by a Saxon while lying sick at Winchester. The dragon represented Uther, now king of Britain, and he would have a powerful son, overlord of vast territories. Uther adopted the style 'Pendragon', meaning 'Dragon's Head'.

Soon after his accession he held court in London. Among the guests were Gorlois, Duke of Cornwall, and his beautiful wife Ygerna. Uther was smitten with ungovernable desire for her. When his interest grew obvious, Gorlois withdrew from the court without asking leave, taking Ygerna with him. Uther treated this act as an insult and marched to Cornwall with an army to ravage the ducal lands.

Gorlois immured Ygerna in his fortress at Tintagel, on a coastal headland accessible only by a narrow, easily guarded approach. However, Merlin turned Uther into an exact likeness of the lady's husband, and he was thus able to enter the fortress past the guards and have his way with her. Thus he begot a son. Meanwhile the real Gorlois had fallen in battle, so Uther was able to resume his true shape and make Ygerna his queen. Their son was

Arthur, the same whom Merlin had prophesied as the Boar of Cornwall, and prophesied again when he expounded the celestial dragon.

Some say that Uther and Ygerna afterwards had a daughter, Anna; others, that Arthur was their only child, but Ygerna had previously borne three daughters to Gorlois, namely Morgause, Elaine, and Morgan le Fay. Uther went on reigning and contained the Saxons without ever decisively beating them. His health declined, and when he drank some medicinal spring-water, a Saxon poisoned the spring and he died, so that Arthur succeeded him while still very young.

96. Ygerna's husband draws her away from Uther, who has designs on her.

Merlin, as known to literature, is a creation of Geoffrey of Monmouth, but he was not created out of nothing at all. Semi-historical tradition told of a Briton named Lailoken, who was crazed as a result of a battle in Cumbria about 575, and wandered through the forests of southern Scotland, an inspired madman. The Welsh called him Myrddin and credited him with prophecies of Celtic resurgence. Geoffrey Latinised 'Myrddin' as *Merlinus* and composed a long series of 'Prophecies' which he ascribed to him, and put in the *History* in the Dinas Emrys episode. Some had a genuine Welsh basis, some were purely Geoffrey's. Some could be fitted to real events, some were unintelligible.

Medieval commentators tried to interpret them, to the eventual amusement of Rabelais.

In the *History*, Geoffrey identified the seer with the young prophet who confounded Vortigern's magicians. This involved a manifest difficulty with dates, and he tried to reconcile the two figures in his poetic *Life of Merlin*, not 6 very successfully. On the face of it he simply made a blunder the first time, through lack of knowledge, and accidentally contrived a composite wonder-worker out of two characters more than a century apart. This would have been very like what he did with Old King Cole, though far more momentous in the outcome. However, there are indications that 'Myrddin' could refer in a general 7 way to prophetic inspiration, so that an inspired seer was a Myrddin-man or simply a Myrddin. Geoffrey may have picked up stories of more Myrddins than one, and wrongly imagined that two of them were the same person. Reincarnation has also been invoked. 8

97. (opposite) Tintagel: in Tennyson's poem. Merlin finds the infant Arthur on the beach below the castle.

98. Merlin reads a prophetic text to Uther, while Ygerna watches them from the battlements.

99. Tintagel Castle, associated with the story of Uther, Ygerna, and the begetting of Arthur.

Carmarthen in Welsh is Caer-fyrddin, the Myrddin-town, with the *m* changing to *f* in keeping with Welsh rules. Geoffrey's implication that it was named after the seer is, however, incorrect. The Welsh comes from a British form *Moridunon*, the Sea-Fort, in Latin *Moridunum*. It has been argued that Myrddin was a fictitious character invented to account for the Welsh name when its derivation was forgotten, but this fails to explain why 'Myrddin' should have acquired connotations of prophecy or been applied to an actual seer in Cumbria. It is interesting that the sacred source of the Stonehenge bluestones, in the Prescelly Mountains, is not enormously far from Carmarthen. The area may have had some association with an ancient god, a giver of inspiration and magical powers, the Myrddin of 'Myrddin's Precinct' as the first name of Britain. Merlin, as he develops in legend, is a transitional figure with a foot in both worlds, a Christian after his fashion, yet also a kind of Druid.

9   The castle of Genoreu, where Geoffrey makes Vortigern meet his death by fire, is an Iron Age hill-fort above Ganarew, near Monmouth, known as Little Doward. If there was a fifth-century reoccupation, the buildings would probably have been made of wood, and liable to be set alight in a siege. Across the valley, in the hillside opposite, is King Arthur's Cave. The reason for that name is obscure.

As observed, Aurelius Ambrosius is based in a vague way on Ambrosius Aurelianus, though there is no serious evidence for his having been a king. After the Saxons' phase of widespread raiding, around the middle of the fifth century, 10   they remained for a time within their authorised settlements. Ambrosius Aurelianus organised a counter-attack which was a major feature in a partial

British recovery. When Geoffrey portrays Aurelius as temporarily turning the Saxon tide, this is his version of the counter-attack. But he puts the fall of Vortigern and the rise of Aurelius not very long after the British visitation by Germanus and Lupus in 429, whereas Vortigern may have survived much longer; and while, to judge from the *Historia Brittonum*, Ambrosius Aurelianus was active in 437, his main anti-Saxon effort cannot even have started so early.

The British recovery itself is beyond reasonable doubt. The notion of a total collapse before an exterminatory Saxon onrush, with no real pause or reversal, is a nineteenth-century fiction of Anglo-Saxon enthusiasts – a modern myth, regrettably not yet defunct. It is based on a selective reading of Gildas, adopting his jeremiads about the raiding, but ignoring his testimony to the shift in fortunes that ensued. Even the relevant part of the *Anglo-Saxon Chronicle*,   11 though a list of alleged victories, implies a slow and piecemeal advance and leaves plenty of room for British victories too. Archaeology shows that in the fifth century there were far too few Saxons in the country to carry out the annihilating campaigns once ascribed to them, and while the settlers were widely spread, most of ex-Roman Britain was still British in 500 and even later.

So much for that. Uther is shadowy. He is briefly mentioned, and dubbed   12 'Pendragon', in a Welsh poem earlier than Geoffrey. The word does not mean 'Dragon's Head' but 'Head Dragon', and probably denotes military leadership. It is a personal epithet, applied at first to no one else. The Pendragonship as an office held by several men in succession is a much later literary fiction.

Tintagel, where, according to Geoffrey, Merlin opened the way for Arthur, is   13 on the north Cornish coast. From the village a ravine runs down to a cove. Rocky promontories rise on both sides of this, and the southerly one, on the left as you face the sea, is the place Geoffrey intends. It is almost an island, joined to the mainland only by a ridge, which, though now crumbled, would always have been hard to traverse against opposition.

Ruins of a castle, on the mainland and on the headland itself, do not go back beyond the middle of the twelfth century. However, imported pottery discovered by excavation has proved the presence of a wealthy establishment in the fifth and sixth. It was at first explained as a monastery, but further finds have suggested a princely stronghold and a considerable settlement. Traditions of this would account, at least partially, for Geoffrey's choice of locale. Aware that Tintagel was important at about the right time, he has Arthur begotten and presumably born there. His knowledge of real Cornish historical lore, whatever its exact content, is implied further by his putting Arthur's origin in Cornwall at all, when his natural inclination would surely have been to put it either in Wales or in a famous city such as London or Winchester.

Tennyson, wishing to get rid of Uther's scandalous exploit but keep its Cornish scene, proposes alternatives. One is a tale which a character in his *Idylls of the King* attributes to Bleys, a senior companion of Merlin. According to this, Uther died childless at Tintagel. Bleys and Merlin, having witnessed his death, went outside for fresh air, and then:

> . . . from the castle gateway by the chasm
> Descending thro' the dismal night – a night
> In which the bounds of heaven and earth were lost –
> Beheld, so high upon the dreary deeps
> It seem'd in heaven, a ship, the shape thereof
> A dragon wing'd, and all from stem to stern
> Bright with a shining people on the decks,

And gone as soon as seen. And then the two
Dropt to the cove, and watch'd the great sea fall,
Wave after wave, each mightier than the last,
Till last, a ninth one; gathering half the deep
And full of voices, slowly rose and plunged
Roaring, and all the wave was in a flame:
And down the wave and in the flame was borne
A naked babe, and rode to Merlin's feet,
Who stoopt and caught the babe, and cried 'The King!
Here is an heir for Uther!' and the fringe
Of that great breaker, sweeping up the strand,
Lash'd at the wizard as he spake the word,
And all at once all round him rose in fire,
So that the child and he were clothed in fire.
And presently thereafter follow'd calm,
Free sky and stars.

The plan of the *Idylls* requires that Arthur's origin should be doubtful, and the story of the child from the sea, though hearsay which Merlin refuses to confirm, adds mystery to doubt.

While Geoffrey introduces Merlin and magic, he has no hint of anything so spectacular. His Uther and Ygerna, having produced their son, simply reign as king and queen. He has a remarkable phrase to the effect that they lived together as equals, in Latin *pariter*. This may be yet another of his touches suggesting awareness, however distant and confused, of the nature of Celtic sovereignty. [14]

1. GM (1), 71–86, and (2), 167–88.
2. Loomis, ed., 319; Wilhelm (2), 214–22 (excerpt from Prose *Merlin*).
3. Ashe (5), 94; Rhys, I, 148, and II, 470.
4. GM (1), 86–100, and (2), 188–211.
5. Bromwich, 469–74; Loomis, ed., 20–30, 75–9; Stewart (2), passim; Tolstoy, 21–9, 101–17; Westwood, 373–4.
6. GM (3), passim; Loomis, ed., 89–91; Stewart (1), passim.
7. Bromwich, 469.
8. Ibid, 214.
9. Ashe (5), 13, 108; GM (2), 187 fn 1; Tatlock, 72–3.
10. Gildas, chapter 25; Morris, 95–7.
11. *Anglo-Saxon Chronicle*, years 449 to 577; Campbell, 19.
12. Bromwich, 520–3.
13. Alcock (1), 249–51; Ashe (5), 198–203; Thomas (2), 421–36.
14. GM (1), 98, and (2), 208.

Arthurian Britain

36 Arthur the Warrior

Concerning Uther's redoubtable son, the Welsh, who claim him as a hero of their own stock, have many tales and poems. They say he rose to leadership of the Britons at a time when their former Roman land, under stress of the long Saxon ordeal, was tending to break apart among regional rulers. It is not clear where his own home territory was, but it was not in Wales itself. He had a residence at Kelliwic in Cornwall, and others elsewhere.   1

In concert with the Britons' kings, or sub-kings, he won twelve victories   2 as war-leader against the Saxons. The first battle was at the mouth of a river, the Glein; the next four by another river, the Dubglas, in Linnuis; the sixth by the river Bassas; the seventh in the Caledonian Wood or Forest of Celidon; the eighth in Fort Guinnion; the ninth in the City of the Legion; the tenth on the bank of the River Tribruit; the eleventh on the hill of Agned; the twelfth on Mount Badon. Thanks to Arthur the Britons at last enjoyed a real breathing-space, in which he and other heroes performed memorable deeds.

As to whether he was himself one of the regional rulers, or a national commander-in-chief, or a high king like Vortigern, or all of these, some of the Welsh say or imply one thing, some another. Certainly he became proverbial for prowess in war. He had a sword called Caledfwlch and a spear   3 called Rhongomyniad. At Badon he slew 960 of the enemy single-handed. Yet his confidence in his own leadership carried him too far. On Tower Hill in London the head of Bran had long lain buried as a magical protection for   4 Britain. Arthur dug it up, arguing that Britain should not rely on such talismans, but solely on the war-effort under his command. This was one of the reasons why, after his departure from the scene, the Saxons advanced again.

Whatever his exact status, he always had a band of warriors attached to him personally. The foremost were Cai, or Cei, and Bedwyr. Cai, though apt to be churlish, was a loyal and valiant henchman till Arthur made fun of him in a satirical verse, at which he took umbrage. (Arthur's verse-making   5 gave him an honorary place among bards.) Bedwyr was noted for his skill

6　with a spear, though some say he had only one hand. Besides these, Arthur's retinue grew to more than two hundred, and he used to assemble them and hold court as the supreme prince of Britain, presiding with his wife Gwenhwyfar. Such was his prestige that a force called Arthur's Men aided British kings without his personal presence and continued in being after his passing.

Arthur was a Christian, and bore Christian emblems into battle, such as a cross, or an image of the Virgin Mary. Some Welsh monks, however, later recalled him as rapacious and overbearing, and told of incidents proving

7　him so, at least towards other monks. When St Cadoc gave sanctuary for a long time to a man who had killed three of Arthur's soldiers, Arthur disputed his right to do so and claimed a hundred head of cattle as compensation, stipulating that they must all be red in front and white behind. The saint miraculously changed the colour of an ordinary herd, but when Arthur's men drove them across a ford, they turned into bundles of fern. On another occasion Arthur burst into St Padarn's cell near Aberystwyth and tried to carry off a fine tunic. Here too a miracle subdued him.

Arthur and his companions were renowned for wonderful adventures, of a more creditable kind. In the course of these they confronted giants and

8　monsters. He had a fierce encounter himself with the giant Ritho, who lived on Snowdon and had made himself a cloak out of the beards of chiefs he had slain. Ritho sent Arthur a challenge, promising that if he won possession of his beard, he would add it to the cloak at the top, in a place of honour.

9　Arthur, however, vanquished the giant. Another time, he pursued a colossal serpent in Somerset, which was ravaging the land near Dunster. In this case he was unsuccessful till he enlisted the aid of St Carannog, a grandson of Cunedda, who banished the monster as St Patrick banished the snakes from Ireland; though Carannog's biographer accuses Arthur of confiscating the saint's altar and refusing to give it back till he promised to help. Cai fought

10　Palug's Cat, a speckled feline that had swum ashore in Anglesey, grown to an alarming size, and eaten 180 warriors.

11　Many of the Arthurian fellowship took part in the bride-seeking of Culhwch, a young cousin of their leader. Culhwch sought the hand of Olwen, the daughter of Ysbaddaden, the Chief Giant. Ysbaddaden, who was under a spell and doomed to die when his daughter married, tried to avert the wedding by requiring her suitor to carry out preposterous tasks. Arthur and his companions helped to fulfil the giant's conditions. One of the tasks involved hunting the enormous boar Twrch Trwyth. The hunt ranged far over western Britain. In the course of it, Arthur's dog, Cabal, set

12　his foot on a stone and left a paw-print. The stone still lies on a heap called Cabal's Cairn.

13　A more uncanny adventure took Arthur and some of his followers into the Otherworld. They voyaged over the waters of Annwfn in his ship Prydwen, seeking a magical cauldron in the custody of nine maidens. On the way they had to pass a series of fortresses. The quest was perilous and only seven returned.

14　Arthur had a son, Llacheu. There is disagreement as to whether Llacheu was legitimate, but, in any case, he is said to have died before his father and certainly did not succeed to whatever office Arthur held. An illegitimate son,

15　Gwydre, met his death in the hunting of Twrch Trwyth. Another, Amr,

100. A mounted figure representing a dark-age boar hunt.

served Arthur as a squire, but Arthur personally slew Amr and buried him, in a tragedy of which the record has perished. Arthur, therefore, seems to have outlived the offspring whom the Welsh recognise. There may, however, have been others. As for his own grave, a poem listing the burial places of various heroes makes Arthur exceptional: his grave is a mystery. 16 17

To speak of the 'Welsh' tradition of Arthur is a simplification, if perhaps an admissible one. Descendants of the Celtic Britons maintained their identity for centuries, not only in Wales itself but in parts of northern England and southern Scotland, as also in Cornwall (West Wales, as it was sometimes called) and Brittany. Though the British language broke up into Welsh, Cornish and Breton, all the peoples concerned had a share in the formation of Arthur's legend. The term 'Cymry', 'fellow-countrymen', originally applied to the northern Welsh-speakers as well as those in Wales proper. As for the large portion of Britain which the Anglo-Saxons transformed into England, the Welsh dubbed it Lloegyr, and referred to its transformation, inexactly, as the loss of Lloegyr by the Cymry. In medieval romance, Arthur is associated with an ill-defined 'Logres' rather than Wales.

The Welsh stories of him, like those of Vortigern, embody a hazy awareness of post-Roman realities. The unique Arthurian legend is rooted in a unique train of events, the Arthurian fact, as it has sometimes been called. Unlike Rome's other provincial peoples, the Britons became independent before the barbarians moved in, and fought back in places when they did, with temporary success. By 468 they had recovered to a point where a British army could safely go to Gaul in support of one of the last western emperors. At the close of the fifth century (it is worth repeating) most of ex-Roman Britain was still in their hands, and they still greatly outnumbered the Anglo-Saxons. Before Arthur's medieval vogue, nearly everything that is in writing about him comes from Wales and portrays him as a leader in this resurgence, and a larger-than-life hero in the British-held regions. Notions of general warfare going on for decades are admittedly too dramatic. Much Anglo-Saxon land-taking was probably creeping ahead peacefully, if not amicably. But there is room for another victorious British leader besides Ambrosius, of great enough stature and importance to have inspired the saga. Cymric bards and story-tellers were not indulging in mere absurdity.

18 The sixth-century tract of Gildas, though it is not historical in intent, and names no fifth-century Britons except Ambrosius, does testify to an overall pattern of disaster and recovery. Gildas mentions a British victory at the siege of Mount Badon, probably a hill-fort in southern Britain, somewhere about the year 500, followed by a phase of relative peace and equilibrium. Early in the ninth century the *Historia Brittonum* identifies the commander at Badon as Arthur and lists the eleven previous battles, so that Badon is made the climax of

19 prolonged campaigning. The list is thought to be based on a lost Welsh poem in Arthur's praise. Its first battle-sites may be in Lincolnshire. The Forest of Celidon, however, was in the southern uplands of Scotland, and the City of the Legion, in this context, is Chester. Celidon implies that Arthur was fighting Pictish allies of the Angles, and Chester that he was combating a foray right across the country. Hence both the locatable actions seem to belong to the period of widespread raiding with Pictish participation, around the middle of the fifth century. Taken with the much later Badon they raise a problem about the time-span, and Arthur's single-handed Badonic slaughter of 960 men shows that legend has already intruded into the record. An appendix to the same work, which is the source for Cabal's Cairn and Amr's grave, also betrays an evolution of fantasy.

20 A tenth-century chronicle, the *Annales Cambriae* (Annals of Wales), again connects Arthur with the Badon success and again does it in terms that sound legendary. It adds the 'strife of Camlann' in which he fell, together with someone called Medraut. Camlann's year is given as 539, a fact that underlines the failure of this Welsh matter to date Arthur: it provides only a long time-range, within which a career that cannot all be historical may fit somewhere.

21 About 600, the northern bard Aneirin composed the *Gododdin*, a series of elegies on some gallant nobles who fell fighting the Angles at Catterick. One line glances at Arthur as a supreme warrior, but it furnishes no clue as to when or where he lived, and it may be a later interpolation, though there is no cogent reason for thinking so. Welsh allusions to his followers are the ultimate inspiration of the knights whom he heads in medieval romance, and a few reappear in that guise, Cai as Sir Kay, Bedwyr as Sir Bedivere. The reference to Arthur's Men, as a force that may have existed independently of his personal

22 leadership and perhaps after his demise, is in a poem about a battle at Llongborth, probably Portchester in Hampshire, where Saxons captured a Roman fort.

Arthurian episodes in the so-called lives of Welsh saints shed a few sidelights but are really anecdotes of a stock type, depicting a proud layman being humbled by a saint's miracle-working or spiritual power. More interesting are the bardic traditions summarised in groups of three in the triads. They supply such items as the exhumation of Bran's head, and Arthur's Cornish residence at Kelliwic, thought to be the hill-fort Castle Killibury, near Padstow. The tale of

Culhwch and Olwen in the *Mabinogion*, besides being richly imaginative and entertaining, is a mine of information on Arthur and his entourage as they were pictured in Wales around the year 1000. Everybody of importance over a span of several lifetimes seems to have gravitated to his court, and he has attracted not only heroic warriors and beautiful ladies but fairy-tale characters of amazing grotesquerie.

There has been much debate as to whether the Welsh matter amounts to [23] evidence for a 'historical Arthur'. One long-popular theory, taking its cue from the battles and the knights, was that such a man existed but was a purely military leader who formed a corps of imperial-type cavalry, gaining the upper hand over the pedestrian Saxons by mobility, surprise and moral effect. Conjectures based on the Welsh matter have diverged so widely, however, that they add up to a proof of its insufficiency. A seldom-noticed crux is that whereas the historical Arthur, on this basis, has to be chiefly the man who won the battle of Badon, [24] there is no trace of his being remembered as such outside the *Historia* and *Annales* themselves.

Three considerations may tell in favour of a real person lurking somewhere. The first is Arthur's name, which is a Welsh form of the Roman Artorius. It [25] suggests a Briton born when the country was not wholly removed from the imperial orbit, and children of the governing classes were still being given Roman names. Moreover, records of several Arthurs up and down Britain in the late sixth century, when Roman names in general had become less common, hint that someone so named had by then been poetised into a national hero. The second point is that in the *Annales*, dozens of other people are mentioned who all seem to be real, so that a wholly fictitious Arthur would be out of keeping with the character of the document. Finally, no one who has explicitly denied Arthur and tried to present him as mythical – as a Celtic god, for instance – has ever explained convincingly where he came from, or how his saga began and took shape. There is no trace of a Celtic god called Arthur or anything like it. The speculations of the 'myth' school have been so ill-supported and contradictory that Arthur perhaps emerges as real by default.

All this historical argument applies strictly to the Welsh matter taken by itself. As will appear, some of it may look more solid when related to data from other sources.

1. Chambers, 91.
2. 'Nennius' (1), chapter 56.
3. *Mabinogion* (2), 100.
4. Bromwich, 89; Westwood, 131–4.
5. Bromwich, 21–2, 279–80, 303–7; *Mabinogion* (2), 128.
6. *Mabinogion* (2), 100–7.
7. Chambers, 81–3, 243–6, 248–9.
8. GM (1), 119, and (2), 240.
9. Chambers, 82–3, 246–7.
10. Bromwich, 304, 484–5; Rhys, II, 504–5.
11. *Mabinogion* (2), 95–136; Wilhelm (1), 30–55.
12. 'Nennius' (1), chapter 73.
13. Chambers, 61–3; Graves (2), 106–8; Loomis, ed., 15–16.
14. Loomis, ed., 14, 267.
15. *Mabinogion* (2), 132.
16. *Mabinogion* (2), 231; 'Nennius' (1), chapter 73.
17. Carley, 157; Chambers, 63; Loomis, ed., 4–8.
18. Gildas, chapter 26.
19. Alcock (1), 38, 55–71; Loomis, ed., 4–8.
20. Alcock (1), 45–55, 67.
21. Alcock (1), 72; Loomis, ed., 3.
22. Ashe (5), 142, 170; Loomis, ed., 13; Morris, 105–6.
23. Alcock (1), 80–8, 359–64; Bromwich, 274–6; Campbell, 27; Dumville, 173–91; Loomis, ed., 1–11.
24. Bromwich, 276.
25. Alcock (1), 73; Bromwich, 274; Lloyd, I, 125; Loomis, ed., 2, 3–4; Tatlock 224–5.

37 Arthur the King

1   Outside Wales, Arthur has been regarded as definitely King of Britain, with a reign that can be set forth in approximate order. He succeeded his father, it is said, at the age of fifteen. His campaign against the Saxons, revealing his military flair, soon followed. The battles were hard fought but successful. Wielding an all-conquering sword, forged in the enchanted island of Avalon, Arthur gave the Saxons the *coup de grâce* on a hill beside Bath and reduced them to complete submission. Those who survived no longer had a domain of their own in Britain. Then he went on to defeat the Picts and Scots, who had been the Saxons' allies.

After this came national rebuilding and reorganisation, restoring Britain to all its earlier dignity, and Arthur's marriage to Guinevere, she whom the Welsh call Gwenhwyfar. She was a very beautiful lady of Roman descent. Because the Irish had aided the Picts and Scots, he invaded Ireland and conquered it. He also conquered Iceland. Then at last the Britons won through to the Arthurian peace. It was a prosperous and happy time, and it lasted twelve years or more. Arthur's courage and generosity endeared him to his subjects. He founded an order of knighthood, enrolling distinguished men from other countries besides Britain. His fame grew to be so awesome, and spread so far, that the rulers of foreign lands feared that he would conquer them too.

Finally, he did form a project for creating a continental empire, and began with Norway and Denmark. Rome, however, still held the western part of Europe. Arthur invaded Gaul and confronted the tribune Frollo who governed it. He slew Frollo in single combat, and formed Gaul into provinces under his own knights, Kay taking charge of Anjou, Bedivere of Normandy.

Nine years after his Gallic victory, Britain was the richest and most civilised country in Europe. He held a Whitsun court at Caerleon with much splendour, feasting, and revelry. But while the court was still assembled, envoys came from the western Roman ruler, Lucius, demanding the former tribute, which Arthur had never paid, and the restitution of conquered lands. The King refused and took the offensive, shipping an army to Gaul, and contemplating the notion of taking over the Empire himself like Constantine the Great . . .

That, in fact, was the beginning of the end, as will be told in its place. But even as to the rest, there is much more to be said.

2   This sums up Arthur's 'official' biography as it was composed by Geoffrey of Monmouth. It gave him quasi-historical status, and supplied the framework for Arthurian romance, though many elaborations and rearrangements were to follow. Geoffrey's account was accepted in varying degrees by most medieval

101. Arthur arrives at
Caerleon to hold court.

102. Arthur fighting
the Roman ruler
Lucius.

103. Marriage of Arthur and Guinevere, an illustration to Malory's version of the legend.

chroniclers in England and Scotland. They were too credulous. No early historian mentions such a towering monarch in Britain, and his empire-building is disproved by authentic records of the countries he is supposed to have conquered. Further – in keeping with general medieval practice – the story is distanced from any possible history by updating. Thus, Arthur's warrior-fellowship becomes an order of chivalry which could not have existed in the fifth century. It is in that spirit that the Cai and Bedwyr of Welsh legend are turned into Sir Kay and Sir Bedivere. Likewise, the semi-barbaric Arthurian assemblage of *Culhwch and Olwen* becomes the courtly gathering at Caerleon, a royal occasion on twelfth-century lines, foreshadowing the imagery of Camelot.

Yet even in the account of King Arthur, as in most of his work, Geoffrey is making use of history, or what he would like to think is history, whether or not it comes from his alleged ancient book. He shows specific knowledge of the *Historia Brittonum* and other Welsh matter in his narrative of the war against the Saxons – the hill at Bath, for instance, is Badon, though the battle is moved back in time – and in one or two later episodes. Admittedly this material underlies only a fraction of the whole. In determining what else he drew on, and what clues to the origins it may supply, the issue of date is vital. A fatal weakness of the Welsh matter in this respect is the lack of a chronological fix. It never gives anything to calibrate Arthur with known history outside Britain, such as a statement that he was born when so-and-so was emperor, or waged his first war when so-and-so was pope. The unverifiable datings which it offers, or suggests, are incompatible and stretch his career beyond any credible limit.

Geoffrey, on the other hand, does date Arthur after a fashion. He gives a chronological fix for Vortigern with his reference to the visitation by Germanus and Lupus in 429. After this, the sequence of events and the family relationships put most of Arthur's reign in the third quarter of the fifth century, and so does the continuance of a fragile Roman hold on Gaul. More important still, Geoffrey gives a chronological fix for Arthur himself, the only one of serious weight that he gets anywhere. Three times an emperor Leo is mentioned during his Gallic campaigning. This can only be Leo I, emperor at Constantinople from 457 to 474. Further if less certain clues narrow the range. For instance, Leo's western colleague Lucius seems to have been suggested by an emperor Lucerius who is mistakenly introduced, in a chronicle Geoffrey may have read, at the end of the 460s. It looks as if Geoffrey got the idea for Arthur's second and final Gallic war from non-Welsh records of something that happened then.

Something did. At the right time, a man described as the King of the Britons is briefly, but reliably, glimpsed playing a part in the last turmoil of the western Empire. Continental documents show that he took an army to Gaul in 468 and advanced into the central part of the country. Betrayed by a Roman governor, and defeated by the Visigothic king Euric, he withdrew with a remnant of his army into the nearby domain of the Burgundians, probably early in 470. No more is said of him. But he is referred to in two places as *Riothamus*, which Latinises a British title or honorific denoting (probably) a high king like Vortigern, while leaving open the question of his personal name. Here then, arguably, is Arthur's original or part-original, and once the clue is grasped, other indications begin to emerge. The preface to *Goeznovius*, mentioned in connection with Maximus and Conan, apparently refers to the same Briton and calls him Arthur. Several medieval chronicles imply a tradition that Arthur belongs in the 460s.

Geoffrey exaggerates wildly, and changes the nature of the war for his hero's greater glory, but he has several themes and incidents that echo the career of this documented King of the Britons. What has obscured the issue is the fact that at the very end of his Arthur story, Geoffrey offers what looks like a precise date for the King's passing, and it is 542. Not only, however, is it inconsistent with everything before it and therefore likely to be an error, it has been satisfactorily explained as a very specific error, due to a confusion between different year-reckonings. On this basis the correct reading is 470, the year in which the King of the Britons, the man styled Riothamus, does fade from view.

104. Arthur and the emblems of the thirty kingdoms subject to him.

Naturally a question arises as to whether this Briton is Arthur in the full sense: that is, the inspirer of the Welsh tradition itself, the starting-point of the whole legend, and not merely a person whom Geoffrey ingeniously wove into it. The obstacle to any judgment is that nothing is known of his activities in Britain, at least as Riothamus, before he took his army to Gaul. He would fit in as Vortigern's successor, a high king with a personal domain in the south-west, to judge from his continental contacts. Perhaps he claimed authority over the infant British colonies in Armorica. He could have won at least some of the twelve Arthurian victories, or presided over the war-effort that led to their winning. Ambrosius could have been a general in his service, and regent, to speculate further, during his absence abroad. Archaeology raises a possibility that Arthur-Riothamus, to coin a term, was the lord of Cadbury Castle in Somerset, the reputed prototype of Camelot.

Obviously he cannot cover all the data. The Welsh claim two Arthurian battles, Badon and Camlann, long after he vanishes from the record, and their doubt as to Arthur's status is curious. Yet Arthur-Riothamus, as the starting-point of the legend, remains credible. Bards may have treated him as freely as German minstrels treated Theodoric, the Gothic sovereign of Italy from 493 to 526, who, in the epic *Nibelungenlied*, is demoted into a henchman of Attila the Hun half a century earlier. Or the figure of Arthur may be a composite, superimposing someone a generation or two later on the original king. This is the solution of worse difficulties with Merlin. Or poems about the deeds of the force known as Arthur's Men, if it continued after the king's departure and recruited new members, could have been misconstrued as saying he was present in person when he was not. These are conjectures, but the debate over the Welsh matter has certainly shown that there is no hard evidence for any insular competitor, any 'historical Arthur' to rival this one.

1. GM (1), 101–16, and (2), 212–37.
2. Fletcher, passim; Lacy, ed., arts. 'Chronicles, Arthur in', 'Chronicles in English', and 'Scottish Arthurian Chronicles'.
3. GM (1), 108, 122–3, 130, and (2), 223, 246, 258; Tatlock, 124.
4. Ashe (6), 33 (ref to Sigebert of Gembloux).
5. Ashe (3), 310–23, and (6), 34–40; Lacy, ed., art. 'Arthur, Origins of Legend'; Wood, 261.
6. Ashe (3), 320, and (6), 36–7; Fleuriot, 172–3; Lacy, ed., arts. 'Riothamus', 'Vortimer'.
7. Ashe (3), 304–9, 321, and (6), 37–8; Chambers, 92–4, 241–3; Fleuriot, 277. Cp Fletcher, 82–3, 185; GM (1), xvii.
8. Alcock (1), 18; Ashe (3), 316–7, and (6), 36.
9. Ashe (3), 312, and (6), 34–5, 38–40; Campbell, 37.

38 *Arthur and Merlin*

1   Story-tellers say Arthur's boyhood was spent in the home of a foster-father, a wealthy knight named Ector. It was the wonder-working Merlin who insisted on this arrangement. Ector's own son was Kay, who was afterwards Arthur's seneschal or chief steward. That is how he came into Arthur's life: as an adoptive brother. When Uther died, there was doubt as to who his heir was. Arthur, who supposed himself to be Ector's son, did not know the truth. After a turbulent interregnum, Merlin told the Archbishop of Canterbury to summon the lords of Britain to London, where a sign would be given them about the succession.

    At Christmas they assembled. Outside the city's principal church, someone, presumably Merlin, deposited a huge stone with a sword stuck in it. An inscription proclaimed that whoever could draw this out was the rightful king. None of the lords could. When a tournament was held, Kay forgot to bring his own sword and sent Arthur back to their lodging to fetch it. Unable to get in, Arthur hurriedly and innocently borrowed the one in the stone, without realising that he had done anything special by extracting it. He brought it to Kay, who did know its significance and tried to pretend that he had drawn it out himself, but soon gave up. Ector told Arthur who he really was. Thus, God's approval was shown and Arthur's claim was established, to his own surprise. Many of the lords protested, but when the sword was thrust back into the stone, the obscure lad was still the only person who could extricate it. And that is how Arthur became king while in his teens. With Merlin as an adviser, able to foresee the future, he gradually mastered all opposition and grew to adulthood with a firmly-grounded authority.

2   He used the sword in combat, but presently broke it. Merlin promised to get him another and took him to a lonely lake. An arm rose above the surface, its hand grasping a magnificent sheathed sword. The Lady of the Lake, an enchantress who presided there, approached them and told Arthur it could be his. He rowed out in a boat with Merlin and took the sword and scabbard, whereupon the arm vanished below. The sword was called Excalibur: this was the marvellous weapon which all agree Arthur possessed. Merlin told him that the scabbard had a magical virtue. While Arthur carried it he could never lose blood, however gravely he might be wounded.

3   Long before, Merlin had made a circular table for Uther. Its shape symbolised the round earth and heavens. Also it commemorated the table of Christ's Last Supper and another on which the Grail, the vessel he used on that occasion, had been kept – a mystery destined not to unfold till late in the reign. On Uther's death the table had passed to a local king named Leodegan. Arthur's wife Guinevere was Leodegan's daughter, and she brought it to him as her dowry. When the King founded his order of knighthood, dedicated to high ideals of chivalry and courtesy, he called its members the Knights of the Round Table and each had his place at it. The

primary intention was practical. A round table, with every knight equal, would avert quarrels over precedence and relative honour. But the table's mystical meanings were inescapable.

King Arthur was wise, kind, magnanimous, and capable of strong action, 4 including of course military action, when that was needed. However, the exploits and loves of those about him grew to attract story-tellers more than his own deeds.

105. Frontispiece to Malory's *Morte d'Arthur*, depicting Arthur in the role of a slayer of monsters.

While Geoffrey makes Merlin the sponsor of Arthur's birth, his sponsorship of the reign as well is part of the legend's vast expansion when a wider public embraced it. Tales of Arthur and his people were spread through western Europe during the twelfth century, often by Breton minstrels. Matter independent of Geoffrey found its way to romancers who took up the Arthurian theme.

106. Arthur with Merlin as his chief adviser.

5 Wace, who wrote a French verse paraphrase of his *History*, made room for the adventures related of the King and his followers by explaining that they happened during the long peace after his first cycle of conquest.

The pioneer romancers, notably Chrétien de Troyes, wrote in French, which was spoken by the nobility in England as well as France. But romances were composed in most European languages. The 'Matter of Britain' became a favourite source for aristocratic story-telling in verse and prose, and reached upper-middle-class readers, though it was never popular at the lower social levels. Like Geoffrey, and more so, the romancers followed habitual medieval practice by updating. They made almost no attempt at authenticity, portraying kingship, warfare, costume, architecture, and much else in terms of their own period, however idealised, and working even Celtic mythology into plots reflecting current interests, such as courtly love-conventions. In their hands Arthur's kingdom became a sort of chivalric Utopia, at least to the extent that it resolutely upheld the right principles, and their violation was a departure from a norm that had some reality.

While more or less accepting the main framework, they added countless characters and episodes, and varied the story. Merlin's immensely enhanced role was one aspect of this development. Another was a change of attitude to Arthur's embroilment with the Empire. By contrast with Geoffrey's treatment, it was apt to be minimised or forgotten. In the standard English version by Malory, it remains important, but is put early in the reign and ends 6 triumphantly with no sequel. Malory does not lose sight of Arthur's continental connections, which take him to Gaul again as in Geoffrey, but it happens for a different reason.

Arthur's boyhood seldom attracted the romancers, beyond the bare notion of a secret fostering. Spenser, in *The Faerie Queene*, introduces Prince Arthur before accession, but his allegories have never been accepted as really belonging to the legend. A modern author who does add to it in this phase is T. H. White. *The Sword in the Stone* makes Merlin the boy's tutor, preparing him for his undivulged destiny.

Geoffrey has no hint of a doubt as to Arthur's rights. The test (with the anachronistic archbishop) is another elaboration. Between one version and another the emphasis alters slightly. In an early account the sword is the sword 7 of justice, and Arthur's ability to wield it is a sign of divine endorsement. Later, proof of his identity as heir is crucial. The mechanics of the marvel vary. Malory says the stone had an anvil on top of it, and the sword passed down through this.

107. Winchester: the Round Table in the Castle Hall, actually made in the thirteenth or fourteenth century, and painted in 1522.

The term 'Lady of the Lake' stands for an office rather than an individual. Different ones appear at different times. The Lady has Otherworld aspects, and was perhaps originally a Celtic priestess. Each Lady heads a group of damsels from whom a successor is recruited. Her magic is generally benign.

8 Excalibur is sometimes identified with the Sword in the Stone, but is more usually a replacement. Arthur's Welsh sword Caledfwlch becomes Caliburn in Geoffrey, and 'Excalibur' is an adaptation of the latter. The likeliest derivation is from the Latin *chalybs*, which means 'steel' and can mean an object made of steel, just as, in English, 'steel' can poetically mean a sword.

9 The Round Table is mentioned first by Wace, Geoffrey's French adapter, who claims to have heard of it from the Bretons. Here Merlin is not involved, and the reason for its circularity is the practical one, that of keeping all the knights on an equal footing. Its mystical character as Merlin's creation is expounded later. The manifest difficulty is that while the number of knights is sometimes manageable – twelve, for instance – it swells to 150, and no round table, in the sense of a plain piece of furniture, could have been big enough. Some medieval artists solve the problem by depicting it as a ring, with gaps for servitors to pass through. The hall housing it would still have had to be very large.

10 Winchester Castle has a Round Table, eighteen feet across, painted in segments with places for the King and twenty-four crowded knights. Caxton, who printed Malory's work in 1485, believed it to be authentic. Carbon-dating and other tests have shed some light. It may have been made for Edward III, who, in 1344, contemplated re-founding the Arthurian knighthood. However, it is probably a few decades earlier and festive in its purpose. Medieval monarchs and barons used to stage entertainments called Round Tables at which the guests played Arthurian roles, banqueted, and jousted. The Winchester table may have been made for one of these. If the sponsor was a king, Edward I is the likeliest, since he held or attended five such festivals. Henry III is also eligible in terms of date, but he seems to have disapproved of them. With the enshrining of the Winchester table, and the publication of Malory's masterpiece, the seal was set on an ironic transformation of Arthur – who fought the ancestors of the English – into a king of *England*, conferring an august antiquity on its crown.

1. Malory, I, 3–III, 1.
2. Ibid, I, 23–5.
3. Malory, III, 1; *Queste del Saint Graal*, 99; Wilhelm (2), 16 (excerpt from Wace, *Roman de Brut*), and 233–6 (excerpt from Prose *Merlin*).
4. Lacy, ed., art. 'Arthur, Character of'.
5. Loomis, ed., 97–8; Wilhelm (2), 17 (excerpt from Wace).
6. Malory, V.
7. Lacy, ed., art. 'Sword in the Stone'.
8. GM (1), 104, and (2), 217.
9. Lacy, ed., art. 'Round Table'; Loomis, ed., 99–100; Tatlock, 471–5.
10. Ashe (5), 209–11; Lacy, ed., art. 'Winchester'; Snell, 284.
11. Loomis, ed., 553–9; Westwood, 314–5.

39 *Camelot*

Arthur used to hold court at several places, but in the days of his highest glory, his chief and favourite residence was Camelot. Primarily, it was a castle where he housed the Round Table, but the name was also given to a town adjacent to this. Camelot stood on a plain. A river flowed past it, and a forest spread close. Besides its role as a scene of tournaments and festivities, and of government when the King was present, it had a religious aspect. Knights were baptised there, and, late in the reign, it was the point of departure for the Grail Quest. 1

The name 'Camelot' may have been suggested by Camulodunum, otherwise Colchester, which was conspicuous, as we have seen, in the history of Roman Britain. But Colchester is unlikely to have any real link with the legend's origins, being in a region of early Saxon settlement, near the North Sea coast and outside Arthurian territory. English ideas have been confused by Malory, who regards 'Camelot' as a name for Winchester. The partly-Welsh Henry Tudor, who 2 became Henry VII in the year of the publication of Malory's work, tried to exploit the Arthurian mystique and had his first son baptised in Winchester Cathedral and christened Arthur. The intention was that he should reign as Arthur II. Unfortunately, the prince died young, and his brother came to the throne as Henry VIII. Though Henry cared less for the propagandist myth, it was he, in 1522, who had the design painted on the Winchester Round Table with himself in Arthur's chair.

Probably Malory chose this city as Camelot because he knew it was very old and had once rivalled London as the capital. There was also the Round Table, however it had come to be there. But he was under a misapprehension, and his own publisher Caxton, despite his belief that the Winchester table was the real 3 thing, dissented. The point about Camelot is that it is *not* a capital, in the sense of being the country's permanent centre. It is King Arthur's headquarters, and a capital solely as the heart and focus of his world. No one else reigns there before or after him. If we turn back to the romancers who created it, in the twelfth and thirteenth centuries, we confront a medieval dream-city which it would be misguided to locate on the map. Camelot indeed is in Logres, which sometimes gives the impression of being a western domain specially Arthur's, as distinct from the fiefs of his sub-kings; but 'Logres', derived from the Welsh name for England, is essentially no more specific. While Cornwall has much Arthurian lore, Camelford is ruled out because no medieval romancer would have imagined the King having his chief residence there. At the time when Camelot supposedly flourished, Cornwall was the realm of the ill-natured Mark of the Tristan legend. Geoffrey supplied a hint with his description of Arthur's court at Caerleon, and Chrétien de Troyes, who is the first to name Camelot, pictures it 4 as somewhere in that direction. But he is clear that it is a different place, and his successors lose sight of the proximity.

108. Jousting, a competitive sport popular with the knights who gathered at Camelot.

Tennyson's Camelot is suitably unreal, or rather, belongs to a non-geographic plane of reality. The future knight Gareth approaches it with two companions:

> So, when their feet were planted on the plain
> That broaden'd toward the base of Camelot,
> Far off they saw the silver-misty morn
> Rolling her smoke about the Royal mount,
> That rose between the forest and the field.
> At times the summit of the high city flash'd;
> At times the spires and turrets half-way down
> Prick'd through the mist; at times the great gate shone
> Only, that open'd on the field below:
> Anon, the whole fair city had disappear'd.
> Then those who went with Gareth were amazed,
> One crying, 'Let us go no further, lord.
> Here is a city of Enchanters, built
> By fairy Kings.'

At Gareth's insistence they do go further, and arrive at the gate, where they are bewildered by sculptures that seem to move, and hear strange music. An old man comes out and speaks to them cryptically:

'Truly as thou sayest, a Fairy King
And Fairy Queens have built the city, son;
They came from out a sacred mountain-cleft
Toward the sunrise, each with harp in hand,
And built it to the music of their harps.
For there is nothing in it as it seems
Saving the King; tho' some there be that hold
The King a shadow, and the city real . . .
They are building still, seeing the city is built
To music, therefore never built at all,
And therefore built for ever.'

A moment later the old man admits that this is 'riddling of the bards', prompted by disingenuous words on Gareth's part, and it remains uncertain how any of it ought to be taken.

Tennyson is right to portray a Camelot that defies pinning down. Yet the place's character as a personal centre, not a permanent capital, suggests that it could owe something to traditions about a headquarters of the original Arthur. Here, and here only, the claim of Cadbury Castle enters. Cadbury is an Iron Age hill-fort near Sparkford in Somerset. There was never a castle on the site, in the medieval sense. The hill itself is the castle. It has four lines of bank-and-ditch defences, now largely overgrown with woods, encircling an eighteen-acre enclosure that rises to a summit plateau. In 1542 the traveller John Leland referred to it as Camelot. Local lore of doubtful age is related to this belief. On a certain night of the year, some say Midsummer Eve, the ghosts of the King and his horsemen ride over the hilltop. The highest part is called Arthur's Palace.

Leland's identification used to be dismissed as a guess, inspired by the village name 'Camel' which occurs in the neighbourhood. However, excavations in 1966–70 disclosed a relevant past. Early in the Roman period the inhabitants

109. Cadbury Castle in Somerset, an ancient hill-fort which was reoccupied about Arthur's time and has claims to being Camelot's original.

resisted the conquerors and were forcibly transferred to a new settlement below. After centuries of vacancy, Cadbury was reoccupied and refortified at roughly the date ascribed to Arthur, i.e. in the 460s or later, but probably not much after 500. The topmost bank was surmounted with a fresh rampart sixteen feet thick, made of stones (some taken from Roman buildings) in a framework of wooden beams. Nearly three-quarters of a mile in circuit, this wall protected the whole enclosure, with a gate-house at the south-west entrance. A timber hall of the same period stood on the plateau in the 'Arthur's Palace' area.

Cadbury's massive refortification implies an occupant with great resources of manpower. The use of timber and stones echoes the story of Vortigern's abortive fortress in Wales, which was likewise to have been built of timber and stones. These may have been the approved materials for a high king's stronghold, and post-Roman Cadbury suggests a political rather than a military base, though it could have served as both. British archaeology offers no parallel. Other hill-forts were reoccupied in the same period, and earthworks were refurbished, but there is no known instance of a defensive structure like this, on such a scale, anywhere else in ex-Roman Britain. A few cases of stone-and-timber refortification in Scotland are smaller and have no gate-houses. Cadbury looks like the headquarters of a king with resources unparalleled, so far as present knowledge goes, in the Britain of his time.

Leland is therefore unlikely to have been guessing, since even a modern archaeologist could not have detected the buried structures by inspection alone. Somehow, he picked out the most appropriate hill throughout Britain, the only credible Camelot in the only credible sense. Presumably he heard a tradition with some factual content. It does not follow that it named Arthur. By the sixteenth century a vague tale of a king who lived on the hill would have been enough to suggest him, and Camelot. Nevertheless, the only documented candidate as the royal refortifier is the aforementioned 'King of the Britons' who led an expedition to Gaul in 468–70. His army, stated to have numbered twelve thousand, proves that he had the manpower, and his cross-Channel contact may indicate a presence in the West Country. His peculiar interest lies of course in his candidature as the original Arthur, the legend's starting-point, on quite separate grounds.

1. Lacy, ed., art. 'Camelot'.
2. Ashe (5), 63–5, 211; Kendrick, 36–7; Loomis, ed., 89.
3. Malory, vol. 1, 5 (Caxton's preface).
4. Wilhelm (1), 89 (*Lancelot*, lines 31–4).
5. Alcock (2), passim; Westwood, 5–8.
6. Alcock (3), 358.
7. Ibid, 362–8, 380–5.
8. Campbell, 20.

40 *Guinevere*

'Guinevere' is the same as the Welsh 'Gwenhwyfar', and it means White   1
Phantom. Before her marriage, Arthur's Roman-blooded queen lived for
some years in the household of Cador, who had succeeded to Gorlois's   2
Cornish dukedom. Her father, Leodegan, had another daughter by a   3
different mother. She was a double, called the False Guinevere, and she once
lured Arthur away from the court. The Welsh assert that there were not
merely two so named in his entourage but three, and that these women were   4

110. Guinevere joins
Arthur on their
wedding night.

all in some sense royal. When Arthur married the one he did marry, he acted
5 in defiance of a prophetic warning by Merlin. In the Middle Ages, the
monks of Glastonbury claimed that an inscription marking their shared
6 grave called her his *second* wife, but nothing is known of any predecessor.

Merlin was right to predict trouble. In various ways, sometimes willingly,
sometimes not, Guinevere became involved with men other than her
husband. At a time when Arthur's authority was still open to local chal-
7 lenges, she was abducted by Melwas, ruler of the Summer Land or
Somerset, who kept her in his stronghold at Glastonbury. Arthur came to
recover her with troops from Cornwall and Devon. The marshy terrain
hindered his movements. Before serious fighting could break out, the
Abbot and Gildas (who was then living in the community) negotiated an
agreement and Melwas restored her.

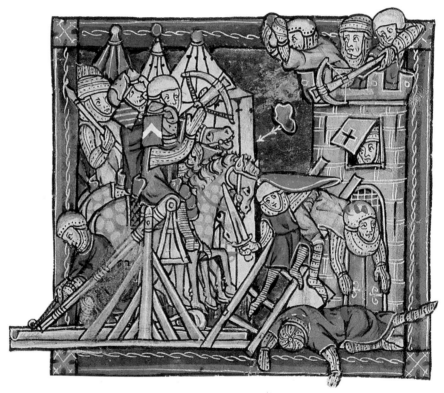

111. Mordred tries to
reach Guinevere, who
has shut herself in the
Tower of London to
escape him.

An enmity destined to be disastrous began, according to the Welsh, when
the warrior chief Medraut raided Arthur's Cornish abode at Kelliwic, looted
8 it, and struck Guinevere . . . or worse. Arthur retaliated. This affray too
seems to belong to a phase when he was by no means supreme in parts of
Britain. Medraut is later called Modred or Mordred, and viewed in a more
sinister light. His sexual designs on the Queen are not only acknowledged
but sometimes alleged to have been successful. When he was left in charge
during Arthur's absence in Gaul, Guinevere is reputed to have become his
9 mistress or even, bigamously, his wife. In Scotland, where chroniclers are
10 more friendly to him, they tell of a voluntary elopement, with Guinevere
joining him in his stronghold on Barry Hill above Strathmore. Those who
have a better opinion of her say nothing of this northern affair or any other

yielding to Mordred. They insist that she only pretended she would comply with his wishes, and then removed herself out of his reach.

Most agree nevertheless that she was unfaithful somehow, whether or not she was abducted as well, and that the infidelity started quite early. As her lover, the commonly accepted person is the famous knight Lancelot, who is also her rescuer in some versions of the abduction. Their amour lasted for years and caused both delight and sorrow for them. Arthur turned a blind eye on it for as long as he could, but it was finally dragged into the open, partly through the machinations of Mordred. The adultery counted as treason and the King was compelled to sentence Guinevere to be burnt at the stake, in Carlisle. Lancelot saved her, but killed several knights who were on guard, causing feuds and partisanships that divided the Round Table.

Some of the stories may be echoes of pagan myth. The strange notion of three royal Guineveres, which is in a Welsh triad, may go back to images of a Triple Goddess. Guinevere's recurring abduction, first located at the possible pre-Christian sanctuary of Glastonbury, sometimes happens in a kind of Otherworld; it recalls the Greek Persephone and the Indian Sita.

112. Guinevere holding hands with Lancelot, her lover throughout most of her husband's reign.

11

12
Her persistent involvement with men other than Arthur may have an ancestry in actual Celtic society. Not only was a pre-Christian Celtic queen her consort's equal, able to wield power herself, and lead armies as Boudicca did: she could also take lovers as a king could take concubines, without being necessarily condemned. A notable instance in the first century AD was the northern queen Cartimandua, whose domestic arrangements appear to have been amicable till she went too far by divorcing her husband and marrying her lover. But when traditions of that remote era reached story-tellers centuries after, who subjected them to the usual updating, the context had changed and they were not equipped to understand. In a medieval, male-dominated society, they could only picture the free and equal woman as a wilful, amoral, disloyal woman. At best Guinevere could be depicted with Lancelot in the artificial and unattractive relationship of 'courtly love'. At worst she became simply an adulteress. For the

13
Welsh she was proverbially the most faithless of wives. Until quite recently a girl of loose morals was apt, in Wales, to be dubbed a Guinevere.

Yet in the romances, traces of the old attitude and ethic may linger, if unconsciously. The Queen is given a lover who is a very splendid figure, and the durable Guinevere-Lancelot liaison is portrayed with some sympathy. The triangular situation has a quality rare in literature. Her infidelity never deprives her husband of stature or dignity, he is no mere cuckold.

In Geoffrey's book the Queen is hardly a character at all. Apart from ceremony, misconduct with Mordred towards the end of the story is almost her

14
only action. Chrétien de Troyes makes her more important, though haughty and unendearing. Her richest medieval development is in Malory, where she is passionate, tragic, ultimately noble. The reader has little doubt of her salvation in a Christian sense. 'She was a true lover, and therefore she had a good end.' Her love for Lancelot was a sin, but not a base sin. It kept something alive in her that enabled her to rise above it at last, and learn a higher love.

If there was an original Arthur, he very probably had a wife, but no more can be said historically. The legend of Melwas, however (told by Caradoc of Llancarfan about 1130), resembles the Tintagel and Cadbury stories in embodying a recollection of Glastonbury being inhabited at about the right

15
time. Excavation has shown that Glastonbury Tor had buildings on it in the sixth century, perhaps the fifth, though it is uncertain whether they were monastic or part of a lay establishment.

1. Bromwich, 380–5.
2. GM (1), 107, and (2), 221.
3. Chambers, 159–60; Loomis, ed., 324.
4. Bromwich, 154–6.
5. Malory, III, 1.
6. Chambers, 113; Giraldus, 287.
7. Bromwich, 381–5; Chambers, 84–5, 263–4; Loomis, ed., 178.
8. Bromwich, 147.
9. GM (1), 129, and (2), 257.
10. Ashe (5), 38–9, 155; Chambers, 191; Snell, 225–6.
11. Malory, XX, 6–10; *Mort Artu*, 118–25.
12. Markale, 123–30, 188.
13. Bromwich, 200; Chambers, 196.
14. Wilhelm (1), 89–156 (*Lancelot*). Cp Loomis, ed., 179.
15. Alcock (1), 251–2; Carley, 5; Rahtz, 130.

41 *Arthur's Principal Knights*

Sir Kay (Cai or Cei), Arthur's early companion and reputed foster-brother, 1
was initially a bold fighter and slayer of monsters, such as the terrifying
Anglesey cat. Mention has been made, however, of his disagreeable side and 2
his taking offence at a quip by Arthur. Royal trust and friendship were not
withheld, but as the King's seneschal, managing the household, he seems to
have deteriorated and made a poor impression. Occasions were recalled
when he was curmudgeonly towards junior members of the court, and
bungled tasks undertaken in a boastful spirit. It would be charitable to think
that it was only his later unpopularity which propagated the story of his
pretending that it was he, not Arthur, who drew the sword from the stone. 3
Thrown back into warfare towards the end of the reign, he proved that he
could still conduct himself honourably.

Sir Bedivere or Bedwyr, the spear-wielder of Welsh tradition, and Arthur's 4
chief early comrade next to Kay, was less conspicuous in a civilian role as
royal cupbearer. However, he and Kay both held responsible posts in
Arthur's reorganisation of Gaul, and both gave him stalwart support in a
fight with a cannibalistic giant on Mont-Saint-Michel. The English tell 5
further that Bedivere was the last knight to remain at the King's side when
the Round Table perished.

Sir Gawain, chief among Arthur's nephews, is usually said to have been a 6
son of his half-sister Morgause, whom Ygerna bore to her first husband.
Morgause married Lot, a northern ruler, and Gawain was their eldest
offspring. He was educated at Rome in the papal household. Later he 7
became a leading member of the Round Table. Because of some un-
explained enchantment his strength used to increase till noon and decline
afterwards. Censorious folk condemned him as a womaniser and cheater,
but he was full of courage and, at his best, a model of chivalry. Once a
repulsive hag got Arthur out of a difficulty by supplying the answer to a
riddle, and demanded Gawain's hand in marriage. When he complied, she 8
told him she could be ugly by day and beautiful by night or vice versa, and
the choice was his. His choice was to let her choose herself, whereupon she
became beautiful all the time. On another occasion, when the gigantic
Green Knight challenged any of Arthur's company to strike a blow at him 9
on condition that the blow should be returned a year hence, it was Gawain
who took up the challenge for the honour of Camelot. He cut off the Green
Knight's head, excusably supposing that the return blow would never be
struck, but the challenger picked it up and rode away. Gawain kept the tryst
and was spared because of his correct conduct when a married lady tried to
seduce him. His most destructive failing was vengefulness. He pursued a
relentless and ruinous vendetta against Lancelot, who had accidentally
killed two of Gawain's brothers when rescuing Guinevere from the stake.
Some say that Gawain was murdered aboard a ship and buried on the coast 10
of Pembrokeshire; most, that he survived till near the end of the reign.

113. Lancelot leaving
Joyous Gard.

114. (opposite)
Bamburgh Castle, on
the site of a British fort
which may be the
original of Lancelot's
Joyous Gard.

11   *Sir Perceval* was one of the young recruits who were drawn to the Round Table after its establishment. He was brought up in Wales by a mother who loathed the chivalric world and tried to keep him in ignorance. At last, however, excited at seeing some actual knights, he set off to seek knighthood himself. Naïve and foolish at first, he gradually matured, though not all the advice which he took to heart was for his good. A warning not to be too forward in asking questions had unfortunate results when he visited the Grail Castle. Nevertheless, his concern with the Grail continued, and he was one of those most nearly successful in the quest which Arthur's companions undertook for that sacred object, Britain's special link with Christ.

12   *Sir Lancelot*, 'the best knight in the world' as admirers called him, was a son of King Ban of Benoic in western France. The Lady of the Lake spirited him away as an infant and brought him up. Hence, he was known as Lancelot of the Lake. When he was eighteen the Lady presented him at Arthur's court, where he rose to supremacy in all knightly pursuits. Among many adventures he delivered a northern castle, Dolorous Gard, from an evil enchantment, and found a tomb with his own name on it. Realising that the castle was his fated home and last resting-place, he took possession and renamed it Joyous Gard. As Guinevere's lover he endured much highhandedness on her part and various clashes for other reasons, which drove him into temporary insanity. But he saved her from an abductor and was generally true to her. He would not respond to the advances of Elaine, the Maid of Astolat, and she died of grief: her body was floated on a barge down-river to Camelot. When Arthur was forced to condemn his wife and Lancelot rescued her, he took her to Joyous Gard, but restored her to the King under a pledge of safety. In consequence of the rift, which divided the Round Table, Lancelot led away many followers to his own French domains, and set up a rival court.

13   *Sir Galahad* was Lancelot's son, begotten during a visit to Pelles, one of the succession of keepers of the Grail. Pelles was of the lineage of Joseph of Arimathea, who had brought the Grail to Britain, and regarded his daughter Elaine (not Elaine of Astolat) as the destined mother of a knight fit to know the Grail's secrets. He led Lancelot to believe Guinevere was in a castle near by, sent Elaine to await him there, and employed a magic potion to delude him into thinking she was the Queen. Thus Lancelot became the father of Galahad. The illicit love that would prevent his own success in the Grail Quest produced the unblemished knight who did succeed. When the potion wore off, Lancelot realised how Elaine's father had tricked him. She would not let him go, and Guinevere's jealous fury when she followed Lancelot to the court was the main cause of his spell of madness. Galahad grew up and came to the court himself. He was handsome, and unsurpassed in jousting and kindred activities, but self-dedicated to chastity and therefore worthy to be the Grail-achiever, as he was soon revealed to be by supernatural signs.

14   *Sir Mordred* or Medraut, like Gawain, is generally reckoned a son of Morgause. Officially he was the King's nephew. Rumour alleged, however, that Arthur himself begot him, unaware of the incest at the time, but still creating his own nemesis. The Welsh say that 'Medraut' was originally loyal. But, for a reason not made clear, he perpetrated his raid on Kelliwic, and after this, and Arthur's reprisal, there could be no lasting amity between

them. While opinions differ as to whether he was successful in his lustful designs on Guinevere, it was out of spite against her and Lancelot that he abetted the exposure of their adultery. An act of blackest treason on Mordred's part was the immediate cause of Arthur's downfall.

The Arthurian legend owes much of its lasting fascination to the perennial dream of a golden age, which comes to its sharpest Arthurian focus in Malory, but is a constant in all the forms which the legend assumes. For the Welsh, the time of Arthur's ascendancy is a heroic epoch of warriors, saints and marvels. For Geoffrey, he is a kind of British Messiah. For medieval romancers his kingdom embodies the aristocratic ideals of the period. For Tennyson, it is a noble attempt at spiritually-inspired monarchy in keeping with Victorian ethics. Even modern novelists, who are more realistic, evoke a state of affairs when a leader of goodwill and integrity was at least briefly supreme.   15

In the romancers' Utopia of justice, knightly virtue, and courtly love, many of the adventures of the Round Table paladins are inspired by a duty to 'right wrongs'. They succour the weak, rescue damsels in distress, slay troublesome monsters, and so on. However, those who stand out as individuals are never abstract paragons, apart from Galahad. They are not entirely consistent, being portrayed by different authors with different ideas; but however we regard or reconstitute them, they have their faults, to put it mildly. The golden-ness of the golden age is more than a resultant of persons living in it, and the character of the King himself, even on the best assessment, is not an adequate reason. Merlin's supernatural sponsorship might be seen as the key factor, but even Merlin has flaws that bring him down. The glory of Arthur's reign is chiefly a matter of aspiration and atmosphere. Yet it is not illusory.

As to the seven picked out here from more than a hundred, the first two belong in any list because of their prominence in the early Welsh layer. 'Cai' is probably the Roman name Caius, a fact that may be thought to favour historicity. In *Culhwch and Olwen*, however, Cai has fairy-tale attributes, such as an ability to hold his breath under water for nine days. The high value Arthur places on him, despite his shortcomings, ensures his continuing importance in Geoffrey and the romancers. Geoffrey makes Bedivere too a leading figure, but he passes into near-eclipse afterwards, till an anonymous English poet gives him his memorable role as the King's last companion, perpetuated by Malory and Tennyson.

Gawain is sometimes identified with another Welsh character, Gwalchmei. Tales of him were current on the continent before Geoffrey. In William of Malmesbury's *Acts of the Kings of the English*, about 1125, he is mentioned as a nephew of Arthur who shared in the struggle against a Saxon onslaught led by Hengist's brother. This would suggest a *floruit* around the middle of the fifth century. The date would fit in with a conjecture that his father Lot is the semi-historical Leudonus, whose stronghold Traprain Law, in Lothian, was a major centre during Britain's last Roman phase but not for very long afterwards. As a literary figure, Lot may be related to the Celtic god Lugh, who had a solar aspect that could account for Gawain's curiously cyclical prowess. The Lug who defeats the Fomorians is an Irish version of this deity. William of Malmesbury records the discovery of Gawain's coastal grave during the reign of the Conqueror. As a result the knight has been fancifully equated with a shadowy Govan whose reputed tomb is in a chapel near the southern tip of Pembrokeshire.   16   17   18

115. Percevel and Galahad as Grail Questers.

Perceval is a literary creation who reaches his zenith in the German epic *Parzival*, the source of Wagner's opera. A Welsh tale entitled *Peredur* has some connection with the Perceval stories. There may be legends in the background about a sixth-century Peredur, who was a northern prince mentioned in Geoffrey's *Life of Merlin*. Distant echoes of Pryderi have been detected.

Lancelot is not in Geoffrey and has no clear prototype. He seems to have been added by French romancers. His British location at Joyous Gard probably owes something to known Welsh traditions of a pre-English fort at Bamburgh on the Northumbrian coast, which was called Din Guayrdi. Lancelot's affair with the Queen is at first simply that, but as the Arthurian cycle develops, the influence of Christian morality grows, making it a sort of time-bomb eventually disruptive of the Round Table. This motif is central in Tennyson, who stresses Christian matrimony as one of the chief pillars of the regime, a symbol of spiritual dominion over baser nature. The disastrous example set by the Queen herself is consequently fatal to the whole scheme, as Arthur makes clear (sanctimoniously, and at great length) in the Idyll *Guinevere*.

Christian influence also underlies the ironic invention of Galahad, who, produced by Lancelot's sin, can accomplish the sacred task which the sin itself prevents Lancelot from accomplishing. His name is taken from 'Galaad' or   20 Gilead in the Bible (*Genesis* 31:48). He represents an attempt to combine chivalry and religion. If a hint has been taken from any historical model, it may be St Illtud, a famous Welsh monastic founder reputed to have been a soldier of Arthur before he embraced the religious life.

Medraut, as noted, makes a brief appearance in the *Annales Cambriae* and may have been real. Geoffrey's 'Modred' form of the name, which becomes the sinister-sounding 'Mordred', is Cornish or Breton, and the raid on Kelliwic also points in a south-westerly direction. His original position vis-à-vis Arthur is far from evident. He may not have been remembered as an opponent at all. When the enmity does emerge, the Welsh version suggests a feud rather than a subject's unruliness. Mordred became the King's traitorous nephew in Geoffrey, and his incestuously-generated son in French romances, though not always.

1. Bromwich, 303–7, 484–5; Lacy, ed., art. 'Kay'.
2. *Mabinogion* (2), 99, 128.
3. Malory, I, 5.
4. Bromwich, 279–80; Lacy, ed., art. 'Bedivere'.
5. GM (1), 117–9, and (2), 237–40.
6. Lacy, ed., art. 'Gawain'.
7. GM (1), 107, and (2), 223.
8. Ashe (5), 68–9.
9. Wilhelm (1), 159–209 (*Sir Gawain and the Green Knight*).
10. Chambers, 17 (quoting William of Malmesbury).
11. Lacy, ed., art. 'Perceval'.
12. Lacy, ed., art. 'Lancelot'; Loomis, ed., 296–302.
13. Lacy, ed., art. 'Galahad'; Malory, XI, 1–3.
14. Bromwich, 454–5; Lacy, ed., art. 'Mordred'.
15. Cp Eckhardt, 120–6.
16. Bromwich, 369–71.
17. Alcock (1), 180–1; Bromwich, 422–3; Morris, 215; Tatlock, 152–3.
18. Chambers, 250; FML, 406.
19. Ashe (5), 37; Morris, 231–2; 'Nennius' (1), chapter 61.
20. Bromwich, 353.

42 *Morgan*

1 Morgan le Fay, or Morgain la Fée, was Arthur's elder half-sister, a daughter of Ygerna by her first husband like Morgause. She had a convent education, but studied magic with Merlin's aid and became proficient. Her principal

2 home was Avalon, the paradisal apple-island where Arthur's sword was forged at a smithy of the fairy-folk. There Morgan was the head of nine sisters. The word 'sister' does not imply that Ygerna bore such an abundance of daughters. What Morgan headed was a sisterhood in the sense of a community. She had powers of healing, shape-shifting and flight. Her companions shared these in some degree, but she surpassed them in beauty and skill, and taught them other subjects, such as mathematics. She had

3 more abodes, including the Castle of Maidens near Edinburgh, and even a Mediterranean retreat in Sicily, where she was called Fata Morgana and gave her name to a mirage phenomenon in the Straits of Messina, for which her lingering magic was, and is, responsible.

She acquired a reputation for sexual rapacity, and was reputed to employ spells to entrap men for her pleasure in a 'Valley without Return'. However, she did marry. Her husband was Urien, one of Arthur's sub-kings, and she bore him a son, Owain. There are those who claim that she and not her sister Morgause was the mother of the doubtfully-derived Mordred.

In several ways Morgan showed friendliness to Arthur, but she was accused of turning against him and using her arts to make trouble. She gave him, it is said, a magical drink that opened his eyes to the Queen's unfaithfulness . . . though perhaps it only cured him of self-deception. In a vengeful mood, due to his execution of one of her lovers, she stole Excalibur and gave it to Accolon, another lover, leaving an ineffectual copy to deceive Arthur. The King recovered the true sword and worsted Accolon in

4 combat. It was Morgan who contrived the challenge of the Green Knight, which Gawain took up, as a somewhat severe test for the Round Table.

Morgan's company of nine may be compared to the nine maidens watching over the cauldron which Arthur sought in the watery Otherworld of Annwfn. Whatever the provenance of these, she is a figure from pagan antiquity. The Celts had myths about sunset islands inhabited by fairy-women, and classical

5 writers mention real and relevant sisterhoods, such as a group of nine wonder-working healers on the Ile de Sein off the coast of Brittany. The head of such a sisterhood might be the priestess of a goddess, and her manifestation. Morgan is

6 certainly divine in her origins, a fact acknowledged by several authors even in the Middle Ages. She may be the same as a Welsh Modron who, in turn, is ultimately the river-goddess Matrona. Her name also hints at influence from an Irish deity, the Morrigan. More or less humanised by romancers, she is given a

7 blood-relationship to connect her with Arthur, and a husband and son, though her family hardly seems close-knit or stable. Urien and his son Owain are

historical persons, who fought against the northern Angles and are praised in the verses of the bard Taliesin. Their introduction into this milieu is a fiction. They lived much too late to be contemporary with Arthur.

Morgan's being the true mother of Mordred, rather than her sister, is an idea of some modern novelists and film-makers. The motive may be a wish to concentrate sinister female power in one woman. But it was not originally sinister. The change in Morgan's character is due mainly to a shift in religious attitudes. Celtic Christians, as will be recalled, had no deep animosity towards the pre-Christian scheme of things. The conversion of a divine Morgan into an enchantress is only one instance of their readiness to adapt the old gods. When Morgan makes her literary début on her apple-island, which happens in Geoffrey's *Life of Merlin*, she is benign and attractive, and early romancers give [8] her relationship to Arthur a kind of 'fairy godmother' quality.

But medieval Christianity hardened, taking a more black-and-white view, so that it had difficulty coming to terms with such a figure. Could a practitioner of un-Christian magic really be good, or even neutral? It was on this principle that Merlin himself, though too great to blacken, was made out to be a devil's son, saved from the full effects of his paternal heredity only by his mother's virtue. As for Morgan, some of the romances made her frankly malignant, in fact a witch, a [9] 'clerk of necromancy' in Malory's words. This mode of thinking did not always apply. The Lady of the Lake escaped serious defamation. Morgan, however, did not, and therefore different portrayals of her do not cohere well. Her treatment foreshadows the delusion underlying the witch-mania of a later period: that anything savouring of magic and especially female magic, even the herbal charms of village wise-women, must be satanic.

116. (overleaf)
Morgan le Fay: a Victorian conception of the enchantress.

1. Malory, I, 2.
2. GM (1), 104, (2), 217, and (3), lines 908–40. Cp Stewart (1), 119–20, 128.
3. Lacy, ed., art. 'Morgan le Fay'; *Man, Myth and Magic*, art. 'Morgan le Fay'.
4. Wilhelm (1), 207–8 (*Sir Gawain*, lines 2446–66).
5. Graves (2), 110, 389; Rhys, I, 331.
6. Bromwich, 458–63; Chadwick (2), 107; Chambers, 272; Ross, 270, 372 n. 57; Wilhelm (1), 207 (*Sir Gawain*, line 2452).
7. Bromwich, 479–83, 516–20.
8. Loomis, ed., 108.
9. Ibid, 535.

43 *Merlin and Nimue*

1   Merlin was lost to Arthur long before the close of his reign. The enchanter became enamoured of one of the Damsels of the Lake, called Nimue or Viviane. He foresaw that this love would be disastrous, yet was powerless to avert his doom. She rejected his advances, but joined him on a long journey through Brittany and Cornwall, on the understanding that he would not use magic to overcome her resistance. On the way she learned many secrets, but was always repelled by what she knew of his devilish parentage. At last she grew tired of him, and employed one of his own spells to shut him in a cave or tomb, or according to one account an enclosure with unseen walls, where she visited him occasionally without ever setting him free. Whatever the nature of his prison, he never escaped in Arthur's time.

2   The Welsh deny Merlin's entrapment; at any rate, his permanent entrapment. They maintain that he is still alive (asleep or waking, it is not certain which) in voluntary retirement on Bardsey Island. His home is a cave or an invisible house of glass. He has with him the Thirteen Treasures of Britain – ancient talismans and magical objects, concealed from the English – and the true throne of the realm, that is, Arthur's.

3   Nimue became the Lady of the Lake, or perhaps succeeded to that position before the end of the Merlin episode. Her chosen male companion was the knight Pelleas. He had been vainly courting a lady named Ettard.

117. (preceding page) Merlin's nemesis in Pre-Raphaelite art.

118. Bardsey Island off north-west Wales, where, according to a Welsh tradition, Merlin still lives.

Gawain, who volunteered to put in a word for him, seduced her himself. Pelleas was plunged into despair. Nimue comforted him, and mischievously cast a spell on Ettard making her change her mind and love him, too late. The now-indifferent Pelleas turned to Nimue instead and they married.

Merlin's shameful fate may resemble the denigration of Morgan le Fay, as a product of medieval Christianity. However splendid the results of a magician's work, he could not be truly good in his antecedents, or fortunate all the way. Not only, therefore, was Merlin's nature made out to be half diabolic: it had to contain the seeds of a nemesis, a betrayal through the forbidden arts themselves.

Since he first appears in Vortigern's reign as a youthful prodigy, even a child, no viable Arthurian time-scheme would allow him to be much past his forties when catastrophe strikes. He is ageing in medieval terms, but far from sexual decay or dotage. A modern reader, picturing him as an old man with a long white beard, may find the episode more unsavoury than it is. That semi-comic image was adopted in Disney's film *The Sword in the Stone*, but not in Boorman's film *Excalibur*. It may be due to Tennyson's *Idylls of the King* or Doré's illustrations to them.

Tennyson distinguishes Vivien, as he calls her, from the Lady of the Lake, and makes her a mere seductress whose ruin of Merlin is part of a spite against the court. Through most of the poem he shows no love or desire for her and seems to be almost past it. But at the end, after she has been wheedling and manoeuvring for hours:

> The pale blood of the wizard at her touch
> Took gayer colours, like an opal warmed.

And he yields, and tells her the fatal spell. This version is in conformity with the theme of 'Sense at war with Soul' which Tennyson makes central to his Arthurian cycle.

1. Malory, IV, 1; Wilhelm (2), 252–66 (excerpt from the *Suite du Merlin*).

2. Ashe (5), 27–8; Bromwich, 474.
3. Malory, IV, 21–3.

44 *Tristan and Isolde*

1   Tristan was a prince of the land of Lyonesse. His uncle, Mark, ruled over Cornwall in Arthur's time, an autonomous sub-king. As a youth Tristan went to live at Mark's court. After some years, the Irish king, Anguish, demanded a tribute of Cornish slaves. He sent over his wife's brother Morholt to press the claim, which Mark refused, though in much trepidation. Morholt was a man of immense bulk and physical prowess. Confident that no one could match his strength, he agreed to settle the issue by single combat. Mark needed a champion for Cornwall, and his nephew Tristan volunteered, fought Morholt on an island, and killed him. A tiny piece of metal broke off his sword and lodged in the Irish warrior's skull. It was still embedded when the corpse was borne home. Isolde, Anguish's daughter, took it out and kept it, hoping that some day she might use it to identify the sword's owner and take vengeance for Morholt's death.

   In due course Tristan paid a visit to Ireland, and was hospitably received by the king and queen, who did not know what he had done. He distinguished himself by slaying a dragon. The monster gave him a wound, and Isolde, who was an expert healer, undertook to nurse him. While he was in a bath she examined his sword in an adjoining room, noticed a notch, and found that her fragment of metal matched it. Her first impulse was to rush in and stab him as he lay in the bath, but, aware that his dragon-slaying and other feats had made him *persona grata* with her parents, she let the matter drop. However, her attitude to Tristan could not remain emotionally neutral.

   His uncle, Mark, asked for Isolde's hand in marriage, and she consented. Tristan escorted her to Cornwall. Her maid Brangaene had brought a love-potion to ensure a happy relationship with Mark, but before the ship reached port Tristan and Isolde drank it, not realising what it was, and fell hopelessly and irremediably in love. The royal wedding proceeded nevertheless. Mark had taken over the castle at Tintagel, and he lived there, and at other residences, with Isolde as his consort. Tristan continued in attendance and managed to spend furtive hours with her. Mark was suspicious, but never quite sure what was going on. Some of his courtiers knew, and tried to convince him of his wife's adultery, but the lovers contrived their trysts too cleverly. Once he hid in a tree to spy on them when they met below. They saw him reflected in a pool and kept their talk innocent, so that he fancied the accusation to be false. When he finally faced the truth about their love, he allowed them to move to a retreat in the woods. Even then he was willing to be tricked into believing that there was no sexual relationship, or that if there had been, it had ceased.

   After various developments his powers of self-deception gave out. Isolde was kept at court and Tristan went into exile. In Brittany he met another Isolde, a princess, nicknamed 'of the White Hands'. Convinced that his amour was finished for ever, he married her, but memories were too strong

119. Tristan and Isolde on board ship, Isolde wearing a crown as an Irish princess.

and the marriage remained unconsummated. When he was wounded in a battle he sent a ship to the Irish Isolde in Cornwall, entreating her to come over and cure him. Uncertain whether she would, he arranged a signal. If, when the ship returned, she was aboard, the crew would hoist white sails; if not, black ones. Isolde embarked gladly and the sails were white. But as the ship neared the Breton coast, Tristan was too ill to get up and look. His Breton wife, who knew about the signal, jealously told him the sails were black. Despairing, he died. When the first Isolde arrived and found what had happened, she died also. The bodies were conveyed back to Tintagel, and Mark allowed them to be buried close together. A vine grew from Tristan's grave and a rose-tree from Isolde's, and the branches entwined.

Tristan was as gallant a fighter as any in his time, and, according to some, a friend of Lancelot and a respected member of the Round Table, if somewhat irregular in attendance. He was also renowned for talents unusual among the warrior-nobles, being a linguist, a chess-player, a master of the arts of hunting and falconry, and a musician. Isolde was less versatile, but she was intelligent and articulate, and her medical skill made her exceptional among women. As for her husband Mark, estimates vary. An early account tells how he cried out in generous regret, when all was over, that if his bride had only explained about the potion he would have let her go. But in later and longer retrospect he tends to be condemned as a mean-spirited scoundrel, whose failure to deal decisively with the situation was due to cowardice and incompetence, not to a willingness to give anyone the benefit of the doubt. Those who regard him thus even give the story a different end, saying that

4   Mark used a poisoned spear to murder Tristan as he sat unarmed, playing his harp.

Among European love-stories, that of Tristan and Isolde is notable as the first major portrayal of a romantic passion as a law unto itself, taking priority over all obligations, justifying virtually anything that serves its ends. In the earliest and plainest versions, Tristan is not only an adulterer but grossly disloyal to a liege lord who has done him no wrong. Isolde practises shameless deception and even contemplates murdering her maid to hush up the truth. Admittedly their love is ascribed to the potion and has a fated, irresistible quality. But it is never treated as a mere crazy aberration, foreign to the norms of human behaviour, like, say, the spell-induced compulsive dancing that figures in many legends. The potion simply creates for this couple a condition which other lovers are assumed to experience, if seldom so obsessively.

5   Both the names are spelt in a variety of ways. 'Tristan' begins as the Pictish 'Drust'. In southern British usage it can be traced back to the sixth century. It becomes Drustan, Drystan, and, in romance, Tristram. The 'Tristan' form occurs in Welsh and has been familiarised by Wagner. 'Isolde' appears as Essyllt, Iseult, Isolt, Yseut. The Wagnerian choice may be allowed to stand equally. 'Brangaene' is probably the same as 'Branwen' in the *Mabinogion*.

6   Tristan's home country Lyonesse may originally have been Leonais in Brittany, or Lothian in Scotland – Loenois in Old French. However, the Cornish localisation led to its being identified with a land figuring in Cornish folklore, which, reputedly, once covered Mount's Bay and spread south and west around Land's End, out to the present Isles of Scilly. It had several towns and 140 churches. At some unspecified date after Tristan the ocean engulfed it. One of the few survivors was a man named Trevilian, who mounted a white horse and galloped just ahead of the flood. He reached a cave near Marazion and sheltered there to watch the disaster. The Seven Stones reef off Land's End is said to mark the position of one of the lost towns, the City of Lions. Fishermen used to report hauling up bits of masonry and window glass in their nets. When the weather is rough, the church bells of Lyonesse can allegedly be heard tolling under water.

7   Folk-memories covering many centuries went into this legend's making. Medieval inundations may have affected the coastline. Long before that, in the second millennium BC, the floor of Mount's Bay was above water and inhabited. Fossil remains of a sunken forest of beeches can still be discerned. A Cornish name for St Michael's Mount, now an island, is *Carrick luz en cuz*, 'the ancient rock in the wood'. A Roman writer, speaking of events in the time of Maximus, refers to the Isle – not Isles – of Scilly, as if most of them were then joined together. Remnants of huts and walls below the present water-level tell a similar tale. The islets Great and Little Arthur attest the King's Scillonian fame.

8   Lyonesse is one of a number of miniature Atlantises, real or partly-real or fictitious, others being Cantref Gwaelod, a lost Welsh district under Cardigan

Bay, and Lomea, where the Goodwin Sands now are. At Ker-Is in Brittany, drowned church bells also ring.

To return to the Tristan legend, the Irish part has a nebulous historical background in the period when Irishmen harassed western Britain and dominated areas near the coast. Anguish is Aengus of Munster, who reigned during the second half of the fifth century. Many of the adventurers had come from his kingdom. 9

Archaeologically the chief item of interest is the Tristan Stone, a monument near Fowey in Cornwall. It used to stand closer to the Iron Age hill-fort Castle Dore, which was reoccupied in and after the fifth century. The stone's Latin inscription says: 'Drustanus lies here, the son of Cunomorus.' 'Cunomorus' Latinises the name of Kynvawr, a regional ruler and probable occupant of Castle Dore. A belief traceable to the ninth century is that 'Cunomorus' is another name for Mark, in which case Drustanus is not merely someone called Tristan but *the* Tristan. 10

An early poetic version by Béroul brings in place-names belonging to the Castle Dore neighbourhood, and he clearly has some acquaintance with it. Yet if Tristan was Mark's son, not his nephew, Isolde was a young stepmother and the moral position looks even more questionable. Story-tellers could have changed the relationship for the lovers' benefit. It may be, however, that the legend came to be located in Cornwall because of the monument itself, and did not begin there. 11

Whether or not Mark is the same as Cunomorus, he is credible as a real 12

120. Mark kisses Tristan, a design on a tile from a medieval pavement at Chertsey Abbey near Windsor.

121. Land's End,
overlooking the sea
that is now said to
cover Lyonesse.

person. 'Mark' is the Roman Marcus. Moreover, the Welsh state that his father was a great-grandson of Coel, Meirchyawn, i.e. Marcianus; and anyone so called might well have been named after an emperor who reigned from 450 to 457. Mark could have had a second name, and it could have been the one that is inscribed on the monument. However, the evidence is frail. Also, his father seems to have lived in Glamorgan, and he is associated with Wales himself. The Welsh form of 'Mark' is 'March', which means a horse, and a rude Welsh anecdote, far removed in spirit from the matter of Tristan, tells of Mark having a horse's ears (an echo of the Greek legend of Midas, who had a donkey's). Further complications are raised by Mote of Mark, a coastal hill-fort, and 13 Trusty's or Tristan's Hill, both in Scotland. The developed Tristan story includes not only the Cornish and Welsh elements but Pictish, Irish and Breton 14 ones. While the Tristan of the inscription is the only Tristan anywhere near the right period, the tale is too much of a literary composite to pin down historically, or even trace to its origin with any assurance.

At first it had only a slight connection with the Arthurian cycle, possibly none, though a Welsh triad that must be fairly old summarises a curious lost tale of 15 'Drystan', the lover of 'Essyllt', preventing Arthur from commandeering Mark's pigs. Béroul brings Arthur in, but Gottfried von Strassburg, a German poet whose work was the inspiration of Wagner's opera, mentions him only in passing. It is in the longer-drawn prose romances that Tristan becomes a knight of the Round Table. As such, he has numerous adventures that threaten to swamp the love-story, and even that, while still firmly embedded, loses some of its primitive directness because a friend of Tristan's, the Saracen knight Palamedes, loves Isolde too though unrequitedly, and jealousies result. The debasement of Mark's character, also due to prose romancers, corresponds to their glorification of Tristan as a chivalric hero in contrast with him. It makes the amour more pardonable, since Mark does little to deserve anyone's loyalty, and Tristan might claim to be rescuing Isolde from a hateful lot. But the extinction of sympathy for her husband weakens the tragedy.

1. Ditmas (2), 15–57; FML, 134–5; Lacy, ed., art. 'Tristan'; Wilhelm (2), 153–97 (Béroul).
2. Malory, VIII; IX, 10–43; XI, 1–22, 26–35, 50–88; XII, 11–14.
3. Lacy, ed., art. 'Mark'.
4. Malory, XIX, 11.
5. Bromwich, 287, 329–33, 349–50; Loomis, ed., 125.
6. Ditmas (2), 63–4.
7. Ashe (5), 149–51, 183; FML, 142; Thomas (1), 276–94.
8. Rhys, I, 382–9.
9. Morris, 353.
10. Bromwich, 444–5; Westwood, 8–11.
11. Ditmas (2), 64–93.
12. Bromwich, 443–8, 456–7; Chadwick (1), 212; Rhys, II, 572–5; Westwood, 274.
13. Ashe (5), 160, 206; Westwood, 9.
14. Loomis, ed., 122–33.
15. Bromwich, 48; Rhys, II, 499.

45 *The Quest of the Grail*

Somewhere in Arthur's Britain there was a mysterious castle in the possession of a custodian called the Fisher King. He was partially crippled by a wound and the land round about was waste.

1   No one knew where the castle was. When Perceval came to it by chance, and was hospitably received by its lord, he saw a procession of young people bearing strange objects. One of them was a lance with blood dripping from its point. A maiden carried a splendid vessel studded with jewels. It had a supernatural power of nourishment. The Fisher King's father, concealed from view in another room, lived on a single Mass wafer placed in it daily. Perceval, though mystified, had been taught that it was discourteous to ask questions, and did not inquire the meaning of what he saw. He learned too late that he should have done. If he had, the spell would have been broken, the Fisher King's wound would have healed, and the waste land would have become fertile again.

2   Those who profess to know explain that this resplendent object was the Holy Grail, the vessel (bowl or cup) in which Jesus instituted his sacrament at the Last Supper. Soon after that event it came into the hands of Joseph of Arimathea, who used it to collect drops of the sacred blood at the crucifixion. Later, the risen Christ appeared to him and taught him secret words, through which the Grail could be the medium of a special revelation. It kept him alive without ordinary food during a long imprisonment by Jews who had been Christ's enemies. Released at last, Joseph set off with many companions on divinely-guided wanderings. They had the Grail with them, and made a table to set it on, in commemoration of the table of the Last Supper. At length these wanderings brought the Grail to Britain, to the Vales of Avalon, the future site of Glastonbury. However, it did not remain there. It passed to its hiding-place in the elusive castle, which was called Corbenic, and to a succession of keepers collaterally descended from Joseph. One of them was Perceval's host. Another was Pelles, whose daughter Elaine became the mother of Galahad.

3   While Arthur still reigned, it was revealed that this unique link with Christ might be rediscovered by search rather than accident. The question

4   to ask in the castle was understood to be 'Who is served from the Grail?' But to the questing knight, the full achievement would be far more than simply locating it or making a correct response. It would be a supreme spiritual experience, hinted at in the tradition of the secret words taught to Joseph. When someone attained this, the mystery would end or pass into a new phase.

5   The Round Table – made by Merlin in commemoration of the two previous ones, that of the Grail and that of the Last Supper – had a vacant place, the Perilous Seat. Only a knight destined to succeed in the Quest could sit in it with impunity. This turned out to be Galahad, whom Pelles had tricked Lancelot into begetting, so that the Grail-achiever would be

born of Joseph's stock. When Galahad arrived at the court, his vocation was shown by signs, one of them being his sitting down without mishap in the Perilous Seat. The Grail briefly appeared, veiled, in the hall where the knights sat round the Table, and each miraculously received the food of his choice. Inspired by this phenomenon, many of them rode off on the Quest. Arthur was unhappy but let them go.

Several had glimpses – cryptic apparitions, in unexpected places. Gawain came close, but finally failed. Lancelot came closer, but his sin with the Queen disqualified him. It was Galahad's chastity and general saintliness that made him, and him alone, worthy of the full vision. With Perceval and Bors, a cousin of Lancelot, he voyaged over the sea to a distant city called Sarras. There Joseph's son Josephe, revisiting this world, officiated as priest

6

122. Apparition of the Grail at the Round Table, with Galahad occupying the Perilous Seat.

123. A portrayal of the Grail Quest in tapestry.

7   in a Mass said with the Grail; for it had gone out of Britain. He summoned Galahad to look into the sacred vessel, and Galahad looked and saw, and died in ecstasy a few moments later.

Accounts of these happenings differ widely, and no one knows exactly what became of the Grail. It may have been borne away into Asia, or taken up to heaven. The Quest was adverse to the Round Table, as Arthur had foreseen it would be, since it drew away many of his best knights and not all returned.

The problem of the Grail has no single solution, because of the discrepancies among the versions, which seem to reflect older story-telling with no pretence of consistency. Malory's narrative derives from a thirteenth-century French romance that constitutes the main tradition. But the German, in Wolfram von Eschenbach's *Parzival*, diverges sharply and introduces a whole order of Grail-guarding knights who reappear in the *Parsifal* of Wagner.

8   The word itself is the Old French *graal*, meaning a large, deep dish or serving-vessel. What Perceval sees in the earliest romance, by Chrétien de

Troyes, is simply 'a graal'. In some way it is manifestly special, but its nature is not disclosed. The idea that the treasured thing is *the* Graal or Grail, unique and holy and with a history, emerges first in a work by Robert de Boron written about 1200. There is no connection with any known holy-relic legend, and the Grail is never thought of in the same way as objects of popular veneration like the True Cross. Modern claims that some existing artefact 'is' the Grail are misguided. The stories can be read symbolically, or allegorically, or mystically, but not literally.

Antecedents have been suggested in pagan fertility magic, possibly ritual. The Grail-keeper's wound, when specified, is sexual in nature, and the barrenness of the land is linked with his impotence and semi-paralysis. The bleeding lance is also given a Christian gloss, as the lance of Longinus that pierced the side of Christ; but in conjunction with the Grail itself, it hints at a juxtaposition of male and female symbols. Furthermore, the Grail's peculiar properties (its power of bodily nourishment persists even when it is fully Christianised) have a background in Celtic horns of plenty and magical cauldrons. Here the cauldron of Annwfn, tended by maidens as the Grail often is, and sought by Arthur and his followers, may be ancestral. It is interesting that this Welsh Otherworld quest is by water, a fact that links it with Irish romances of mysterious voyages, the *immrama*. One of the Grail stories, *Perlesvaus*, includes a kind of *immram*.

Basically, the Grail is a supernatural source of life, exerting its power when the right person utters the right words. But when the immemorial imagery is absorbed into a Christian myth, evolved by Robert de Boron and his successors, the emphasis changes. As the vessel used by Christ to institute the Eucharist, it becomes involved with the Catholic doctrine of his Real Presence in the sacrament, received in communion, and with spiritual rather than physical nourishment. The supreme vision, which only Galahad attains, is a mystical experience of the Godhead – of the Trinity, and the incarnation of its Second Person in Christ: a face-to-face awareness of the source of eternal life.

Though the Grail is conveyed to the future site of Glastonbury, medieval romancers never state plainly that it was brought to that spot by Joseph in person, even when they speak of his coming to Britain. Conversely, while Glastonbury Abbey claimed Joseph as its founder and the builder of its Old Church, it never claimed that he brought the Grail, and its account of his coming is incompatible with the romances; because the date does not fit, to look no further. Hence Joseph's two roles, as Grail-bearer and founder of Christian Glastonbury, are not combined – at least in the Middle Ages. Eventually Tennyson does it. A frequent academic assumption that the monks merely borrowed from the romancers therefore presents difficulties. Since the official Church always ignored the Grail, perhaps as being a literary figment of doubtful orthodoxy, it may be questioned whether thirteenth-century monks would even have known the romances, or used them if they did. Joseph of Arimathea is a strange person to think of, either as acquiring the Grail, since he was not present at the Last Supper, or as pioneering Christianity in the remote west, since even legend seldom takes him on missions. There may be a single explanation for his different roles in earlier hagiography or speculation, now lost.

9

10

11

124. Tassilo's Chalice, probably made in Anglo-Saxon North-umberland; the Grail is often imagined as a chalice, because of its association with the imagery of the Mass.

1. Loomis, ed., 184–90.
2. Lacy, ed., art. 'Grail'.
3. *Queste del Saint Graal*, 36–42, 99.
4. *Perlesvaus*, 35.
5. *Queste*, 97–100; Wilhelm (2), 233–6 (excerpt from Prose *Merlin*).
6. Malory, XIII, 1–8.
7. *Queste*, 282–4.
8. Lacy, ed., art. 'Grail'.
9. Weston, passim.
10. *Perlesvaus*, 250–7.
11. *Queste*, 304, n. 87.

46 *The Passing of Arthur*

All agree that Mordred caused Arthur's downfall, and most say the catastrophe began while the King was in Gaul (or France, if they call it so). As to the reason for his being there, opinions differ.

1 It will be recalled that Lucius, the western colleague of the eastern emperor Leo, demanded that Arthur should pay the tribute he had withheld, and restore the Roman lands he had occupied. Arthur retorted by gathering a vast army and leading it into Gaul, with notions of taking Rome and becoming emperor himself. On this last point his advisers encouraged him by citing precedents, not only Constantine but Belinus. Lucius opposed the Britons with a cosmopolitan force. Arthur, bravely supported by Gawain, defeated and slew him, and pressed on into Burgundy. He was preparing to cross the Alps when, according to this account, appalling news from Britain recalled him.

2 Widely preferred, however, is a rival account taking his story to the same point by another route. Those who tell it thus hold that while he did wage the Roman war, it was fought and won early in his reign. The expedition that proved fatal was tragically different, and involved Romans only marginally, if at all.

3 It was nothing less than a campaign against Lancelot, brought about indirectly by his long love-affair with the Queen. As already recorded, his rescue of her at Carlisle was not effected without bloodshed, including the death of two brothers of Gawain. The Round Table was split between supporters of Lancelot and supporters of the King. Lancelot led away his knights to the continent, where, using French lands of his own as a base, he made himself ruler of much of the territory Arthur had conquered. Arthur followed with an army and tried to bring him under control. Gawain's unappeasable enmity, due to the death of his brothers, prevented any agreement. It was during a siege that the news arrived which called Arthur back to Britain.

4 On either showing, what had happened was this. When Arthur went overseas he had left Mordred in charge as deputy-ruler, nominally in partnership with Guinevere, but for practical purposes sovereign. It was an odd choice in view of his character and conduct, but the King, it is said, regarded him as his heir in spite of all, and therefore entitled to the position. Mordred, however, waited till Arthur had been abroad for some time and then betrayed him, giving out that he was dead, seizing the crown himself, and making a treaty with the Saxons offering to restore a holding in Britain for them in return for aid. When he also tried to get possession of Guinevere as his wife or mistress, she at least led him to expect her compliance, but those who are friendly to her explain that this was only a subterfuge, and say she shut herself in the Tower of London with a loyal garrison and withstood a siege by Mordred's troops. Nevertheless, he won widespread support by playing on a popular longing for peace, or simply for a change. His only overt opponent was the Archbishop of Canterbury, who knew that his

125. Arthur confronting Mordred in the final battle.

announcement of the King's death was untrue. Threatened with execution, the prelate fled westward and settled in a hermitage near Glastonbury.

Arthur hurried back from the continent. At Dover, Gawain died of a wound Lancelot had given him in single combat. He was sorry for his vendetta, and a reconciliation would now have been possible, but there was no time. The King had to fight Mordred and he had to do it without Lancelot. Mordred's support survived the revelation that Arthur still lived, but after some indecisive successes Arthur crushed the traitor at a place which the Welsh call Camlann. As to its whereabouts there is much dissent. It may have been on the River Camel in Cornwall, which is spanned by a bridge called Slaughter Bridge to this day. Some profess to find it in the Salisbury neighbourhood or on the Plain, adding that Arthur and Mordred held a parley which almost led to a truce, but failed because a knight drew his sword to kill a snake, and the action was misconstrued so that fighting broke out. Mordred perished in the battle; so did nearly all the knights. Arthur himself was mortally wounded. The magical protection of his sword's original scabbard had been lost long before when it was stolen.

126. Bedivere mourns as Excalibur returns to the Lady of the Lake.

7   Near by (strangely indeed, if either of these battle-sites is correct) lay an expanse of open water. Arthur commanded Bedivere, who remained with him, to go and cast Excalibur into it. Being reluctant to throw away such a fine weapon, Bedivere twice falsely told him that he had, but when questioned as to what he had seen he spoke of nothing unusual, and Arthur knew he was lying. The third time, Bedivere obeyed, and a hand rose above the surface, caught the sword by the hilt, and drew it below. Then a boat approached over the water with a number of ladies in it wearing black hoods, among them Morgan le Fay and Nimue. Weeping and wailing, they took the King aboard and bore him away to Avalon, where, he told Bedivere, he would seek healing.

8   The second Roman war as the catalyst of disaster is Geoffrey's idea. The alternative of a continental conflict with Lancelot takes shape in French romance, where the Romans do not quite vanish, but are a distraction only. Malory adopts and improves the campaign against Lucius, but boldly transfers it to an earlier phase, with a triumphant conclusion and many years of peace ensuing. Thereby he makes room for a more impressive golden age, affirming its ideals even as far as a second generation. Yet the inner strains have to assert themselves, the crash has to come, and more bitterly than in Geoffrey's version. The golden age is a doomed golden age, moving steadily towards tragedy, and while Caxton may have been misled when he entitled the whole Malory compilation *Le Morte d'Arthur*, his instinct was not far wrong.

The Tower of London was not an anachronism in medieval eyes, because

127. Arthur lying wounded in Avalon, and the women who brought him there.

Julius Caesar was supposed to have founded it, a belief mentioned by Shakespeare in *Richard III* (Act III, Scene 1). When Mordred besieges it, however, he uses guns – a touch taken up by T. H. White in *The Once and Future King*, where the news of this unspeakable atrocity, the negation of chivalry, convinces Arthur that all is over. The Archbishop of Canterbury is another anachronism, here as in the Sword in the Stone episode, since Canterbury was in Saxon hands, and its see was not created till St Augustine's mission at the end of the sixth century. A statement made by Malory and echoed by Caxton, to the effect that Gawain's skull is in Dover Castle, must raise a query, but Arthur's return Channel crossing makes Dover a logical place for his decease.

9

128. Dozmary Pool in Cornwall, one of Excalibur's supposed resting-places.

10

Arthur's fatal clash with Mordred is a deep-rooted Welsh tradition, but early particulars are lacking. The perishing of Arthur and 'Medraut' at Camlann, as mentioned in the *Annales Cambriae*, occurs also in the triads where it is one of three 'futile battles', an understatement. Historians have been known to claim that this is the only solidly-attested fact about Arthur. But the *Annales* entry cannot be proved earlier than the tenth century, and is so placed that if it is accepted almost everything else must be rejected, with the improbable implication that the entire Arthurian legend grew round an obscure squabble of petty chiefs, unrelated to the Saxon invasion or anything else. As ever, there is the possibility that the Arthur of legend is a composite, and a 'Camlann Arthur' was absorbed into the saga of an earlier leader. The brief Welsh allusions know nothing of a Gallic campaign. That, and the conception of Mordred as a traitorous deputy-ruler, are external motifs combined with the Welsh tradition by Geoffrey, perhaps as an afterthought, since a forecast of Arthur's end which he ascribes to Merlin suggests that he planned at first to have it happen in Gaul. 11 12

Considerations like these add to the likelihood of his having taken hints from the historical 'King of the Britons' called Riothamus. Like Geoffrey's Arthur, that king was in Gaul with a British army towards 470, advanced to the neighbourhood of Burgundy, was betrayed by a deputy-ruler (the imperial prefect Arvandus) who tried to make a deal with barbarians, is last located on the continent in Burgundian country, and fades from the scene after a fatal battle with no recorded death. He is in fact the only documented person who does anything Arthurian, though, of course, Geoffrey's work is a literary construction using and rearranging historical elements, and in no sense a history.

While Camlann made an impression on the Welsh, a much deeper one than the Badon victory, it cannot be pinned down on the map. The name seems to be derived from a British form *Camboglanna*, meaning 'crooked bank', presumably of a river. Hadrian's Wall had a fort so named, perhaps Birdoswald, above the sinuous River Irthing. But Wales itself has two present-day Camlans, and the Arthur-Mordred clash is never placed in the north. The Camel, Geoffrey's choice, is known to have been the scene of a battle, but it was fought between Saxons and Cornish in 823. The Somerset Cam is another candidate, recommended by its closeness to Cadbury-Camelot and by a multiple burial said to have been unearthed in a nearby field. 13 14

The romancers' preference for Salisbury Plain, or, in Malory, 'a down beside Salisbury', is puzzling. Was it suggested by the famous hill-fort Old Sarum? In any case the geography is absurd, because there is no neighbouring sea or open water. Tennyson moves back south-westward, siting Arthur's last battle in Lyonesse – apparently the level part now under Mount's Bay – and drawing on Loe Bar and Loe Pool for his topography.

As for Avalon, Geoffrey says the 'Isle' and is vague as to where it is; Malory says 'Vale' and can only mean central Somerset, a geographical fix that makes a journey by boat from anywhere near Salisbury all the more unmanageable. The Welsh name for the island is *Ynys Avallach*. It is interesting that Geoffrey's *Insula Avallonis* does not precisely Latinise this and is influenced by a real place-name, Avallon in Burgundy. Here again he may have picked up a hint from some account of Riothamus, who, when last visible, is moving in the general direction of the Burgundian Avallon. 15 16

Excalibur's casting-away may have a factual basis. In Denmark, where lakes have become peat-bogs, swords are found which were clearly submerged on purpose and sometimes weighted down with stones. A warrior's sword was very much his personal property, almost an extension of himself, and care was taken to ensure that no one else should ever wield it. But Excalibur's own watery exit may not have been traditional, or generally believed in. Richard I presented Tancred of Sicily with a sword which he alleged was Arthur's and had therefore, by inference, been retrievable. 17 18

Morgan's presence in the boat is noteworthy. Despite all her literary misfortunes, she is still, as in the début Geoffrey gives her, the Lady of Avalon who will take Arthur into her care. The scene of his passing has an air of authentic ancient myth, wafting the hero into an Elsewhere, an inscrutable goddess-realm. A line

129. Llyn Llydaw in Snowdonia, one of several places where legends locate the casting-away of Arthur's sword.

Tennyson puts in Merlin's mouth, 'From the great deep to the great deep he goes,' is well conceived. In the end it has to be faced that while Arthur may have a certain human reality, he is a human being mythified.

1. GM (1), 112–29, and (2), 230–57.
2. Malory, V.
3. Malory, XX, 8–22.
4. GM (1), 129–31, and (2), 257–60; Malory, XXI, 1–3.
5. Ashe (5), 186–91.
6. Malory, XXI, 3–4.
7. Ibid, XXI, 5.
8. *Mort Artu*, 187–90.
9. Malory, XXI, 2, and Caxton's preface.
10. Bromwich, 160–2, 206; 'Nennius' (1), *Annales Cambriae*, Year 93.
11. Lacy, ed., art. 'Camlann'.
12. GM (1), 74, and (2), 172.
13. Alcock (1), 67; Ashe (5), 65–6.
14. Chambers, 184.
15. GM (1), 132, and (2), 261; Malory, XXI, 5.
16. Bromwich, 267; Loomis, ed., 66.
17. *Man, Myth and Magic*, art. 'Sword'.
18. Chambers, 274.

47 *The Survivors*

When the boat had passed out of sight, Bedivere turned away and rode off.
Prompted by Arthur's parting words, he made for the region of Avalon in
Somerset. Near Glastonbury he came to a small valley between two wooded
hills. This was the place to which the Archbishop of Canterbury, ousted by
Mordred, had retired as a hermit. The Archbishop told him that some ladies
had brought a dead man to him for burial. Bedivere took it for granted that
this was Arthur, and that he had died soon after departing. Yet a doubt
lingered as to who the deceased actually was, and many believed that Arthur
was still living, though withdrawn from the world. Bedivere became a
hermit himself and settled in the valley.

When Lancelot, in his French domain, heard of Mordred's treason, he
gathered an army and hastened back to Britain to aid the King. At Dover he
learned that it was too late. He visited Gawain's tomb and prayed for his
soul, full of grief for the quarrel that had divided them and the whole Round
Table. Then he rode westwards looking for Guinevere, and found she had
retired to a convent at Amesbury. She was sadly aware how her love had
disrupted the fellowship and ruined her husband. Lancelot hoped that she
would leave the convent, and go back to France with him, but she bade him

**130. Lancelot meets
Guinevere by Arthur's
tomb – a romantic
improvement of the
medieval account – and
she refuses a farewell
kiss.**

a penitent farewell and refused even a last kiss. They parted in deep sorrow and she devoted herself to works of charity.

Lancelot made his way to the valley near Glastonbury, and joined Bedivere as a hermit. During the next few months, his cousin Bors and several more of his followers drifted into the same retreat, forming a small religious community. When Guinevere was reported to be dying, they went to the convent and found her already dead. They brought the body back with them and gave it burial. Soon after, Lancelot sickened and died himself, in the odour of sanctity and with a smile on his lips. He was buried at his own castle Joyous Gard, in the tomb long prepared.

Most of the little community dispersed. Some returned to their former homes and continued in the religious life. Others went to the Holy Land as crusaders. Bedivere remained in his hermitage and died there.

2   To revert to the time of Arthur's departure, two vengeful sons of Mordred had caused disturbances, but both were slain, either by Lancelot and Bors before their retirement or by Arthur's successor. This was his cousin Constantine, the son of Duke Cador of Cornwall. Constantine restored the hermit-archbishop to his see, prevented any Saxon recovery, and preserved peace for several years, but could never hope to reinstate the Arthurian glories. The unpleasant Mark was reputedly another survivor.

3   When he was sure there would be no opposition, he marched up from Cornwall and spitefully destroyed Camelot.

Early texts have little to say about the final phase. Geoffrey speaks of the Queen

4   entering a convent, though he locates it at Caerleon. Amesbury did have an ancient monastery, pre-Saxon, according to the Welsh. A triad mentions it as the abode of a 'perpetual choir', with monks chanting the liturgy continuously in relays. 'Amesbury' means the place of Ambrose, perhaps Ambrosius

5   Aurelianus. If so, the name is more likely to be due to his having stationed troops there than to his having founded the monastery. There was a women's community later, but it is doubtful whether any existed early enough for Guinevere.

Most of the rest is due to romancers, the fullest version being Malory's, which combines previous romance matter, Glastonbury traditions, and embellishments of his own. The small valley is almost certainly the one separating the Tor from Chalice Hill near by. It has a well in it, now known as Chalice Well and

6   associated by some with the Grail story. The Grail romance *Perlesvaus* does apparently mention this, or rather the original spring, and also describes hermitages thereabouts, in a passage to which the topographical key lies in an old road leading up to the hills from some distance below. As late as 1586 a traveller records a local belief that ruined buildings in this area were once the cells of Joseph of Arimathea and his companions, and an Anchor Inn and Anchor Orchard may have been the last echoes of the tradition of anchorites.

A regional king named Constantine ruled in Dumnonia, the West Country, during the first half of the sixth century. He is one of five such kings whom

7   Gildas denounces in his tract. Historically, all five were living when Gildas was, but Geoffrey, who needs a royal line to span a time interval, makes four of them follow one another as kings of all Britain. By representing Constantine as a son of Cador, who succeeded Gorlois (though in what relationship is not clear) as

131. Chalice Well, Glastonbury, near the place where Malory probably locates the hermitage of Bedivere and Lancelot.

Duke of Cornwall, he gives him a step-cousinly connection with Arthur that permits the crown to pass to him, and thence to the others in the contrived series. Later writers accept Constantine. Agreement seems to be general that while Arthur had illegitimate sons, such as the Amr of Welsh legend and – perhaps – Mordred, he had no legitimate issue alive at the time of his demise, so that the rather remote kinsman Constantine was his nearest heir. Because of this lack, plus the death of most of his knights, there could never be a continuation of the Arthurian kingdom. Mark's destruction of Camelot, a sequel added by only one or two authors, is none the less symbolic and apt.

1. Malory, XXI, 5–13.
2. GM (1), 132, and (2), 261–2; *Mort Artu*, 226–9.
3. Loomis, ed., 330, 351.
4. GM (1), 130, and (2), 259.
5. Morris, 100.
6. Ashe (1), 30–3.
7. GM (1), 132–3, and (2), 262–3; Gildas, chapter 28.

48 *Arthur's Destiny*

1   For many years Arthur's grave – if any – was, as the Welsh poem put it, a mystery: something not to be talked about. One rumour was that it did exist, but his people had kept it secret to prevent its discovery and desecration by Saxons. At last, however, when story-tellers outside the Celtic lands had learned about Arthur and enormously enlarged his fame, the monks of Glastonbury announced that they had found where he was buried, together with his queen . . . or perhaps re-buried after a prior interment nearer the Tor. The secret had been handed down by a few, and a bard had divulged it to King Henry II. Arthur's remains lay very deep in the graveyard of the Abbey, between two memorial pillars. Henry had passed on this information and a search confirmed it.

2   To judge from the report given out, the search took place in 1190 or early '91. Seven feet down the diggers unearthed a stone slab, with a cross of lead under it inscribed in Latin. The inscription said: 'Here lies buried the renowned King Arthur in the Isle of Avalon.' Nine feet farther down they reached a rough coffin made of a hollowed-out log. Inside it were the bones of a tall man, with a damaged skull, suggesting a fatal blow on the head. There were also some smaller bones with a scrap of hair that crumbled when touched, presumably all that was left of Guinevere. The monks transferred the bones to two chests, and, eighty-seven years later, to a black marble tomb in the great new Abbey church that had been built in the interval. One result of their find was that the hill-cluster cradling Glastonbury, known to have been formerly a near-island with lakes and marshes around it, came to be widely accepted as the real Avalon where Morgan once dwelt.

No one challenged Glastonbury with a rival burial site. Whether the King was truly at rest is another matter. Not only did it come to be told that his ghost appeared annually at Cadbury-Camelot, he was reputed to join other spectral figures (such as Gwyn ap Nudd, the lord of Annwfn and Glastonbury Tor) in what was called the Wild Hunt, careering through the
3   clouds summoning the souls of evildoers and unbaptised infants. But in any case, many held that the tradition of Arthur's grave as a mystery referred not to mere secrecy but to the fact that he was not dead, and therefore had no grave, at Glastonbury or anywhere else.

4   According to one such view, when he was borne away in the boat, he was conveyed to an Avalon that was no Somerset hill-cluster but a Fortunate Isle over uncharted waters. This was Morgan's true home, where she governed her sisterhood of nine. She had Arthur placed on a golden bed, examined his wound expertly, and undertook to heal it if he would stay there long enough. She was as good as her word. Both of them are immortal and living on the island. Arthur's cure is said to have been effected by bathing in water
5   from the Tigris, which has its source in the Earthly Paradise. He renews his youth by visits to the Holy Grail, which, of course, departed from Britain during his reign.

But according to a belief of a more popular kind, current in Somerset and among the Cymry of Wales and the north, Arthur lies asleep in a cave. He may be alone, or he may have his knights with him, or his royal treasure, or both. There are caves, too, with treasure or sleeping knights but not the King, who lies elsewhere. Such hiding-places are magically concealed and cannot be found by searching. Cornwall has yet a third version of Arthur's immortality. He turned into a bird, probably a raven, perhaps a chough, and he still flies among other birds.

Those who affirm his continued life affirm also that he will return. He will come back from Avalon, or he will awaken with his knights, or he will shed his avian disguise. Maybe, too, Merlin will emerge from his Bardsey retreat with the true throne of Britain, and enthrone the King for his second reign. In any event, justice and peace will be restored. First to prophesy this return were the people descended from Arthur's – Bretons, Cornish, Welsh, Celtic northerners. They expected him as a Celtic Messiah who would expel the English and other alien overlords. But when the English themselves adopted him, making him a predecessor of their own sovereigns, they gave the prophecy a more general meaning. Arthur, the later story goes, will return to save Britain in an hour of need and renew his golden age.

6

7

8

132. View from Glastonbury Tor, near the Abbey associated with Joseph of Arimathea and Arthur.

Glastonbury's account of the grave of Arthur and Guinevere has often been dismissed as a fraud and a publicity stunt. In 1184 most of the Abbey burned down. Henry II provided money for rebuilding and invited others to do the same, but he died in 1189 and the flow of funds dried up. Something was needed to enhance the Abbey's prestige and attract more donations. The monks certainly publicised the grave. But there is no evidence that they exploited it to raise funds, and this supposed motive for their project, though often stated as a fact, is a modern speculation only.

Today, the site of the marble tomb in the great Abbey church is marked by a notice-board. The actual exhumation occurred in the graveyard south of the Lady Chapel, which was built on the site of the Old Church after this was destroyed in the fire. Modern excavation has established that the monks dug where they said and found an extremely early burial. A disturbance of its stone lining even showed where they dragged the coffin out. They did not fake the grave. The question is whether they faked the cross identifying it as Arthur's. This has vanished with most of the plundered Abbey's possessions, but William Camden, who saw it, published a facsimile drawing in 1607. His drawing is sometimes cited as proof that the cross he saw was a later forgery, and not evidence for anything found at the time, because Giraldus Cambrensis, writing soon after the exhumation, says the inscription mentioned Guinevere and the drawing does not. But as Camden reproduced only one side of the cross, her name may have been on the other, and there is no good reason to doubt that he saw the genuine article. Obviously it could still have been made at the time, as a bogus identification for the grave. Yet the statement, likewise due to Giraldus, that it called Guinevere Arthur's *second* wife, would have been a strange thing for the monks (or Giraldus) to invent; and peculiarities in the spelling and style of lettering indicate that the cross may well have dated from long before 1190.

9

10

133. Drawing by William Camden (1607) of the cross said to have been discovered in Arthur's grave.

Weight must be given to the fact that even in Wales, no one seems to have disputed the Glastonbury claim. While there are several alleged Camelots, several scenes of Arthur's last battle, and so on, all the centuries of legend-making produced, for practical purposes, only the one grave. King Henry's bard would appear to have revealed what was at least an authentic tradition of some antiquity, which, once brought into the open, could not be gainsaid. One objection is definitely wrong – that Arthur was not associated with Glastonbury before. He was. Caradoc's account of the abduction of Guinevere, written about sixty years earlier, brings him to the Old Church and within a few paces of the burial site.

The use of the phrase 'Vale' (or 'Vales') 'of Avalon' for central Somerset, noted in connection with the Grail and the Passing, was doubtless due to Glastonbury's identification with the apple-island, Arthur's last earthly destination, which the words on the cross supposedly clinched. Whether or not this identification was older than 1190, it was easy to make, both because central Somerset is apple-growing country and because Glastonbury undoubtedly had an 'Otherworld' aura. That is reflected in an old name for its hill-cluster, Ynys-witrin or the 'Glass Island', and in the Gwyn story. There is no early trace of Avalon being given a real location anywhere else. Geoffrey leaves it indefinite in his *History*. In his *Life of Merlin*, where he puts Morgan on the island, he gives it qualities borrowed from classical descriptions of the Fortunate Isles or Isles of the Blest, as well as Celtic tales. The boat bearing the wounded Arthur is piloted by Barinthus, a mythical figure who appears also, as someone familiar with western waters, in the Irish legend of the Voyage of St Brendan. In both his versions of Arthur's departure Geoffrey leaves the door open for a belief in his return, but never asserts it himself.

Even with the Glastonbury grave disclosed, Giraldus keeps Morgan in the story by making her a medically skilled lady who owned the Isle and received Arthur as her kinsman, though her efforts to cure him were, in the end, unsuccessful. It is intriguing that the Tor may have been a pre-Christian goddess sanctuary, and that its deity may even have been Matrona, who was semi-humanised as Morgan. Giraldus knows the essential point but turns it round, saying that because of Morgan's nursing Arthur at Glastonbury-Avalon, the 'credulous Britons' invented a 'fantastic goddess' called Morgan who carried him off to an Avalonian immortality. 11

The notion of his not being dead may have begun with a simple reluctance to accept the loss of a national hero, whether this was Riothamus, who does drop out of sight in Gaul, or some other constituent of the figure of Arthur. More recently similar fancies have gathered briefly around Charles Stuart Parnell and Lord Kitchener, and quite elaborately around President Kennedy, who became a sort of retroactive American Arthur with survival legends oddly resembling his. An earlier and closer parallel is the case of King Sebastian of Portugal, who was killed in a Moroccan battle in 1578, with the result that Portugal was annexed by Spain. Since none of the Portuguese remembered seeing Sebastian dead, a patriotic belief that he had made his escape, and would come back as a liberator, went on impossibly long and inspired several pretenders. 12

The main conceptions of Arthur's survival, the Avalon legend and the cave legend, both derive from the Celtic myth of a banished god sleeping in a cave on a western island, the god whom Plutarch identifies with Cronus, in the Roman pantheon Saturn. In classical myth Cronus was not only overthrown by his son – as Arthur is by his alleged bastard Mordred – but, before his banishment, was 13

14   lord of a golden age. Virgil even poetically predicts his return and a new golden age, a new Saturnian reign.

A version of the cave legend is part of the Arthurian lore of Cadbury-Camelot. The King sleeps in an underground chamber in the hillside, with gates that occasionally open so that a passer-by can catch a glimpse of him. There are at least fifteen locations of the folk-belief, in one form or another, through Wales and up to Melrose in Scotland. During the Middle Ages and later, much the same was told of other heroes, such as the German emperor Frederick. Arthur was possibly the prototype. Throughout Europe the sleeper is a historical human being in a large majority of cases, and the few exceptions are at least regarded as human beings, not as fairy-tale characters. Hence this motif, though ultimately myth-derived, tells in favour of Arthur's reality in some sense.

15   A Cornish belief in a living Arthur was noted in 1113 by some French clerics visiting Bodmin, who were struck by the parallel with popular Breton lore. However, the nature of his survival seems not to have been specified. Cornwall's story of his transformation into a bird was known, curiously enough, in Spain.

16   Cervantes touches on it in *Don Quixote* before anyone mentions it in writing in England. Many years afterwards a sportsman on Marazion Green, about to take a shot at a raven, was dissuaded by an old man who warned him that it might be Arthur.

The idea of the King's second coming seems to have begun in Brittany, and spread to Cornwall and then to Wales. It has reinforced the fascination due to

17   his golden-age quality. Because of his tragic fall the golden age perished, yet because of his immortality it is not truly lost: he is still somehow 'there', and it can be reinstated for a fresh start, with intervening corruption swept away. His legend gives symbolic expression to a deep-rooted pattern of belief which has been traced influencing religious and political movements as well as mythology. In the case of Arthur himself, the 'Tudor myth' that represented Henry VII's part-Welsh dynasty as restoring the true British kingdom has already been mentioned. Poets and friends of the court applied it to at least four of Henry's descendants. With Elizabeth I it was taken quite seriously and helped to glamorise her reign.

Spenser makes out Elizabethan England to be, in effect, Arthurian Britain resurrected. So far as *The Faerie Queene* can be said to have a date, its story takes place when Arthur is a young prince, and Merlin appears in it as a character. He delivers himself of a long prophecy of Britain's future, partly based on Geoffrey, and closes with a salute to the Tudors. It introduces them by an allusion to the family's ancestral island of Mona – that is, Anglesey. Elizabeth is foretold as rescuing the Low Countries from Spain and defeating Philip II, symbolised by a castle, which was part of his royal arms as king of Castile

> Tho when the terme is full accomplishid,
>   There shall a sparke of fire, which hath long-while
>   Bene in his ashes raked vp, and hid,
>   Be freshly kindled in the fruitfull Ile
>   Of Mona, where it lurked in exile;
>   Which shall breake forth into bright burning flame,
>   And reach into the house, that bears the stile
>   Of royall maiesty and soueraigne name;
> So shall the Briton bloud their crowne againe reclame.

> Thenceforth eternall vnion shall be made
>> Betweene the nations different afore,
> And sacred Peace shall louingly perswade
> The warlike minds, to learne her goodly lore,
> And ciuile armes to exercise no more:
> Then shall a royall virgin raine, which shall
> Stretch her white rod ouer the Belgicke shore,
> And the great Castle smite so sore with all,
> That it shall make him shake, and shortly learne to fall.

(III, iii, 48–49)

Merlin apparently foresees what will happen after that, but Spenser of course cannot, so he cuts the prophetic utterance short.

The Tudor myth faded out during the seventeenth century, yet as late as 1757 Thomas Gray, in *The Bard*, imagines a Welsh poet making much the same prophecy to Edward I. Edward's descendants will fight each other to the death in the Wars of the Roses, and then will come the new dispensation:

> But O! what solemn scenes on Snowdon's height
>> Descending slow their glittering skirts unroll?
> Visions of glory, spare my aching sight,
>> Ye unborn ages, crowd not on my soul!
> No more our long-lost Arthur we bewail: –
> All hail, ye genuine kings! Britannia's issue, hail!

And Elizabeth duly makes her appearance with the future nobility of the realm:

> In the midst a form divine!
> Her eye proclaims her of the Briton-line:
> Her lion-port, her awe-commanding face
> Attempered sweet to virgin-grace.

Gray's Welshman foreshadows Shakespeare and even Milton as products of the true-British renaissance.

1. Carley, 157; Chambers, 63; Loomis, ed., 13. Cp also Chambers, 17 (quoting William of Malmesbury).
2. Ashe (1), 58–70; Carley, 147–50; Giraldus, 281–8.
3. Loomis, ed., 70; Westwood, 8, 156–7.
4. GM (3), lines 908–40.
5. Loomis, ed., 68, 415–6.
6. Ashe (5), 83–4; Loomis, ed., 69–70; Westwood, 8.
7. FML, 144; Westwood, 7.
8. Loomis, ed., 64–5.
9. Carley, 149, 178.
10. Ashe (1), 69–73.
11. Chambers, 270, 272.
12. Hole, 147; Westwood, 136.
13. Plutarch (1), chapter 26, and (2), chapter 18; Rhys, II, 493–4.
14. Ashe (2), 53.
15. Chambers, 18, 249.
16. Westwood, 7, citing *Don Quixote*, I, 13.
17. Ashe (2), 91, 93, 101, 105–6, 134–5, 210–1.

49 *The Arthurian Landscape*

Arthur's renown left a widespread impression on the face of his country. Quite early it was told how a heap of stones in Buelt was Cabal's Cairn, called after Arthur's dog, and a stone on top bore Cabal's paw-print, because he set his foot there during the hunting of the boar Twrch Trwyth. The stone, it was rumoured, could not be removed – a day later it always reappeared on the heap. Early too is the report of a tomb in Ercing near a spring, the burial place of Arthur's son Amr, who was slain and buried there by Arthur himself: a tomb with the property of being a different size at every attempt to measure it – six feet long, or nine, or twelve, or fifteen.

By the early twelfth century (and very likely before, who knows?), rock formations and prehistoric stone huts were known by Arthurian names. Arthur's Chair and Arthur's Oven were pointed out west of Exeter before the major explosion of his fame. Many things of the same kind, and many others also, now scatter his name and legend over Britain. Some are megaliths, some are earthworks, some are natural features, even hills. Six stones are called Arthur's Stone, eleven are called Arthur's Quoit; four hills are called Arthur's Seat. There are five earthwork Round Tables.

Several of the related stories evoke him as a giant like Bran. On King's Crags in Northumberland he sat and threw a boulder at Guinevere on Queen's Crags, half a mile off. It struck her comb and lies on the ground between, the tooth-marks still showing. On another occasion, walking through Carmarthen, he felt a pebble in his shoe and tossed it away. It flew seven miles and landed on high ground in the Gower peninsula, where it remains, as Arthur's Stone. It weighs 25 tons and rests on several smaller stones. At Midsummer Eve and All-Hallows Eve the whole group go down to the sea to drink or bathe. At full moon, girls used to place honey-cakes dipped in milk on the great stone, crawl round it three times on hands and knees, and await the lovers whom its magic would attract.

Such tales of the King are retrospective, but the cave legend is concerned with his continuing life. Where he lies sleeping underground, or his knights lie sleeping, there may be a guardian who admits visitors. The outcome, for the visitor, is apt to be unhappy. At Alderley Edge in Cheshire the guardian is Merlin himself. At Craig-y-Ddinas in Glamorgan, the last Welsh abode of the fairy-folk, a Welshman was ushered into the cave by an English wizard. They entered by a tunnel with a bell hanging from the roof. He saw the King and many knights, with weapons ready to hand, and a heap of gold and a heap of silver. The wizard told him he could help himself to the gold or the silver, whichever he preferred, but must be careful not to touch the bell as he left. If it rang, a knight would wake and ask if it was day, and he must then reply 'No, sleep on.' He loaded himself with so much gold that he walked clumsily and hit the bell, with the result predicted. Giving the correct answer, he escaped, but some time later when he had squandered the gold he returned for more, hit the bell, and forgot the formula. Several more of

the knights woke up. They took back the gold, gave him a beating, and threw him out, and he never found the entrance again.

Near the Eildon Hills on the south side of Melrose, a horse-dealer, Canonbie Dick, was stopped on several evenings by a stranger who bought horses from him and paid with obsolete coins. The purchaser was the poet Thomas the Rhymer, an initiate into the ways of Elfland. One night, warning Dick that he must on no account show fear, he led him through a door in the hillside into a vast, torchlit subterranean chamber, full of slumbering knights and horses, among them the ones Thomas had bought. On a table lay a sword and a horn. Thomas told Dick that he must choose

134. 'King Arthur's Cave' near Whitchurch, Hereford.

whether to draw the sword or blow the horn. The right choice would give him power in the future kingdom. Dick thought drawing the sword might seem aggressive and blew the horn, but this was wrong, because it was the act of a man summoning help and therefore showed fear. With a sound like thunder the knights began to stir. Now Dick was terrified indeed. A wind blew him out into the open, the door closed behind him and disappeared, and he died soon after. Such tests are imposed in several of the Arthurian caves, and the victim, so far as anyone knows, has always failed.

Other characters from the King's circle – Merlin, Guinevere, Lancelot, Kay, Mark, Tristan – are likewise found up and down the land. After Arthur himself, though a long way after, Merlin is the most prominent. Besides his Bardsey retreat there are sites around his birthplace, Carmarthen: a hill, a cave, a wood, a stone. He has two graves, one at Marlborough in Wiltshire, one at Drumelzier in Peebles. At Tintagel his ghost haunts Merlin's Cave, under the headland where the castle is.

With most of these local associations, it is hard to decide how early they are. Four, but only four, can be documented before Geoffrey.

The cairn and the tomb are mentioned in a ninth-century list of 'Marvels of Britain' appended to the *Historia Brittonum*. Buelt was a Welsh district, still recalled by Builth Wells. Ercing, its name derived from the Roman Ariconium, extended over Herefordshire. Arthur's dog Cabal is mentioned elsewhere, and is something of a puzzle, because the Latin *caballus* means a horse, and in one or two variants the footprint is made by the hoof of Arthur's steed. Cabal's Cairn has usually been located on the hill Corngafallt near Rhayader. The Twrch Trwyth episode in *Culhwch and Olwen* does not bring the hunt to this part of Wales, but there may have been different versions. In the Ercing legend the spring is Gamber Head, the source of the Gamber, and the tomb may have been a barrow, Wormelow Tump, now regrettably effaced and no longer measurable. Nothing else is known of the tragedy of Arthur's son Amr, or Amhar, and very little is said about him at all, doubtless because he was held to be illegitimate.

Arthur's Chair and Oven were seen by the French priests who heard of Arthur's survival at Bodmin in 1113. En route, according to Hermann of Tournai who tells the story, they had travelled west from Exeter and were informed by their guides soon after leaving the town that they were entering King Arthur's country. Hermann is imprecise. The Oven has been doubtfully identified as the King's Oven on Dartmoor.

As for the many cases where the connection is completely undatable, some of the 'stones' and 'quoits' are Neolithic structures. The one on the Gower peninsula is the capstone of a burial-chamber which has lost its earth covering, like Kit's Coty House. So is another Arthur's Stone on a ridge overlooking the Golden Valley in Hereford. One of the best Round Tables is a circular earth platform at Mayburgh in Cumbria, about 150 feet across, with a girdling ditch and a bank outside, as at Avebury. It may be about equally old, and its purpose is unknown. A Round Table under the walls of Stirling Castle, in Scotland, is a mound at the centre of what was once a Stuart formal garden, the King's Knot.

Most famous of the four Arthur's Seats is the one beside Edinburgh, but the Dumbarrow hill near Letham in Tayside has its interest. The Arthurian name is a by-product of a Perthshire legend about the King, Guinevere and Mordred, which was inspired by misunderstanding of traditions concerning Pictish events. The reason for any hill being so called is that it has a double top with a dip between, giving a vaguely saddle-like effect. That is the case with an Arthur's Chair in the Brecon Beacons, between the two highest points, Corn Du and Pen y Fan. Giraldus Cambrensis mentions it in the twelfth century. As at Craig-y-Ddinas there is fairy lore, localised at a lake below, Llyn Cwm Llwch.   17

The background of the cave legend has been discussed. Sir Walter Scott recorded the Melrose version. While the cave is normally enchanted and inaccessible, there are two real Arthur's Caves, one near Monmouth and one in Anglesey. However, it is by no means clear that he was ever asleep in either.   18

Some of the stories are late and literary. Thus, Excalibur is cast away in at least five places, and the best known is Dozmary Pool, on Bodmin Moor; but its real folklore inhabitant is the ghost of Jan Tregeagle, a cruel magistrate condemned   19 to spend his after-life on impossible tasks, one of them being to bail out the pool with a limpet shell. The Excalibur notion here may be due to the Arthurian vogue started by Tennyson.

More than 150 of these sites have been catalogued. Most have no claim to any sort of authenticity, and the explanation is often as obscure as the date. While other characters have attached themselves to the landscape (Robin Hood, for example), Arthur outstrips every rival but one. The Devil is said to be more

135. Stirling's 'Round Table', actually a mound at the centre of what was once a formal garden of the Royal Stuarts, called the King's Knot.

widespread, but no one else is. Arthur's frequency is proof of his fame, and the distribution is eloquent in another way. Considering how long the medieval romance-image, 'King Arthur and the Knights of the Round Table', has been the standard one, it is striking how slight its relation is with the Arthurian map, how little impression it has made. The majority of the sites are in places which the romances could never have suggested. Moreover, while Arthur's kingdom in romance includes the more English portion of Britain, nearly all the Arthurian topography is outside. Most of it belongs to the West Country, Wales, Cumbria, Scotland – to areas where Celtic people clung to an identity longest, and sometimes still do. Its roots are not in the medieval literature, but in the senior and elusive Arthurian saga.

1. 'Nennius' (1), chapter 73.
2. Ibid.
3. Ashe (5), 13–14, 18; Chambers, 18; Westwood, 8.
4. Ashe (5), 19–25; Snell, 114, 161, 183, 200–1, 203, 224, 225.
5. Ashe (5), 186; FML, 352; Snell, 209.
6. Ashe (5), 22–4; FML, 402.
7. Ashe (5), 2–4; FML, 358.
8. Ashe (5), 88–9; Chambers, 222–3; Rhys, II, 458–61.
9. Ashe (5), 156–8; Snell, 213–7; Westwood, 369–71.
10. Ashe (5), 69–72, 98–9, 153–5; Snell, 217–8.
11. FML, 144.
12. Ashe (5), 86–7; Chambers, 188; Rhys, II, 538–9; Snell, 158–9; Westwood, 274–5.
13. Ashe (5), 107.
14. Chambers, 249; Westwood, 8.
15. Ashe (5), 174; Snell, 200–1.
16. Ashe (5), 174–6; Snell, 223–4.
17. Ashe (5), 42–4; FML, 382; Giraldus, 96; Rhys, I, 20–3; Snell, 158.
18. Ashe (5), 13, 165; Chambers, 223; Rhys, II, 457–8.
19. Ashe (5), 96–8; FML, 138–9.

50 *Taliesin*

One passenger on the boat carrying Arthur to Avalon (if that is where he went) is said to have been the bard Taliesin. Though the King's victories did not long postpone Saxon dominance, the Welsh held out after Lloegyr had crumbled, and their poets and story-tellers transmitted Britain's heritage. Taliesin was not the first bard, but he was chief among five who established the lasting Welsh tradition. The others were Aneirin, Talhaern, Bluchbard and Cian. The Welsh are uncertain when Taliesin flourished. Some make his adult life overlap Arthur's, so that he could indeed have gone on the Avalonian voyage. Most, however, put him later, at the same time as the other four. A wonderful tale is told of his birth, his naming, and his public début.

A witch named Ceridwen had an ugly son. Knowing no charms to make him handsome, she resolved to make him wise. She prepared a cauldron of inspiration which had to be kept simmering for a year and a day, and dropped herbs into the brew at prescribed seasons. To gather the herbs she had to go far, and while she was absent a boy, Gwion, watched the cauldron and stirred it. As the year drew towards its close, the cauldron's fierce bubbling shot three drops of the liquor on to Gwion's fingers. He licked them off, and at once had more than mortal knowledge and power, realising, among much else, that Ceridwen planned to kill him as soon as the work was finished. The loss of the three drops had in fact spoilt it, and there was no way he could mollify her.

When she came back, he fled and she chased him. He changed himself into a hare; she changed herself into a hound. He dived into a river as a fish; she pursued as an otter. He flew as a small bird; she became a hawk. Then he turned into a grain of wheat, and Ceridwen became a black hen and swallowed him. She reverted to human shape but was now pregnant, and in due course gave birth to Gwion. The child was so beautiful that she could not kill him with her own hand, so she tied him up in a leather bag and threw him into the sea. He was rescued by Elphin, nephew of Maelgwn, king of Gwynedd in North Wales. Elphin called the child Taliesin meaning 'radiant brow', and fostered him.

While the foundling was still a boy, Maelgwn imprisoned Elphin at Degannwy near Llandudno. Taliesin came there to rescue him, and achieved this, rather like Merlin at his confrontation with Vortigern, by outdoing the royal poets – bards of an earlier vintage. He cast a spell on them so that they could say only *blerwm blerwm*, flipping their lips with their fingers. Assured of an uninterrupted hearing, he recited a riddling poem which no one could expound.

As preserved, it has forty lines. Nearly all of them are, or appear to be, statements by Taliesin about himself. But it may be that each statement refers to a different person, and if all are identified they contain some message, in the manner of an acrostic. These lines are a fair sample:

My original country is the region of the summer stars . . .
I was with my Lord in the highest sphere,
On the fall of Lucifer into the depth of hell;
I have borne a banner before Alexander;
I know the names of the stars from north to south;
I have been on the Galaxy at the throne of the
    Distributor;
I was in Canaan when Absalom was slain;
I conveyed Awen to the level of the vale of Hebron . . .
I was instructor to Eli and Enoch . . .
I have been three periods in the prison of Arianrhod;
I have been the chief director of the work of the tower of
    Nimrod . . .
I have been in Asia with Noah in the Ark,
I have witnessed the destruction of Sodom and
    Gomorrah.

With more in the same style.

Taliesin moved north, to the court of the Cumbrian king Urien or Urbgen. Among his adult poems, and likewise obscure, is *The Spoils of Annwfn*, the one that relates Arthur's raid on the Otherworld in quest of a wonder-working cauldron . . . another cauldron, perhaps a hint towards the Grail. Three of his fellow-bards are scarcely more than names. But Aneirin, 'of flowing verse' as he was dubbed, also flourished in the north, joined an attack on the Angles at their stronghold Catraeth, and got home safely when only a handful did – 'because of my fine songs', to quote his own explana-
4   tion. He still perished by violence, though, being the victim of one of the 'three unfortunate assassinations', when Heidyn (otherwise unknown) killed him with a hatchet.

5   To see the Welsh bards in their context we need to trace the aftermath of the 'Arthurian' phase. During the first half of the sixth century, much of Britain was in a sort of equilibrium. The Saxons were consolidating and multiplying, but they had suffered a military check at Badon, and the Britons still outnumbered them. Apart from minor encroachments in Hampshire, there is no clear sign of a further forward movement or a continuation of warfare.
6   The Britons survived in most areas, and remained in control of the greater part of the ex-Roman territory. British colonisation overseas was reaching a level where Armorica was turning decisively into Brittany, the 'Lesser Britain'. The Church was prospering in Wales, thanks largely to St Illtud's monastic school at Llantwit Major in Glamorgan. Welsh missionaries strengthened the hold of Christianity in western regions, and helped to organise the new Breton society, as indeed they had been doing ever since its scattered beginnings.

The ecclesiastic Gildas is the one contemporary witness. His prose is influenced by Late Roman rhetorical style; many memorial inscriptions confirm the continuing vitality of Latin, 'our language' as he calls it. He speaks of the
7   Britons as 'citizens', implying some kind of nominal Roman-ness, even yet. But he shows also that a political break-up has gone beyond retrieval. Complaining that the Britons have forgotten the lessons of their ordeal and semi-recovery,

136. David, from
the Jesse Tree in St
Dyfnog's Church,
Llanrhaedr.

and have taken to fighting among themselves, he castigates five independent
kings for their sins and misrule. They are Constantine of Dumnonia, meaning
the West Country (this is the one whom Geoffrey turns into Arthur's successor); Aurelius Conanus, probably ruling in the Gloucester area; Voteporix in
south-west Wales, perhaps a descendant of Irish chiefs who found a niche in the
imperial system; Cinglas in central Wales and Maelgwn in the north – Gwynedd
– both of them said, though not by Gildas, to be of the stock of Cunedda. The
last of these is the same Maelgwn at whose court young Taliesin gives his
virtuoso performance.

Gwynedd was the most important of the regional kingdoms and retained
somewhat more of the Roman inheritance. One of Maelgwn's residences was
indeed at Degannwy. Another, at Aberffraw in Anglesey, found its way into the
tale of Branwen. Both are archaeologically confirmed. Gildas mentions this   8
king's sycophantic poets. Maelgwn is said to have claimed hegemony over other
rulers, but the time for that was past. The imperial structure was gone, the
remnant of Romanised urban life was fading away. Over a great deal of Britain,
people had returned to the land or reoccupied the old hill-forts.

Though a northerner by birth, Gildas seems out of touch with the British
north beyond Wales. It too is known to have been divided among several
kingdoms – Elmet in Yorkshire; Rheged, centred on Cumbria; a domain in
Scotland, its capital at Dumbarton (the 'Fort of the Britons'), which became
Strathclyde and proved highly durable; and Manau Guotodin by the Firth
of Forth.

Towards the middle of the sixth century an outbreak of plague hit the Britons   9
severely, but was less deadly for the Saxons, who imported less of the foreign
merchandise that brought it. Henceforth the two populations were more nearly
balanced. Renewed Anglo-Saxon progress began the definite formation of
England, Angle-land. The strongest resistance came from Rheged in 570–90,   10
under the leadership of its king Urien and his son Owain. Both are drawn
anachronistically into Arthurian romance, where Urien becomes a husband for
Morgan le Fay, and Owain becomes the knight Yvain. Owain's name is linked
with the Giant's Grave, a strange composite monument in a churchyard at
Penrith.

137. The Giant's Grave, Penrith, Cumbria, supposedly marking the burial site of Owain.

During these developments the British language had evolved and disintegrated. Welsh was its chief derivative, spoken not only in Wales but in the north. Those who spoke it were to be known as Cymry. Other derived languages were Cornish and Breton. Taliesin may have been a native of Powys, but he and the other four pioneers of Welsh poetry, all listed in the *Historia Brittonum*, were associated chiefly with Rheged and its patriotic court and nobility. So was the prophet Myrddin or Lailoken, who became a constituent of Merlin.

A Welsh bard was credited with inspiration denied to most humans, but he was not an independent versifier or seer, he had a professional position. It was only under royal or aristocratic patronage that a learned, creative class could find a stable subsistence. These bards resembled a body of literary men in Ireland called *filid*. When Druidism expired, the *filid* took over the Druids' scholarly functions. Like them, the Welsh bards were official minstrels composing laureate verses for employers, but also far more. They were custodians of saga, tradition, genealogy, custom. Power and property rights might depend on their pronouncements. At the kings' courts they were held in honour. One result, with the passage of time, was that royal secretaries and codifiers of law worked in consultation with them, and Welsh law codes acquired a rich and expressive vocabulary. Another result was that they were not only story-tellers themselves but inspirers of story-telling in others. Popular entertainers took notice of them, and expanded the bardic traditions into tales such as those of the *Mabinogion*, often with a high degree of literacy.

To Taliesin, 'chief of bards', many poems were eventually ascribed, as well as *The Spoils of Annwfn*. His name has the usual spelling variants. Geoffrey introduces him in *The Life of Merlin*, where it is he who gives the account of Avalon and Arthur's voyage thither. A few of the poems (not the *Spoils*) are authentic, being the oldest in any living language of Europe, apart from Greek. They extol the valour and generosity of Urien and Owain. While the wording is curt and simple, the verse-forms are already sophisticated, implying a prior development and a technique for recitation to music. It is a pity we have nothing from the earlier poets at the court of Maelgwn.

Aneirin's role in the Catraeth campaign is attested by himself. Catraeth was the Roman fort of Cataractonium, its name surviving today in Catterick. A composite British force assembled in Manau Guotodin about the year 600, and marched south to make a brave but suicidal assault on the Angles who held the place. Aneirin, having made his escape from the disaster, composed a number of laments for the fallen, grouped under the title *Gododdin*. Though these poems do not tell the story directly, they are full of information on the British nobles and their life-style. It is in one of them, unless the passage is an interpolation, that we have the earliest allusion to Arthur by name. A warrior is praised for having fought well, 'though he was not Arthur': he was great, though not of course equal to the man proverbially the greatest.

Taliesin shifts about chronologically like Merlin, and is sometimes found long before his true date. In *Culhwch and Olwen* he is at Arthur's court. In the French paraphrase of Geoffrey by Wace he lives before Christ and prophesies his advent. In the tale of Branwen he is one of the survivors of Bran's Irish expedition. Charles Williams, in his poetic cycles *Taliessin through Logres* (1938) and *The Region of the Summer Stars* (1944), plants the bard in the Arthurian milieu as a key character.

As to his legendary beginnings, his mother Ceridwen may be another Celtic goddess, and her cauldron of inspiration may be another Grail antecedent. His riddling list, asserting his existence in many places and periods, is not old enough to be authentically his work but is still fairly early. It has been explained as referring to reincarnation; if that could be admitted, it would account for his accompanying Bran, prophesying Christ, and attending on Arthur – three further manifestations would be neither here nor there. Robert Graves in *The White Goddess* offers a solution best described as cryptographic. Perhaps, however, the boy-poet is simply making fun of bardic pretensions to super-human knowledge. The nearest thing to a modern parallel is an American ballad published by John and Alan Lomax in *Folk Song USA*. Here is a sample:

> I was born about ten thousand years ago,
> There ain't nothin' in this world that I don't know;
> I saw Peter, Paul and Moses playin' ring around the roses
> And I'll whip the guy that says it isn't so.

138. Llyn Geirionydd where there is a monument to Taliesin.

I saw Satan when he looked the garden o'er;
I saw Adam and Eve driven from the door;
And from behind the bushes peepin', I saw the apple they were eatin'
And I swear I was the guy what et the core . . .

I was there when Alexander crossed the sea,
And I always cheered him on to victory –
And when King Darius died, I was fighting by his side,
So he gave his cha-ri-ot to me . . .

I saw Nero fiddling when he burnt up Rome;
I told him it looked like his future home;
When he had the nerve to swear, I dragged him from his chair
And broke a Pilsner bottle on his dome.

This piece of impudence is attributed to students at a college in an eastern state. The presumed target of ridicule is the know-all teacher. Maelgwn's entourage might have prompted the same sentiments.

1. GM (3), lines 908–40.
2. 'Nennius', chapter 62.
3. *Mabinogion* (1), 471–94. Cp Bromwich, 510; Graves (2), 27–8, 80–1; Rees, 229–31; Rhys, II, 613–4.
4. Bromwich, 70, 74.
5. Alcock (1), 114–5; Morris, 114–5, 200–22.
6. Chadwick (2), 61–7.
7. Gildas, chapters 23, 26, 28–36. Cp Morris, 201–7.
8. Gildas, chapter 34; Lloyd, I, 128–31; Morris, 206; Sheldon, 77.
9. Morris, 222–4.
10. Ashe (5), 168–70; Bromwich, 479–83, 516–20.
11. Chadwick (2), 86–100, 193–5.
12. Bromwich, lxxxii-lxxxiv; Loomis, ed., 12, 44.
13. Alcock (1), 13–14; Bromwich, 509–11; Morris, 231–2, 235–6; Parry, chapters 1, 2.
14. Alcock (1), 15; Blair, 44; Bromwich, 271–3; Fraser, 24.
15. Alcock (1), 15; Loomis, ed., 3.
16. *Mabinogion* (2), 37, 101; Loomis, ed., 98; Tatlock, 469.
17. Ross, 290.
18. Graves (2), 81–121.

Excursus III

The Western Paradise

Taliesin's account of the Avalon voyage, in Geoffrey's *Life of Merlin*, is the first literary version of the Passing of Arthur. Geoffrey's French adapter, Wace, shows no sign of having read it, but a little of it reappears in an English adapter, Layamon. Here the wounded Arthur appoints Constantine as his successor, and adds:

> 'I will fare to Avalun, to the fairest of all maidens, to   1
> Argante the queen, a fay most fair. She shall make my
> wounds all sound, make me all whole with healing
> potions. Then I will come again to my kingdom and dwell
> with the Britons with great joy.'

Argante is Morgan, slightly re-styled. Layamon continues:

> Even with the words, there came from the sea a short boat
> gliding, driven by the waves, and two women therein
> wondrously clad. They took Arthur at once and bore him
> in haste and laid him down softly and moved away.

The story is already changing. In particular, it has lost Taliesin as a participant. Romancers change it further, and by the time it comes through to Malory it differs widely.

If we turn back to Geoffrey's version, three facts are worth examining.   2
First, that Taliesin is the narrator; second, that the island belongs to a group of women, who in this context are 'Otherworld' figures; and third, that the boat's pilot is Barinthus, 'to whom the waters and the stars of heaven were well known' . . . and he too drops out in later narratives. Geoffrey is not offering mere invention, but an adaptation from senior Celtic matter, not all of which had survival value for romance. The same might be inferred from indications that when early romancers in France speak of Morgan, they are   3

drawing on Breton sources. In Britain the Celtic antecedents of the Avalon episode are scanty and fragmented, but the three significant features lead back to more enlightening matter in Ireland.

There is, of course, no way of telling whether the real Taliesin had any share in the story's making. *The Spoils of Annwfn*, with its nine magical maidens reached by water, looks like evidence, but – it must be reiterated – is not truly his. He is a pointer nevertheless to a bardic source, perhaps with druidical conceptions behind it. As presented by Geoffrey he calls Avalon the Apple-Island, *Insula Pomorum*. This is the usual etymology of the name, which in Welsh is *Avallach*. Doubt has been cast, but none can be cast on the way Taliesin takes it.

4   He gives 'Fortunate Isle' as an alternative, and the debt owed to classical 'Fortunate Isles' is manifest:

> It produces all things of itself. The fields there have no need of farmers to plough them, and Nature alone provides all cultivation. Grain and grapes are produced without tending, and apple trees grow in the woods from the close-clipped grass. The earth of its own accord brings forth not merely grass but all things in superabundance, and people live there a hundred years or more.

The Greeks told of an Elysium over the western ocean, which, to judge from a comparison of Homer and Hesiod, was originally the same place. It was the domain of Cronus, and there departed heroes beloved of the gods lived on, without care, exempt from death. This would be appropriate to Arthur. But Taliesin's classical imagery is blended with Celtic myth, and Ireland

5   supplies proof of that in the shape of an island paradise known as Emain Ablach, 'rich in apple-trees'. *Ablach* is equivalent to the Welsh *Avallach*.

Once Irish mythology is opened up, it becomes clear that this is only the beginning. The Celts of Erin had ideas of the paradisal west going far beyond anything Greece could offer. Their imagination was far more active in bestowing substance and location. Their western Otherworld was multiple and diverse and, indeed, by no means all paradisal. It was a varied archipelago in the realms of sunset with no known limit. One of its happier regions was Tir na nOg, the Land of the Young. Another was Mag Mon, a kind of Elysium itself.

Avalon's femininity links up with a special feature of this wonderful west. Here too we may detect a hint from classical sources, from the sisterhoods of healers and magic-workers in such places as the Ile de Sein. But here too is a Celtic element. Layamon and others, by calling the Avalonian women 'fays' or fairy-folk, make their character clear. This is consistent with the basic divinity of Morgan herself, and we are still at a stage where she has not been de-mystified by a family relation to Arthur. The western isles of the Irish included a Land of Women, with an Otherworld quality which actual sisterhoods would never have evoked by themselves. The Land of Women is more than a sexual fantasy of male story-tellers. Its inhabitants do not resemble the houris of the Islamic paradise. They have an aura of wise enchantment conducive to well-being and happiness, possibly a legacy from an older goddess-world. The same applies to the Avalonian Morgan and her sisters.

Much of the foregoing is illustrated in an Irish tale, *The Voyage of Bran*. It   6
was written about 700, perhaps at the monastery of Bangor on Belfast
Lough. A mixture of prose and verse, it is the oldest and simplest known
specimen of the literary form called the *immram*, concerning voyages to
extraordinary islands, including the paradisal places of myth. The hero of
this tale, Bran son of Febal, is a humanised version of the Celtic god who
also underlies Bran the Blessed. If this is indeed the god whom Plutarch's
Britons located on a remote island, his myth may partly explain the
derivative hero's Atlantic journeying.

Long ago, we are told, before the coming of Christ, Bran was walking
along a western sea-shore. Suddenly he heard music of enchanting sweet-
ness, and saw an apple-bough covered with white blossom. He took hold of
it and carried it to his hall. Thereupon a strangely-garbed woman appeared,
and sang of a realm across the sea which knew no death, nor decay, nor care,
only human joys going on everlastingly:

> 'There is a distant isle,
> Around which sea-horses glisten . . .
> A delight of the eyes, a glorious range,
> Is the plain on which the hosts hold games . . .
> There is nothing rough or harsh,
> But sweet music striking on the ear,
> Without grief, without sorrow, without death . . .
> The sea washes the wave against the land,
> Hair of crystal drops from its mane.
> Wealth, treasures of every hue,
> Are in Ciuin, a beauty of freshness,
> Listening to sweet music,
> Drinking the best of wine.
> Golden chariots in Mag Rein,
> Rising with the tide to the sun,
> Chariots of silver in Mag Mon,
> And of bronze without blemish . . .'

An entire New World, the singer declared, stretched beyond the horizon for
an adventurer to discover:

> 'There are thrice fifty distant isles
> In the ocean to the west of us;
> Larger than Erin twice
> Is each of them, or thrice.'

She turned to depart, and as she did so the white branch, which had come
from an apple-tree in Emain Ablach, sprang across from Bran's hand to hers.
Resolving to go the way she had pointed, he launched three boats, each with
a crew of nine. The company rowed out west for two days and nights. Then
the sea-god Manannan approached them over the waves in his chariot.
(This is the Manannan whose Welsh humanisation is Pryderi's friend
Manawydan.) He foretold certain future events including the advent of
Christ, but not the voyagers' own destiny, though he encouraged them to
press on and assured them that marvellous islands lay close ahead, including
Emain Ablach, which was his own favourite home.   7

**139. Cliffs at Moher,
County Clare.**

They passed by and made their first landfall at the Island of Joy. A crowd of people stood laughing on the beach. One of Bran's followers disembarked, joined the crowd, began laughing himself, and took no notice of calls to return to the boat. So they left him and continued. Soon they reached the Land of Women, of which they had had inklings from both the singer and Manannan. Its queen escorted them ashore, throwing a ball of thread which clung to Bran's hand. They entered a great house with a bed for every man and his chosen partner, and there they lived for a year, or so it seemed, and feasted on inexhaustible food.

At last one of the party grew homesick and Bran agreed to leave. The queen told him to pick up the comrade left on the Island of Joy, but said he would regret his return, and warned him not to set foot on Erin. He persisted, and reached the Irish coast. Many people were gathered at that place, and Bran told them who he was, but they knew him only as a character in an ancient tale. Centuries had slipped by during the spellbound sojourn across the ocean. The voyagers were back in the mortal world, and when the homesick man did step ashore he crumbled into a heap of ashes. Bran spoke to the people of his wanderings and turned seaward again, and further the story does not tell of him.

Geoffrey's Avalon episode reflects a belief apparent in *The Voyage of Bran*, that the islands were, under certain circumstances, attainable. While myths could affirm their existence, the notion of actually reaching them was prompted by technology. The Irish invented the curragh or skin-boat, an 8
improvement on the coracle, pointed at both ends. A light, seaworthy craft made of greased ox-hides drawn over a wooden frame, it could be rowed or sailed. Bran's three boats are curraghs. In real life the most daring users of this vessel were monks. From the sixth century onwards, groups of them 9
were venturing forth from Ireland on 'sea-pilgrimages', partly with missionary aims, but more in search of island retreats where communities would be safe from warfare and persecution. They reached the Orkneys about 579, the Shetlands in 620, the Faeroes about 670, and Iceland towards 795. A sea-pilgrim named Cormac, caught in prolonged storms, was blown into the arctic far enough to encounter 'loathsome stinging creatures' which were quite probably Greenland mosquitoes swarming low over the water.

Reports of these voyages helped to inspire the fully-fledged *immrama*. The most important was *The Voyage of Mael Duin*, a fantasy elaborating 10
the hints in *Bran*. Mael Duin and his companions visit no fewer than twenty-nine islands. Extravagant fairy-tale imagery in such yarns may owe something to seafarers' hallucinations induced by thirst.

Alongside these developments, the traditions of sea-pilgrimage acted more directly to create another legend, overlapping the *immrama* with influence going both ways. Arthur's voyage to Avalon is linked with it by that third notable feature, the identity of the pilot. Barinthus is taken from the *Navigatio Sancti Brendani*, the story of St Brendan's Voyage, composed 11
between 900 and 920. Brendan, who flourished in the sixth century, was a pioneer of the Irish monastic seafaring. He travelled widely and crossed to the Inner Hebrides, acquiring a nickname, 'the Navigator'. His clerical biographers gave him a career full of legend and miracle. That happened with many saints, but Brendan's case was special, because, owing to his reputation, he was credited more with sea-marvels than with land-marvels. The tale of his tremendous and fabulous Voyage became a popular medieval theme, and was even counted as a branch of the Arthurian cycle.

In the *Navigatio*, the fullest and most sophisticated of the Irish versions, Barinthus visits Brendan at Ardfert in Kerry and tells him of a voyage he has made himself, westward to the 'Land Promised to the Saints'. This country contains the Earthly Paradise of Christian belief, and thus replaces or reinterprets the pagan ones. Since the Bible locates Paradise eastwards in Asia, it must be supposed that the author knows the world to be round (as well-read Irishmen did) and imagines Barinthus doing what Columbus intended to do: reach Asia by sailing west. Brendan decides to go in search of the Land and sets sail with seventeen companions. They wander about the ocean for years, with long spells ashore on islands, and finally reach their goal and explore inland. An angel tells them that they are on the borders of Paradise. This country will one day be made accessible as a haven from persecution, and will later be open to all Christendom, but now they must go back. They comply.

The *Navigatio* is not a record of a real voyage, and nothing follows from it as to anything St Brendan actually did. It has been described as a Christian *immram*, and so in a sense it is. But it is much more. Unlike (say) *Mael Duin* it gives indications of distance, direction, even climate, from which a reader can often judge roughly where the monks are meant to be. Moreover, the author's descriptions of places which they visit show knowledge of the Faeroe Islands and Iceland, and he has a fairly convincing iceberg . . . which *Mael Duin* annexes and makes preposterous. Other places that are at least arguable are St Kilda, Rockall, Greenland and the Newfoundland Banks. Two passages can be read as giving distorted images of the Bahamas and Jamaica.

In the Middle Ages the *Navigatio* carried enough conviction to plant islands of St Brendan or 'Brandan' on several maps, and Columbus took them seriously. The author's knowledge can be largely accounted for from earlier sources, and his work is a sort of fantasia on ideas about the North Atlantic. But his implied map is remarkably good, and since the *Navigatio* antedates the Norse Vinland voyages, enthusiasts have inferred an Irish discovery of America, or Irish awareness of an older discovery, even a prehistoric one. However that may be, Geoffrey's allusion to Barinthus suggests that he read this work, and he echoes it faintly in another way. Before Taliesin describes Avalon he describes a series of other islands, some of them real. Thus Geoffrey gives Avalon itself an air of geographic validity. His Avalon passage is a further piece of evidence, if a slightly disguised one, for Celtic Christians' assimilation and adaptation of pre-Christian mythology; while Ireland's legendary Navigator shows the same process directly.

1. Layamon, *Brut*, closing passage: in Loomis, ed., 109, and Wilhelm (2), 28.
2. Cp Stewart (1), 119–20, 128, 204–5.
3. Loomis, ed., 108.
4. Ibid., 92–3.
5. Bromwich, 267–8; Loomis, ed., 66.
6. *The Voyage of Bran*, ed. cit. See also Jackson (1), 173–5, and Rees, 314–6.
7. Rees, 39.
8. Ashe (9), 67–9.
9. Ashe (9), 34; Morris, 355, 383–4.
10. Ashe (9), 54–5, 57–9; Joyce, 79–122; Rees, 318–22; Rolleston, 309–31.
11. Ashe (9), 73–119, 183–9, 293–7; Morris, 384–5.

The Birth of Scotland

51 The Beginnings of the Reign of the Scots

Dalriada, the kingdom in Argyll, was named from the Dalriadic Scots who had emigrated from Ireland and founded it. Many of their kinsfolk had stayed behind, not electing to cross the North Channel. It was a man of part-Dalriadic stock, native to Ireland, who followed in the migrants' footsteps during the sixth century and raised their kingdom to importance. 1

Born in Donegal about 521, Colum, or Columba as he is known, was early destined for the Church. He attended a school conducted by St Finnian at Moville on Strangford Lough. At that time the Irish clergy were the most learned in western Europe, and Columba received a good education and became an ardent scholar. Some years later, when he was a priest himself, he borrowed a manuscript from his former teacher and made a copy. Finnian, when he got the original back, demanded the copy too. In the absence of printing, a manuscript embodied much work and was an object of value. The dispute was adjudicated by the high king Diarmaid, who decided in favour of the schoolmaster: 'To every cow her calf, and to every book its son-book. The copy you have made, Colum, belongs to Finnian.' Columba was resentful, and grew much more so when the king's soldiers killed someone he was sheltering, thereby violating the rights of sanctuary. Fighting broke out between supporters of Columba and supporters of Diarmaid. Columba was blamed for the bloodshed, and resolved to expiate his guilt by self-imposed exile. 2

Tall and energetic, with a voice 'so loud and melodious it could be heard a mile off,' he had no trouble in attracting companions. In 563 he embarked with twelve in a curragh, like St Brendan and the other sea-pilgrims, not to mention Bran. The party landed on Hi, or Iona, a little island off Mull. The Dalriadic king Conall granted him possession and he founded a monastery, which was to be one of the most famous and influential in Christendom.

From there, Columba and his disciples went out on missions in Dalriada and among the Picts.

One of his most eventful journeys was to the Pictish king Bridei, a son of Maelgwn of Gwynedd, invited in to rule because of a problem over the royal succession. He was a formidable figure, and had conquered most of the West Highlands. Columba's visit involved travelling up the Great Glen and Loch Ness. Formerly, the tale goes, there was no such loch, only a pleasant valley. In it was a well that supplied unlimited water when its cover was off, and stopped when it was put back. One day a woman who heard her child scream, and ran to see what the matter was, dropped the cover instead of replacing it. The water overflowed, flooding the valley. The people fled crying 'Tha loch nis ann!' ('There is a lake there now!') and that is why it was called Loch Ness.

Beside the river that enters the loch at Fort Augustus, Columba told one of his monks to swim over and fetch a boat from the farther bank. Midway in the crossing, the monk was pursued by a terrible, roaring water-monster. Columba sternly commanded it not to harm him, and it fled. While the Loch Ness Monster has been sighted many times since, even to the present day, it has never hurt anyone. The saint also had trouble with a relative of Bridei who tried to raise a contrary wind by magic, while the missionaries were sailing up the loch. Their boat simply went its way with the wind against it. In Inverness, where the heathen monarch lived, he wanted to shut them out, but when Columba made the sign of the cross the gates opened by themselves. After that Bridei treated him with respect and he converted many Picts.

On another occasion he met Aedan, king of Dalriada. Aedan had named one of his sons Arthur; the fame of the British hero had spread beyond

140. (opposite) Christ's Temptation, a page in the Book of Kells, the work of monks at a monastery in Ireland founded by St Columba, and one of the masterpieces of Celtic Christian art.

141. A container for a relic of St Columba, the Monymusk Reliquary, made about the year 700 and reputedly carried into battle by the Scots at Bannockburn.

British lands. Columba made the sad and correct prophecy that this prince would fall in battle and not succeed Aedan. So no second Arthur reigned.

Columba returned once or twice to Ireland. At a synod in 575 he vetoed a proposal for abolishing the order of *filid* or poets, and established that no military service should be imposed on women. But Iona was now his home. Its graveyard became Scotland's royal cemetery. Sixty kings, Scottish, Irish and Norwegian, are buried here, including Macbeth. The graveyard is dedicated to Oran, Columba's brother, of whom strange, scarcely Christian stories are told. According to one of them, when Columba first arrived, he wished he could consecrate the ground with a burial, and Oran voluntarily died. According to another, the monastic church could not be built because the walls kept collapsing, and it was necessary for someone to be buried alive there . . . a problem reminiscent of Vortigern's in Snowdonia. Oran had been arguing with his brother about the nature of heaven and hell. He broke off, agreed to be the victim, and descended into a pit which was lightly filled. After twenty days the pit was opened and Oran's head spoke:

> 'Heaven is not what it is said to be;
> Hell is not what it is said to be;
> The saved are not for ever happy;
> The damned are not for ever lost.'

Columba, convinced that a deceiving demon was speaking, quickly had the sinister thing buried again.

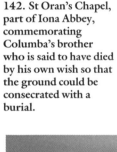

142. St Oran's Chapel, part of Iona Abbey, commemorating Columba's brother who is said to have died by his own wish so that the ground could be consecrated with a burial.

He died in 597. Iona remained the northern centre of Celtic Christianity, evangelising not only Picts and Scots but Northumbrian Angles. Some would have it that the Celts were separate from the universal Church, differing fundamentally in doctrine and practice, and not admitting Roman authority or the supremacy of Peter's successors. But they are mistaken.

During St Columba's last years the northern British were losing ground to the Angles, led by a strong king, Aethelfrith. They appealed for help to 7 Aedan, the same who had chosen Arthur as a name for his son. In 603 he marched south and fought the Northumbrian army at an unidentified place called Degsastan, Degsa's Stone. He inflicted heavy losses but was finally routed and driven back. Welsh tradition branded him as crafty, perhaps even with a hint at treachery, for no obvious reason. After Degsastan, says the English historian Bede, 'no king of the Scots ever dared to make war on the English.' Bede wrote in 731 and his statement remained valid many years, but not permanently.

For a century Dalriada was under direct Pictish rule. But in a way this helped the Scots, by making it easier for them to spread through Pictland seeking their fortunes. In 839 Dalriada broke free again, and in 843 the whole Pictish edifice collapsed. This was when the Dalriadic king, Kenneth 8 MacAlpine, created the Scottish realm. He claimed the throne of Pictland on the ground that he was fractionally Pictish himself. At Scone, during a conference about the succession, he invited the leading Picts to a banquet and seated them on benches that were disguised trap-doors, held up by bolts which could be pulled out. When they were all in place Kenneth's retainers withdrew the bolts, and the nobles tumbled into pits where the Scots slaughtered them. By the 'Treachery of Scone' Kenneth removed every rival and emerged as ruler of the whole of Albany. He clinched his triumph by adopting Scone's mystique and bringing the Stone of Destiny there. Successors annexed Strathclyde and the country to the Border.

History is breaking in. Geoffrey of Monmouth carries on, ending with the 9 Welsh king Cadwaladr in 689, but his last chapters are uninspired and uncreative. The main reason is that he finds himself in the territory of Bede, and the historian's facts are too much for him. So also with St Columba. Picturesque and fantastic stories abound, but they are outgrowths from the career of a real 10 person, whose real life-story can be reconstructed. The chief myth promoted by his work at Iona and its sequels is a much later one, arising from Catholic –Protestant disputes: the myth of an independent Celtic Church that was crushed and swallowed up by Roman aggression.

Celtic Christianity certainly had a character of its own. Profoundly important 11 was the way it left the door open for the adaptation of pagan deities and motifs. There was much more. It was differently organised. Having grown up in areas with few towns, it was not centred on urban sees but on religious communities serving tribes. Abbots rather than bishops were the dominant figures, especially in Ireland and in the sphere of Iona. Monks counted for more than secular clergy, nuns had a corresponding status, and women generally ranked somewhat higher than elsewhere, as they had in pagan Celtic society.

Because of a period of near-isolation, the Church in Celtic lands diverged. But it remained, if tenuously, part of the Catholic body in communion with

143. St Columba's Cave, one of many places associated with him.

12 Rome. St Augustine, sent by Pope Gregory to convert the Anglo-Saxons, acknowledged as much by inviting the Welsh bishops to cooperate in his mission, and they might have done if he had shown a little more tact.

Celtic otherness, in spirit, in atmosphere, and in religious practice, did give rise to problems. This Christianity was plainer and simpler than the continental kind, less formal and patriarchal. The monastic life was more austere, yet in some ways more easy-going: each member of a community had a private cell

13 and a certain freedom to wander. Censorship was rarer. Celtic Christians not only had the advantage in erudition, they had books which Rome condemned and tried to suppress. Such features in themselves were hardly definite enough to antagonise. But on various matters of practice there were sharp differences, sometimes because the Celts had changed, sometimes because they had not kept up with Roman changes.

When Rome re-asserted itself in the British Isles, the principal test issue was the method of fixing Easter. Tempers ran high, and the Easter controversy was a rallying-point for rival attitudes. Rome won at the Synod of Whitby in 663 when the Celtic spokesman conceded that Peter, not Columba, had been entrusted by Christ with the keys of heaven. Conformity gradually ensued, in Scotland, in Ireland, belatedly in Wales and Cornwall. It can be argued that this

14 was a pity. It cannot be maintained, on the basis of any authentic document, that Rome took over a hitherto separate church, or that the Celts were proto-Protestants, or that they stood for a religion incompatible with the Roman

communion. (An academic theory on these lines is presented as the hobby-horse of one of the more unbalanced dons in Angus Wilson's *Anglo-Saxon Attitudes*.)

On the political side the swift débâcle of the Picts, after a phase of power, is 15 curious. One reason was that several generations of Scots had taken service with Pictish kings and received lands in payment. Scottish families were numerous in the Forth valley and in Fife. A disputed succession may indeed have given an opening. Such problems were inherent in the Picts' monarchy, because their custom of tracing hereditary rights through the mother was combined with actual rule by men. Often the crown could not pass incontestably from father to son. If Bridei was a son of Maelgwn, the explanation of this partly-Welsh sovereign may lie in royal Pictish blood on his mother's side. So, likewise, with Kenneth, who apparently had a Pictish grandmother. Whatever the truth about his massacre, that alone could not have worked such a sweeping change. Doubtless he had support from the Scots in the kingdom, and these may have won over a sufficient number of Picts. Probably, also, he made use of Iona-affiliated clergy. As soon as he could he began appointing priests of that disposition to posts of influence, and he transferred the remains of Columba to Dunkeld. He was buried at Iona himself, however, as were his successors.

The early demise of the Scottish Arthur, which Columba foretold, has two English echoes. On the death of Richard I, the rightful heir was Prince Arthur of Brittany, but he died as a prisoner of John, his uncle, and never reigned. After Bosworth came Henry VII's attempt to annex legendary glories by bestowing the name Arthur on his heir-apparent, and in this case too the prince died. Britain has not yet produced another King Arthur.

1. Alcock (1), 130–1; Morris, 180.
2. Butler, art. 'Columba', June 9th.
3. FML, 445.
4. FML, 445; Westwood, 410.
5. Adomnan, I, 9.
6. FML, 525.
7. Alcock (1), 131; Bede, I, 34; Bromwich, 264–6; Morris, 181–3.
8. Mackenzie, 207–8.
9. GM (1), 132–47, and (2), 262–84.
10. Bede, III, 4; Mackenzie, 128–33; Morris, 169–74, 181–2, 192–3, 387–8; Prebble, 23.
11. Chadwick (1), 257–9; Hodgkin, I, 247; Morris, 356–88, 397–8; Sheldon, 123.
12. Bede, II, 2; Gougaud, 215. Cp Butler, art. 'Columbanus', November 23rd.
13. Duckett, 20.
14. Bede, III, 25; Duckett, 78; Gougaud, 196–7; Hodgkin, I, 299; Sheldon, 177, 185, 199.
15. Mackenzie, 206–20; Morris, 196–7.

52 *Fingal and Ossian*

Despite their vigour and success, the Scots were slow to create their own mythology. Story-tellers looked back to the ancestral homeland. They recalled folk-wanderings, still a live issue in 1320 when the Declaration of Arbroath was sent to the Pope, and they adopted two long-departed Irishmen into their saga-making, a warrior and a poet, father and son.

Finn mac Cumaill, colloquially Finn MacCool, was and is the hero of a body of Irish tales and poems, the Fenian Cycle, so called from *fiana* meaning 'warrior bands'. They are located mainly in central and southern Ireland. Finn is said to have flourished in the third century AD. When his mother was in a late stage of pregnancy, an enemy killed his father Cumaill. His mother gave birth soon after and the boy was called Demne, but he was later renamed Finn, 'fair' – that is, fair-haired and pale-skinned. As a youth he was tutored by a poet who caught the Salmon of Knowledge and told Finn to cook it, forbidding him to eat any of it. During the cooking Finn touched the fish, burned his thumb, sucked it, and acquired superhuman knowledge. Henceforth he could find the answers to many questions by chewing his thumb.

He gathered a war-band or *fian* around him. To achieve membership as a *féinid* – in later parlance, a Fenian – a candidate had to pass rigorous tests. In one of them he was buried up to his waist and given a shield and a stick. Nine warriors threw javelins at him, and if he failed to ward them all off, he was rejected. In another test he had to run through the woods with the Fenians in pursuit, all of them skilled at tracking by the sound of twigs and similar clues. If they caught him he was not admitted to the fellowship. The applicant also had to be well educated, familiar with twelve poetic classics.

Finn's warriors fought for a high king, Cormac mac Airt, but the arrangement was voluntary, and did not reduce them to the status of mercenaries. Often they went their own way, living off the country by hunting. They fought on foot, not in chariots like the nobles of Ulster. Their chief martial exploits were in defence of Ireland against the Norsemen. Finn himself was loved for his valour and generosity. He performed mighty individual feats, killing giants, goblins, serpents, and huge wild boars.

Besides having preternatural knowledge he was a shape-shifter, and so were several people related to him. He wore a magic hood, and could turn himself into a dog or a stag by wearing it at different angles. His hounds (one of them named Bran) were his cousins. He also had several wives – they were tested like the warriors, in this case by being asked riddles – and one of them took the form of a doe. When her child was about to be born she was told that if she licked it, it would be a deer, but if she could refrain, it would be human. Human it was, but she brushed its forehead with her tongue and a tuft of fur grew. This child was Oisin, 'little fawn'. He became a poet and accompanied the war-band on its adventures, but left to voyage to the Otherworld country of Tir na nOg, the Land of the Young, staying there in a spellbound timelessness for many years.

Finn died at the age of 230. Oisin returned to Ireland, too late to see his father alive, and wandered about nostalgically recalling the past. Another survivor, Cailte, or according to some Oisin himself, had the good luck to meet St Patrick and told him of the glories of Finn and his company. It was partly thus that the missionary saint – himself British, not Irish – learned what he knew of Erin's past. He interceded for the souls of Finn and his chief followers, and secured their salvation. Oisin's final departure was to the Otherworld; though a cluster of stones in Antrim is pointed out as his grave.

When the Scots reshaped the saga in their new country, Finn became   4

144. Finn's work? The Giant's Causeway in Northern Ireland, formed by columnar basalt.

5   Fingal and Oisin became Ossian. They transplanted some of the tales and added more. Fingal's Cave, in the basaltic island of Staffa, is so called because the hero used Staffa as a base for defence of the Hebrides against the Norse. Ossian too has a cave, high up in a mountainside above Glen Coe. Stories of both, and short pieces of Gaelic verse ascribed to Ossian, were handed down by the Highlanders and remained orally current into modern times. In the eighteenth century, the poet's fame was enhanced by the publication of longer works given out as his. Some believed it, but they were wrong.

6   Aside from all this, the Scots did in time create a rich body of folklore and fairy-tale, drawing in Pictish matter as well as their own. It peopled the land with extraordinary beings – kelpies or water-horses, giants in caverns, invincible swordsmen and archers, blind seers and snow-maidens, trees that sang and stones that talked: not to mention innumerable witches.

Finn, or Fingal, is the nearest thing to a Gaelic equivalent of the Welsh Arthur. No Irish records are early enough to establish anything for or against his existence. His longevity can be paralleled in legends of persons who did exist, such as Charlemagne, but his alleged military context tells against him. The Norse were not a menace to Ireland or Scotland till long after the third century. In this respect he is unlike Arthur, who, whether historical or not, is given the plausible setting of the Saxon invasion and British resistance to it.

7   Finn may have divine antecedents. Some of his mythic affinities are interesting. For instance, he is a descendant of Nuadu. The Welsh character Gwyn is a son of Nudd. As noted, Nuadu and Nudd are cognate forms of the Celtic deity known in Britain as Nodons; and as 'Finn' means 'fair', so 'Gwyn' means 'white'. Are they ultimately the same? Intriguing also is the act by which Finn acquires knowledge. It is like the act by which the boy Gwion, who becomes Taliesin, does likewise.

Fingal's Cave, the inspiration of Mendelssohn's overture, is one of the Scottish additions. The tales, songs and poems transmitted orally preserved Ossian's fame as a poet, and some of his attributed verses may at least be ancient. But the epics and other narratives that caused a stir in the eighteenth century were largely fabricated. In 1760 a Scottish schoolmaster, James Macpherson, began offering the public what he claimed were translations of Ossian's originals. His output aroused furious debate. People who knew the Highland lore were sometimes willing to give him the benefit of the doubt. Dr Johnson was not. When a pro-Macpherson clergyman asked whether he thought 'any man of a modern age' could have written these productions, he replied: 'Yes, sir, many men, many women, and many children.' No one ever saw the alleged manuscripts. Macpherson certainly made use of traditional Gaelic fragments, but equally certainly, he invented much more.

His 'translations' are in a tiresome rhythmical prose. A fair specimen is the opening of the epic *Temora*, quoted (inexactly) and derided by Wordsworth in a supplement to the *Lyrical Ballads* preface, but praised by Edgar Allan Poe in a literary essay:

> The blue waves of Erin roll in light. The mountains are
> covered with day. Trees shake their dusky heads in the breeze.
> Grey torrents pour their noisy streams. Two green hills, with
> aged oaks, surround a narrow plain. The blue course of a

stream is there. On its banks stood Cairbar of Atha. His spear
supports the king; the red eye of his fear is sad. Cormac rises
in his soul with all his ghastly wounds.

Despite the fraud, pseudo-Ossian had a considerable influence on the Romantic
movement. Some of the characteristic rhythms are echoed in Blake's unrhymed
verse. Napoleon kept the book by his bedside.

145. Fingal's Cave in
Staffa, which figures in
the Scottish saga of the
transplanted Irish
hero.

The native Picto-Gaelic mythology, as it has been called, seems to have begun
taking shape in the eleventh century. Scotland's witch-lore is much later than
that, and owes a debt to King James VI and I, who had a great deal to say on the
subject. *Macbeth* may have been prompted by the royal interest. Burns's *Tam o'
Shanter* is closer to popular folklore. In the version of the Arthurian cave legend
preserved by Scott, the chamber under the Eildon Hills is entered through an   8
odd-looking hillock, the Lucken Hare, and this was a witches' rendezvous.

Scotland of course has many heroic legends, but they are attached to historical   9
figures in the Middle Ages and later, such as Wallace and Bruce, Chroniclers
adapt Geoffrey, sometimes re-interpreting him from a patriotic viewpoint,   10
making 'good' characters 'bad' and vice versa. But no chronicler offers a real
Scottish counterpart to his work.

1. Prebble, 112–4.
2. FML, 519; *Man, Myth and Magic*,
   art. 'Finn'; Rees, 63–4, 250–1,
   266–7; Rolleston, 252–308.
3. Rolleston, 266–76.
4. Ebbutt, 248; FML, 517–9.
5. FML, 450.

6. Prebble, 30–1.
7. Chadwick (2), 197.
8. Ashe (5), 158; Westwood, 369–70.
9. Ebbutt, 248; FML, 519–23.
10. Kendrick, 65–8; Lacy, ed., art.
    'Scottish Arthurian Chronicles'.

146. A view along the
Wansdyke, called
Woden's Ditch by the
Saxons, a post-Roman
earthwork running
across parts of Avon
and Wiltshire —
possibly for frontier
demarcation rather
than defence.

The English Inheritance

53 *Woden's Brood*

As British resistance weakened, the chiefs of Anglo-Saxondom consolidated their hold and pressed forward. Seven regional kingdoms took shape, so that incipient England has been spoken of as a Heptarchy. Nearest the continent was Kent, founded by Hengist under Vortigern's auspices, a realm of Saxons and Jutes. Westward from it was Sussex, and west of that was Wessex. North-east of London was Essex. Those three names denoted the domains of the South Saxons, West Saxons, and East Saxons. Beyond Essex was the kingdom of the East Angles. In the midlands was Mercia, and all the Anglian north was Northumbria.

Since the first rulers were heathen, they could claim loftier antecedents than their British counterparts, who, being Christian, could no longer say that their reputed ancestors were gods, even when they were. Saxon royal pedigrees, with a single exception, were traced to the head god Woden, [1] whom Scandinavians knew as Odin. The exception was the East Saxon dynasty, and that was descended from another god, Seaxnot. Woden gave [2] his name to Wednesbury, and to several places where his worshippers settled before their Christianisation, such as Wednesbury and Wednesfield. A famous British earthwork is called the Wansdyke, Woden's Ditch, because, when the Saxons reached it, they believed it to be superhuman.

Folk-memory did not reach far back. The royal pedigrees had few generations, and put Woden himself in the third or fourth century AD, with almost no history for the years between. However, while the kingdoms' creators lacked a cohesive tradition or common purpose, they recognised a unity in the Roman-formed country they had come to, and expressed this in a title. Whichever Anglo-Saxon king was respected as paramount was the Bretwalda, the Britain-ruler. That distinction passed from kingdom to [3] kingdom – from the South Saxon ruler to the West Saxon, from him to the king of Kent, from Kent to East Anglia, and then to Northumbria and Mercia and finally to Wessex again. At first the Bretwaldaship was hardly more than honorary, but with the passage of time it became a focus of power. Wessex, when it emerged as supreme, made England politically one.

4 Present royalty is descended from the West Saxon house, and thus from its founder, whose name was Cerdic.

On the face of it, Woden in the genealogies is an ancestor-deity, as the Welsh Beli originally was. Yet they make him so recent that a real person may be involved, perhaps a patriarchal chief named after the god, like Brennus. All these kings claimed divine descent to assert a god-given right to whatever they had acquired in Britain. Most of the founders had been self-made, not the heirs of

5 kings before the migration. Only the Mercian dynasty had an ancestor, Icel, who can be traced on the continent as a person of authority in the fifth century.

6 The Heptarchy is an approximation. Smaller kingdoms came into being and disappeared, taken over or merged with others. While there is no evidence anywhere for a mass genocide of Britons, the ethnic mix varied. Kent was more solidly 'English' than most areas. Northumbria, at the other extreme, was created by dominance of the new stock over a population not vastly altered. Wessex absorbed many Britons as it expanded, and gave them a recognised status in its laws, though not an equal one. But whatever the differences, the Anglo-Saxons' ascendancy was a constant. Their language became the norm everywhere – Cornwall was the only part of England where another vernacular survived – and it evolved into English with very little assimilation of British

7 words, though the old language persisted in geographical names, notably the names of rivers.

8 The Bretwaldaship, an unusual institution, had a touch of mystique. Its movement from one holder to another depended for many years on consent rather than force. The third Bretwalda, Aethelbert of Kent, was by no means the strongest of the kings. His contemporary Aethelfrith of Northumbria was a major conqueror, yet was never Bretwalda. This may have been because the Bretwaldaship did not at first extend past the Humber, but an implication remains of some sort of agreement, some hazy notion of proprieties and spheres of influence: Aethelfrith could not break into the system. Aethelbert's Bretwaldaship may have been due to his reigning over the most civilised part of the country, with continental contacts lending prestige. The next Bretwalda was Raedwald of East Anglia, and in his case the wealth and foreign connections of

9 his court, spectacularly revealed by the Sutton Hoo ship-burial, may have been decisive. The point is that power alone was not.

After Raedwald, however, the Bretwaldaship changed. Supremacy was confined to the three largest kingdoms, first Northumbria, then Mercia, then Wessex. The Bretwalda became more of an overlord, and the lesser kingdoms were absorbed. The final triumph of Wessex, and the descent of its dynastic title

10 right through to the House of Windsor, give that dynasty's origin a special interest. Its beginning was on Southampton Water, where the founder Cerdic is said to have planted himself late in the fifth century. His settlers and their immediate heirs, though attested archaeologically, seem to have been few. However, they pushed north and asserted control over larger Saxon bodies, forming a kingdom that grew swiftly from the 560s onward.

The early West Saxon annals are most confused, and almost nothing is known of Cerdic himself. Some writers have made him an opponent of Arthur, and involved him in the battle of Badon. This is fancy. But there is one intriguing fact, which no Saxon chronicler or genealogist would have invented. His name is not Saxon but British, and several Britons are on record who bore it. While he is given a Woden pedigree as a matter of course, the name hints at a family connection with Britons. An early term for the West Saxons was 'Gewisse', which meant 'allies' or 'confederates', but was taken to mean 'Gewis's people'; Cerdic therefore has a Gewis in his pedigree. Geoffrey of Monmouth, however, transfers the word to Wales and says Vortigern was the ruler of the Gewissei. He does not mention Cerdic, yet there are indications, as we have seen, that in using this word he is trying to handle a tradition about a title Vortigern held, and it may now appear that it was supposed to have passed from him to the West Saxon dynasty, perhaps through an unmentioned offspring of his Saxon marriage. 11 12

Quite seriously, Cerdic could have been a noble of mixed blood, with a foot in both camps. He might have recruited a following in Gaul. Emigrant Britons on the lower Loire were in contact with more-or-less subdued Saxon settlers. Cerdic, let us say, assembled a combined British-Saxon band in that area, and returned to Britain to carve out a domain based on his British status. Tiny at first, it grew into Wessex, and eventually into England and the United Kingdom. Modern royalty may be descended not only from the West Saxon sovereigns but, farther back, from Britons of the 'Arthurian' world. 13 14

1. Blair, 194–8.
2. Copley, 66–8; Ekwall, 496, art. 'Wansdyke', and 503, art. 'Wednesbury, Wednesfield'.
3. Bede, II, 5.
4. Barlow, 3; Moncreiffe, 32.
5. Morris, 272.
6. Blair, 20–1, 199; Copley, 48–9.
7. Jackson (2), 221–3.
8. Blair, 49–54, 199–203; Campbell, 53–4; Morris, 329–30; Sheldon, 141.
9. Campbell, 32–3.
10. Alcock (1), 116–8; Barlow, 3.
11. Copley, 39, 135, 140–1; Morris, 103–4; Oman, 224–5.
12. GM (1), 62, and (2), 151.
13. Campbell, 37.
14. Cp Moncreiffe, 12.

54 *Beowulf*

Like the Scots, the Anglo-Saxons had their own minstrelsy. But with them, too, the first hero of legend in the new lands came from the legacy of the old. And he was not even one of themselves.

Beowulf is the only long Anglo-Saxon poem drawing its inspiration from pre-Christian antiquity. Its setting is in Denmark and thereabouts. In unrhymed alliterative verse, it begins by telling how the Danish king Hrothgar built a splendid hall. He named it Heorot. But when he had assembled his court in it, a frightful, half-human monster called Grendel started a series of raids, killing and eating Danish noblemen. Grendel lived in a cave under a lake. Wandering over the fens, he had seen Heorot and conceived a hatred for its lights, music and revels. The raids were his response, and he carried them out with impunity, because a devilish spell made him impervious to weapons.

Over a stretch of years he invaded Heorot many times, always after dark, and the Danes became afraid to go there except in daylight. At last Beowulf, a nephew of King Hygelac of the Geats, arrived by sea with fourteen companions and offered his help. Tall and handsome, a swimmer of unrivalled prowess, he had already dealt with water-monsters and believed he could defeat Grendel by strength alone. Hrothgar gave him leave to attempt it. That night the Geats lay down in the hall and waited. Grendel entered, slew one of them so quickly that Beowulf could not stop him, and devoured the corpse. Then he turned to Beowulf. The prince seized him in a wrestling grip. A fearful struggle ensued. The other Geats could do nothing to aid their leader, because their swords were useless against the demon. Eventually, Grendel wrenched himself free, leaving his arm in Beowulf's grasp. He staggered back to the pool and reached his cave, but the wound was mortal.

The Geats hung the severed arm from the roof as a trophy. When the Danes saw it they rejoiced. The king and queen rewarded Beowulf's party with many gifts. No one, however, had reckoned with a second monster, Grendel's mother, who also dwelt under the lake and now came out to avenge her son. She carried off and killed one of Hrothgar's most valued thanes. Hrothgar asked for Beowulf's further help, and rode with him along the water-hag's tracks, with a number of Danes and Geats following. One of the Danes lent Beowulf a sword called Hrunting.

The lake was a sinister place, with serpents writhing in it, and the head of the recent Danish victim lying on its rocky bank. Beowulf dived in, going down and down. Suddenly Grendel's mother fastened her claws on him and dragged him into the cave, a sort of huge bubble enclosed by rock and lit by a fire. He soon found that the sword Hrunting made no impression on her. He attempted a wrestling hold as he had with her son, but stumbled and fell, and she broke free and attacked him with a knife. His chain mail saved him. Springing to his feet again, he caught sight of another sword, a gigantic one, taken in some earlier combat. Against this weapon the ogress had no defence, and he snatched it and cut her head off. Exploring the cavern in the firelight, he found the corpse of Grendel and cut the head off that too, to take back to Hrothgar. The blade of the sword melted in the venomous blood and he returned with the hilt only.

Most of the group at the lakeside had despaired of seeing him again, but he surfaced at last. Amid renewed Danish acclaim he took his leave and went home. Time passed. Beowulf became king of the Geats, and reigned prosperously for half a century. When he was not far short of a hundred years old he perished with glory, defending his people against another monster. This was a winged dragon that lived in the chamber under a burial-mound, guarding treasure stowed there by the last of the family possessing it. A runaway serving-man had crept into the chamber while the dragon lay sleeping and stolen a cup. The dragon began making forays and devastating the country with its fiery breath.

Guided by the thief, Beowulf traced it to its lair and approached behind a specially-made iron shield. He had eleven warriors with him. When the dragon emerged, however, they all fled except for a youth, Wiglaf. With his aid the old king managed to kill the beast, but he was fatally wounded, and, having no son to succeed him, presented Wiglaf with his own armour and weapons and a gold necklace. Wiglaf brought some of the treasure out of the mound, and Beowulf looked at it, but died a moment later. The young man decided that it had been won at too high a price and no one deserved to have it. When the cowards returned he upbraided them scathingly. Under his direction the king's body was laid on a funeral pyre and cremated, and the treasure was buried with his ashes under a tumulus called Beowulf's Barrow, visible from far out to sea. So ends the tale.

Unlike Finn, Beowulf was never acclimatised in Britain. A transfer of his Grendel exploit to Hartlepool, in County Durham, did not find favour. 1

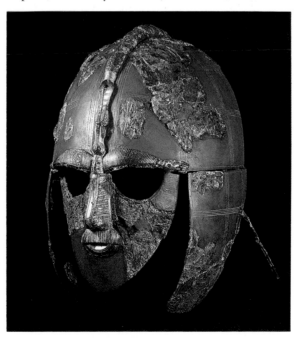

147. A helmet such as Beowulf might have worn, from the Sutton Hoo treasure, found in what is thought to be the ship-burial of a Saxon king.

2 *Beowulf* survives in a manuscript of about 1000 AD. Its date of composition is a matter of controversy. The Anglo-Saxon poet, like the Welsh author of the Pryderi tales, shows a personal Christianity in various touches and asides. He cites *Genesis* and even makes out that Grendel was descended from Cain. But his subject is pagan, and if his descriptions of artefacts are compared with items at Sutton Hoo and elsewhere, it is clear that knowledge of pre-Christian crafts-

3 manship, as of the early seventh century, has gone into the poem's making. King Hygelac can be dated after a fashion and puts the action earlier still. He is one among a number of named persons who occur in other contexts, though Beowulf himself does not. They include (not as a contemporary) a certain

4 Hengest, possibly the Hengist with whom Vortigern made his fatal deal. Scandinavian parallels confirm the authenticity of the background. It is by no means certain, however, who the Geats are. They are generally located in southern Sweden, but they are not Swedes.

Heorot means 'stag'. The derived English word is 'hart'. Its explanation here may lie in royal symbolism. The abortive Hartlepool transfer was prompted by

5 the first syllable of the place-name itself, basically *heorot*, with an allusion to stags on the headland.

So far as documentary evidence goes, *Beowulf* stands alone. The Anglo-Saxons in Britain never developed a real mythology. When the eighth-century poet Cynewulf composed narratives he turned to Christian themes, such as St Helen and the True Cross. Even such borrowing was restricted in scope. No Anglo-Saxon took the slightest notice of Arthur or anyone else in Welsh tradition. It was not till after the Normans turned Anglo-Saxondom into a different realm, in a new relation to the continent, that the island's heritage began flowing together in England.

6 The Anglo-Saxons did make a contribution to Arthurian folklore. This was the Wild Hunt. Originally a gallop among the clouds by Woden and his Nordic companions, it became, in Britain, a more elaborate affair. Among the new huntsmen were Gwyn ap Nudd with his white, red-eared hounds, and Arthur himself in some spectral guise. The Wild Hunt spread to the continent as the *Chasse Artu*. The huntsmen summoned ghosts of the dead and the souls of unbaptised infants. Their visitations, especially with hounds (Gwyn's or others), could be portentous of doom.

While the substance of Arthur's literary legend owed the Anglo-Saxons nothing, several of the poets who enlarged it in English did adopt the alliterative verse-form, as in *Beowulf*. Though modified, this is the essential metre of three masterpieces: Layamon's *Brut*, his epic rehandling of Geoffrey of Monmouth; the marvellous fairy-tale *Sir Gawain and the Green Knight*; and a pre-Malory *Morte Arthure*. England's annexation of the Celtic hero did not, after all, involve a total setting-aside of ancestral Englishness. That was still a presence in format if not in matter. Moreover it was Malory, not any French or German romancer, who gave the legend a definitive form and handed it on to future generations.

1. FML, 122.
2. *Beowulf*, ed. cit., introduction, xi–xix; *Man, Myth and Magic*, art. 'Beowulf'.
3. *Beowulf*, note, 118–9.
4. *Beowulf*, note, 116–7; Blair, 15; Copley, 133.
5. Ekwall, 222, art. 'Hart'.
6. Hole, 141–2; Loomis, ed., 70; Westwood, 8, 33–4, 75, 154–7.

55 *The Saints and the Kings*

Gregory, a Roman monastic founder, afterwards pope, was walking one day through the city's slave market. He noticed some fair-haired, blue-eyed lads and asked what country they had come from. They were heathen Angles from Deira, the southerly portion of Northumbria. 'Not Angles but angels,' Gregory commented, 'if they had the Faith.' He planned a mission and even set out himself, but was prevented, first by a message from the Pope saying he was needed in Rome, later by his own election to the papacy.

As pope he dispatched a mission led by another monk, Augustine, which arrived in the island in 597. Augustine made his first contact with King Aethelbert of Kent, at that time Bretwalda. Aethelbert's queen, Bertha, a Frankish Christian princess, had ensured that he would be granted a hearing. Aethelbert received the clergy in the open, because he feared that if he met them indoors they could use magic against him. With growing trust, however, the king housed them at Canterbury and finally adopted the new religion. While he made no attempt to impose it on his Kentish subjects, they gradually conformed. Augustine founded a Canterbury bishopric which was to become the Church's headquarters in England. Progress, however, was slow and slight. Aethelbert arranged a conference with the Welsh bishops, but they had little interest in evangelising the old enemy,

148. St Martin's Church, Canterbury: when Augustine arrived, there was a former British church dedicated to the same saint, which Aethelbert's Christian queen used as her oratory.

and Augustine's attitude estranged them. They declined to cooperate in expanding his mission. Overtures to other kings by his aides and successors established only limited bridgeheads.

Many suppose that St Augustine converted England. Many even suppose that there were no Christians in this island before 597. The latter belief is manifestly false, and the former, though not manifestly so, is false none the less. Augustine's only solid success was in Kent, and England's Christianisation came from several sources, over nearly a hundred years.

2   The most promising extension from Kent, which happened in 625, was almost totally abortive. A priest from Canterbury, Paulinus, travelled north as chaplain to Aethelbert's daughter, who was marrying the Northumbrian king Edwin, the fifth Bretwalda. After much wavering, Edwin summoned a council to debate a change in religion. He was persuaded when a councillor compared human life to the flight of a sparrow through firelight in a hall – from darkness into darkness again – and urged the value of a doctrine that shone light into the obscurity before and after. But Edwin and his nobles had not been Christian very long when a Welsh invasion threw the north into anarchy. Edwin fell in battle, the queen and Paulinus fled, and hardly any of the neophyte Christians remained. The northern Angles' true conversion was due to Celtic monks from Columba's community, led by the humble and endearing St Aidan. They came at the invitation of King Oswald, who had taken refuge in Iona during the invasion, become a Christian there on the Celtic model, and returned to clear out the Welsh.

3   Oswald reigned at Bamburgh, formerly Din Guayrdi, perhaps the home of Lancelot. Once, when he and Aidan were at dinner, the king's almoner reported that a number of his poor subjects were outside. Oswald handed the almoner a silver dish and told him to give them the food on it, and break up the dish itself so that each could have a fragment of silver. Aidan touched the king's right hand and exclaimed, 'May this hand never perish!' and it never did; after his death it was enshrined in a silver casket and remained uncorrupted. Oswald died fighting Welsh and heathen Mercians in Shrop-

4   shire, where Oswestry, Oswald's Tree, commemorates a cross he set up. Miracles were worked by earth from the spot where he fell, and pilgrims carried so much away that they scooped out a pit. Oswald was revered as a saint in many places. He is the celestial patron of Zug in Switzerland.

5   The differences between Romans and Celts, notably over the fixing of Easter, came to a head in 663 at the Synod of Whitby. This was held at a religious community of Celtic type, with inmates of both sexes under an abbess, St Hilda. Oswald's brother Oswy, who had followed him as king of Northumbria, presided. Wilfrid, abbot of Ripon and a strong advocate of Roman ways, appealed to the practice of the Church everywhere else, in conformity with the Pope, St Peter's successor. As he put it, 'The only people stupid enough to disagree are these Scots and their obstinate adherents the Picts and Britons, who inhabit only a portion of these two islands in the remote ocean.' Colman, for the Celts, cited St Columba and others.

Arguments and precedents were tossed back and forth, till Wilfrid quoted Christ's words to Peter, appointing him as the gatekeeper of heaven. Oswy turned to Colman: 'Is it true that Our Lord said this to Peter?' Colman acknowledged that it was. Oswy persisted: 'Did he say anything like that to

Columba?' 'No.' 'Then,' said Oswy, with a smile of relief at having found a way to close the dispute, 'I must rule in favour of Peter, or he may not let me in.' So Rome won. Peripheral rumblings and mutterings lingered on, but the Church in England was henceforth united in its administration and practice, and governed from Canterbury.

Meanwhile, the slowly advancing West Saxons, themselves Christianised, had reached Glastonbury. The British monastery passed peaceably into their hands. It was the first institution in which the old and new people came together, with Christian continuity from 'Arthurian' times. Kings of Wessex made it a temple of reconciliation. After a while it attracted Irish scholars. The way was prepared for that fusion of traditions which gave the medieval Abbey its role in the formation of Arthurian legend.

Glastonbury's first major patron was King Ine, a successor of Cerdic. In the ninth century it was a successor of Ine, Alfred the Great, who set England on course towards political unity, for which religious unity had laid the foundation. Alfred's name, 'Elf-rede', hints at inspiration from good

149. Saxon stone carving in Sompting Church, Sussex.

fairies. When he was crowned in Wessex, the other Anglo-Saxon kingdoms had been overrun by marauding Danes, and little remained of Wessex itself.

8   It was told in later days how Danish victories reduced Alfred to a wandering resistance leader; how he refused to give up; how he spied out the camp of the Danish chief Guthrum disguised as a minstrel; how he took refuge in Athelney in the Somerset marshlands near Glastonbury; how, when deep in thought, he let a cottager's fire burn some cakes which she had set him to watch, not knowing who he was; how the Virgin Mary appeared to him with words of encouragement; how he raised a final army, routed Guthrum at Ethandune, and forced him to retreat; how he commemorated the struggle by having a White Horse cut, or even two; how he recovered southern England and founded a navy. Let it be added that because he kept Wessex in being when the rest of the kingdoms were effaced from the map, his heirs were able to extend their domain with no rivals, and to become sovereigns of a united England, destined, for better or worse, to draw the Welsh and Scots into a united Britain.

What may be called the 'St Augustine delusion' is the last of the modern myths requiring notice, and one of the stubbornest. In its crude form it really does assert that there were no Christians in Britain till 597, and then Augustine arrived, and converted all of the population that mattered. The crudity is sometimes toned down, but much of the delusion persists. An ironic feature is its stark contradiction of the other myth about Britain's early Christianity, that a separate and admirable Celtic Church flourished over most of the British Isles, till intrusive 'Romans', who had never had any jurisdiction before, enslaved and perverted it.

Neither account is anywhere near to being true. Augustine's Kent was at one pole of the conversion process, Aidan's Northumbria at the other, and the rest of the kingdoms were subjected to various influences over a long period, some from Kent itself and the continent, some from the north, some from Ireland. The *Historia Brittonum* claims that despite the Welsh bishops' holding back, a
9   Cymric northerner named Rhun, a son of Urien, played a leading role in the first Northumbrian mission and officiated in some way at the baptism of Edwin.

Anglo-Celtic Christianity had much to be said for it, and the uniformity following Whitby brought both gain and loss. Thanks largely to the re-doubtable Wilfrid, rapid advances were made in art and architecture. The
10   appointment in 669 of a learned Greek, Theodore of Tarsus, as Archbishop of Canterbury, helped to give the Church a firm structure and intellectual force. In the early eighth century, Bede of Jarrow was easily the foremost scholar in Europe. But the freer, more imaginative Celtic spirit lost ground. The preva-lence of the continental outlook, with its fierce rejection of the old gods and all that went with them, may be part of the reason why the Anglo-Saxons fell so far short of Celtic achievement in the creation of mythology.

11   Alfred the Great was genuinely extraordinary. Besides his dogged resistance to the Danes, and final triumph at Ethandune (probably Edington near Westbury, where the horse is), he gave the crown of the West Saxons a new kind of lustre, and impressed himself on history as a personality. When at peace, he lived in a modest-sized manor at Cheddar, not only hawking and hunting but acquiring enough expertise in both pursuits to give advice to his falconers and kennelmen. He collected Anglo-Saxon poems and songs, welcomed travellers,

150. Statue of Alfred the Great in Winchester.

and listened to their reports of distant countries. To promote his subjects' education he founded a school for the sons of nobles (sending his own to it) and brought foreign scholars to his court, including a Welshman, Asser, who became his biographer. Part of his programme was to inform the people about their own past, and to this end he sponsored a compilation of traditions which was the first version of the *Anglo-Saxon Chronicle*. He learned Latin, and presided over the translation of important books into 'the language which we can all understand' – an obvious thing to do, yet nobody had done it, and it was many years before anything comparable was done abroad.

He issued a code of laws drawn from the best of Kent and Mercia, as well as Wessex. Those he added himself were humane, limiting the custom of blood-feud, for instance. It will be remembered that according to Geoffrey of Monmouth, he copied laws from the ancient Britons; not so, but proof of the prestige which his code still possessed in Geoffrey's time. That had been shown already by its adoption or imitation in other parts of England and Wales. To plan his work he invented a kind of clock, a graduated candle inside a transparent casing, which admitted air but kept out draughts so that the candle burned at a regular rate.

Several Welsh princes placed themselves under Alfred's protection or became allies. Thanks to the Danes' extinction of the other kingdoms, and their own waning, his son and daughter established their rule in Mercia, and his grandson Athelstan took over Northumbria. Athelstan routed a coalition of Scots, Irish and Norse, and was uncontested sovereign of the whole of England.

Alfred deserved the honour of a national epic, yet no one composed it. As a hero of legend Arthur leaves him so far behind that there is no comparison. The few Alfred legends, such as the anecdote of the cakes – probably bannocks – and his acceptance of the housewife's rebuke, suggest that he was recalled as not only 'great', but human, good-natured, and free from pride. Still, he had to wait a

151. Silver penny of Alfred.

long time for a poetic celebration with any value. It came at last in G. K. Chesterton's *Ballad of the White Horse*, which conserves popular fiction about the Uffington horse being Alfred's, by acutely postulating a pre-Alfred original which he restored. The *Ballad* is a perceptive and colourful mini-epic, with passages as fine as any poetry in English inspired by Arthur. Alfred's companions in the poem rightly include representatives of Celtic and Roman traditions as well as Anglo-Saxon.

152. Made for the king: the Alfred Jewel, found at Athelney in 1693, perhaps part of a bookmark.

1. Bede, I, 22–3, II, 1–3; Butler, arts. 'Gregory the Great', March 12th, and 'Augustine, Apostle of England', May 28th; Campbell, 45; Morris, 389–90; Sheldon, 114.
2. Bede, II, 9–14, 20, III, 1–3; Hodgkin, I, 286; Morris, 390–2; Sheldon, 141.
3. Bede, III, 6; Butler, art. 'Aidan', August 31st; Campbell, 46; Duckett, 106; FML, 337.
4. Bede, III, 9; Butler, art. 'Oswald', August 9th; Ekwall, 352, art. 'Oswestry'; Sheldon, 160–3.
5. Bede, III, 25; Butler, art. 'Wilfrid', October 12th; Campbell, 46–7; Hodgkin, I, 299; Morris, 394–5.
6. Campbell, 51; Duckett, 13–17; Hodgkin, I, 315, and II, 642; Sheldon, 164; Slover (1) and (2), passim. Cp Carley, 87–112.
7. Carley, 6; Duckett, 45.
8. FML, 77, 148, 513–4; Kightly, 99–105; Westwood, 3–4, 150.
9. 'Nennius', chapter 63.
10. Bede, IV, 1–2; Blair, 136; Duckett, 32: Hodgkin, I, 305; Morris, 395–6.
11. Ashe (7), 205–9; Blair, 351; FML, 168; Hodgkin, II, 648.
12. GM (1), 26–7, 31, and (2), 94, 101.
13. Ashe (7), 209–10; Blair, 81, 87; Kightly, 105.

Epilogue

William Blake, in his conception of the giant Albion, ranged far beyond
accepted legend. By making this island the source of the primeval world-
order, he was able to present the giant as a symbol of humanity, Primordial
Man. Yet he did not turn him into a pure abstraction. He kept in touch with
the mythologies he transcended, and, in particular, with a leading figure in
the mythology of Britain. He wrote:

> The giant Albion, was Patriarch of the Atlantic; he is the
> Atlas of the Greeks, one of those the Greeks called Titans.
> The stories of Arthur are the acts of Albion, applied to a
> Prince of the fifth century.

That last sentence has an air of profundity, but what does it mean? Blake is
referring to several things, but pre-eminently to an aspect of Arthur that we
have glimpsed more than once. A major reason for his recurrent spell, in a
variety of guises, has been his golden-age aura. Other legends express the
same dream, but the Arthurian golden age has an extra dimension. The
King is gone . . . but he is not gone for ever. He is asleep in his cave, or
immortal in his magical island; he will return, and presumably bring the
golden age back.

That Blake saw Arthur in this light is manifest from what he does with his
Albion, chiefly in the prophetic book *Jerusalem*. He depicts the symbolic
giant's career in such a way that Arthur's departure-and-return story
becomes a reflection of it. Wise and glorious in his primary state, Albion
goes spiritually astray and sinks into a deathlike sleep, in which he lingers for
aeons. This is externalised in the ills that beset humanity through loss of
vision: the apostasy of the sages, and their decline into historical Druidism,
prototype of oppressive religion; war, division, perverted science, and, in
Blake's time, the factory system and the iniquities of wealth. But at last light
breaks in, Albion awakens, humanity is reintegrated, the world is reborn in
love and forgiveness.

Even apart from Blake, Arthur himself, in this aspect, is a distinctive
contribution to world mythology. There is nobody else quite like him – no
human hero, at least. Other legendary sleepers, who may or may not wake
up, are very probably imitations of him, and in any case they do not carry his
golden-age quality. What Arthur stands for is the idea of a long-lost glory or
promise, plus a belief (as may be repeated here) that it is not truly lost; that it
can be reinstated for a fresh start, with intervening corruption swept away.
Belief of that kind is a real and potent motive force which is seldom given
due weight as a factor in history. It has inspired, or helped to inspire, several
of the most radical movements for change.

Thus, the sixteenth-century Christian reformers, both Catholic and
Protestant, held that the Church once had its golden age of apostolic purity.
Cumulative abuses had corrupted it, but the Reformation, however con-

ceived, would abolish them and recapture the pristine rightness. Or again, Rousseau gave the French Revolution a driving mystique by his doctrine of a virtuous, long-ago natural society ruined by bad institutions, but capable of being restored by good ones. Engels and Lenin invigorated Marxism by adding what was not at first part of it, a classless idyll of 'primitive communism' at the dawn of history, which the Revolution could restore on a higher level by ending the long succession of class tyrannies. In India, under British rule, nationalists who favoured westernised progress made no headway with the masses. The leader who did rouse them was Mahatma Gandhi, who condemned westernisation and evoked a wiser pre-conquest India of village communes and handicrafts, and the need to re-create it.

More recently the same motif has appeared again in the work of some women prehistorians, drawing on the poetic insights of Robert Graves, but also on the work of so accomplished an archaeologist as Marija Gimbutas. Their view was foreshadowed some time ago by the 'Goddess' interpretation of the megaliths. Once, they claim, there was a 'matristic', Goddess-oriented epoch when both sexes had their proper status, and society had a basic balance and rightness. This was brought to an end by the advent of a patriarchal, male-dominated age of gods. Suitable enlightenment through an informed women's movement can bring the lost rightness back.

These phenomena, and others like them, have nothing explicit to do with Arthur, and many of those concerned would reject such an association. The point, however, is that Britain has evolved a myth embodying a *way of looking at things* which has deep roots in human nature. Some might speak of an archetype. It may be reasonable, it may be misguided. It certainly calls into question the humanistic idea of progress. Yet it remains a fact, recurrent in history. Why this should be so, is a matter for debate. Perhaps we should see it as an affirmation of life against death, against a sense of things-closing-in, which is all too frequent and natural. The glory did exist once; therefore it is not a mere phantasm, an impossibility; it can exist again. To have created a myth expressing that affirmation, however irrelevant its literary trappings may seem, is a unique achievement for Britain's story-tellers. Was it an accident? Or did it grow, as Blake implies, out of the whole character and life-span of Albion? Certainly, when he traced that life-span in the same terms, with an apocalypse of awakening at the last, he was creating a myth himself, in full harmony with the materials that came to his hand.

153. Blake's cosmic Albion lying in his deathlike sleep, lamented by his daughters.

1. This epilogue summarises the theme
    developed in Ashe (2).

And there was heard a great lamenting in Beulah: all the Regions
Of Beulah were moved as the tender bowels are moved: & they said:

Why did you take Vengeance O ye Sons of the mighty Albion?
Planting these Oaken Groves: Erecting these Dragon Temples
Injury the Lord heals but Vengeance cannot be healed:
As the Sons of Albion have done to Luvah: so they have in him
Done to the Divine Lord & Saviour. who suffers with those that suffer;
For not one sparrow can suffer. & the whole Universe not suffer also,
In all its Regions, & its Father & Saviour not pity and weep.
But Vengeance is the destroyer of Grace & Repentance in the bosom
Of the Injurer: in which the Divine Lamb is cruelly slain:
Descend O Lamb of God & take away the imputation of Sin
By the Creation of States & the deliverance of Individuals Evermore Amen

Thus wept they in Beulah over the Four Regions of Albion
But many doubted & despaird & imputed Sin & Righteousness
To Individuals & not to States, and these Slept in Ulro.

Bibliography

In the references to this Bibliography, two abbreviations are used. FML means 'Folklore, Myths and Legends of Britain'. GM means 'Geoffrey of Monmouth'.

Adomnan, *Life of St Columba*, ed. with trans., Alan Orr Anderson and Marjorie Ogilvie Anderson (Thomas Nelson, 1961).

Alcock, Leslie:
  (1) *Arthur's Britain* (Allan Lane, the Penguin Press, 1971).
  (2) *'By South Cadbury is that Camelot . . .'* (Thames and Hudson, 1972).
  (3) 'Cadbury-Camelot: a Fifteen-Year Perspective' (*Proceedings of the British Academy* LXVIII, 1982).

Anglo-Saxon Chronicle, ed. G. N. Garmonsway (Dent, 1933; Dutton, New York, 1953).

Ashe, Geoffrey:
  (1) *Avalonian Quest* (Methuen, 1982, and Collins/Fontana, 1984).
  (2) *Camelot and the Vision of Albion* (Heinemann, 1971; St Martin's Press, New York, 1972).
  (3) 'A Certain Very Ancient Book', *Speculum*, April 1981 (The Medieval Academy of America, Cambridge, Massachusetts).
  (4) *The Glastonbury Tor Maze* (Gothic Image, Glastonbury, 1979; revised edition, 1985).
  (5) *A Guidebook to Arthurian Britain* (Longman, 1980, and Aquarian Press, 1983).
  (6) 'The Historical Origins of the Arthurian Legend', in *The Vitality of the Arthurian Legend* (a symposium, Odense University Press, Denmark, 1988).
  (7) *Kings and Queens of Early Britain* (Methuen, 1982).
  (8) *The Land and the Book* (Collins, 1965).
  (9) *Land to the West* (Collins, 1962).

Atkinson, R. J. C., *Stonehenge and Avebury* (HM Stationery Office, 1959).

Barlow, Frank, *The Feudal Kingdom of England* (Longman, 1955).

Bede, *History of the English Church and People*, trans. Leo Sherley-Price (Penguin, 1955).

Beowulf, trans. Marijane Osborn, with introduction by Fred C. Robinson (University of California Press, 1983).

Béroul. See Wilhelm.

Blair, Peter Hunter, *An Introduction to Anglo-Saxon England* (Cambridge University Press, 1956).

Bolton, J. D. P., *Aristeas of Proconnesus* (Oxford, Clarendon Press, 1962).

Bord, Janet and Colin, *Mysterious Britain* (Garnstone, 1972).

Brewer's Dictionary of Phrase and Fable (Cassell, 1959).

Bromwich, Rachel, *Trioedd Ynys Prydein*: the Welsh Triads, with translation and notes (University of Wales Press, Cardiff, second edition, 1978).

Brown, Theo, *Trojans in the West Country*: West Country Folklore Series No. 4 (Toucan Press, Guernsey, 1970).

Butler, Alban, *Lives of the Saints*, rev. and ed. H. Thurston and D. Attwater, 12 vols (Burns Oates & Washbourne, 1926–38).

Caine, Mary, *The Glastonbury Zodiac* (Grael Communications, Torquay, 1978).

Campbell, James, ed., *The Anglo-Saxons* (Phaidon, Oxford, 1982; Cornell University Press, Ithaca, N.Y., 1982).

Carley, James P., *Glastonbury Abbey* (Boydell, Woodbridge, Suffolk, 1988).

Chadwick, N. K.:
  (1) *Early Brittany* (University of Wales Press, Cardiff, 1969).
  (2) ed., *Studies in Early British History* (Cambridge University Press, 1954).

Chambers, E. K., *Arthur of Britain* (Sidgwick and Jackson, 1927, and reissue, 1966; Barnes and Noble, New York, 1964).

Chippindale, Christopher, *Stonehenge Complete* (Thames and Hudson, 1983).

Copley, Gordon J., *The Conquest of Wessex in the Sixth Century* (Phoenix, 1954).

Cross, Tom Peete, and Slover, Clark H., ed. and trans., *Ancient Irish Tales* (Henry Holt, New York, 1936; reissue, Barnes and Noble, New York, 1969).

Dames, Michael:
  (1) *The Avebury Cycle* (Thames and Hudson, 1977).
  (2) *The Silbury Treasure: the Great Goddess Rediscovered* (Thames and Hudson, 1976).

Devereux, Paul, and Thomson, Ian, *The Ley Hunter's Companion* (Thames and Hudson, 1979).

Ditmas, E. M. R.:
  (1) *Traditions and Legends of Glastonbury*: West Country Folklore Series No. 14 (Toucan Press, Guernsey, 1979).
  (2) *Tristan and Iseult in Cornwall* (Forrester Roberts, Gloucester, 1969).

Dobson, C. C., *Did Our Lord Visit Britain?* (Covenant Publishing Company, 1936; revised edition, 1986).

Dodds, E. R., *The Greeks and the Irrational* (University of California Press, 1953).

Duckett, Eleanor Shipley, *Anglo-Saxon Saints and Scholars* (Macmillan, 1947).

Dumville, David, 'Sub-Roman Britain: History and Legend', *History* 62 (1977).

Ebbutt, M. J., *Hero-Myths and Legends of the British Race* (Harrap, 1910).

Eckhardt, Caroline D., 'Prophecy and Nostalgia', in Braswell, M. F., and Bugge, J., eds., *The Arthurian Tradition* (University of Alabama Press, 1988).

Ekwall, Eilert, *The Concise Oxford Dictionary of English Place-Names* (Oxford University Press, 1936; revised edition, 1959).

Fletcher, Robert Huntington, *The Arthurian Material in the Chronicles* (Ginn, Boston, 1906; second edition, Franklin, New York, 1966).

Fleuriot, Léon, *Les Origines de la Bretagne* (Payot, Paris, 1980).

Folklore, Myths and Legends of Britain (Reader's Digest Association, London, 1973).

Fraser, Maxwell, *Wales* (Robert Hale, 1952).

Geoffrey of Monmouth:
   (1) *Historia Regum Britannie*, ed. Neil Wright (D. S. Brewer, Cambridge, 1985).
   (2) *The History of the Kings of Britain*, trans., with introduction, by Lewis Thorpe (Penguin, 1966).
   (3) *Vita Merlini*: The Life of Merlin, ed. and trans. J. J. Parry (University of Illinois Press, Urbana, 1925).

Gildas, *De Excidio Britanniae*, ed. and trans. under the title *The Ruin of Britain* by Michael Winterbottom, in *History from the Sources*, vol. 7 (Phillimore, Chichester, 1978).

Giraldus Cambrensis (Gerald of Wales), *The Journey through Wales* and *The Description of Wales*, trans., with introduction, by Lewis Thorpe (Penguin, 1978).

Gougaud, Louis, *Christianity in Celtic Lands* (Sheed and Ward, 1932).

Graves, Robert:
   (1) *The Greek Myths*, 2 vols (revised edition, Penguin, 1960).
   (2) *The White Goddess* (amended and enlarged edition, Faber, 1952).

Grinsell, L. V.:
   (1) *The Druids and Stonehenge*: West Country Folklore Series No. 11 (Toucan Press, Guernsey, 1978).
   (2) *The Folklore of Stanton Drew*: West Country Folklore Series No. 5 (Toucan Press, Guernsey, 1973).
   (3) *Legendary History and Folklore of Stonehenge*: West Country Folklore Series No. 9 (Toucan Press, Guernsey, 1975).

Guthrie, W. K. C., *The Greeks and their Gods* (Methuen, 1950).

Hadingham, Evan, *Ancient Carvings in Britain: a Mystery* (Garnstone, 1974).

Hawkins, Gerald S., *Stonehenge Decoded* (Fontana, 1970).

Henry of Huntingdon:
   (1) *Historia Anglorum*: The History of the English, ed. Thomas Arnold (Longman, Rolls Series, 1879).
   (2) *Chronicle*, i.e. the *Historia Anglorum*, trans. Thomas Forester (Bohn, 1853).

Higgins, John. See *Mirror for Magistrates*.

Historia Brittonum. See 'Nennius' (1).

Hodgkin, R. G., *A History of the Anglo-Saxons*. 2 vols (Oxford University Press, 1935 and 1952).

Hole, Christina, *English Folklore* (Batsford, 1940).

Holinshed, Raphael, *Chronicles of England, Scotland and Ireland*, vol. 1 (J. Johnson and others, 1807).

Jackson, Kenneth H.:
   (1) *A Celtic Miscellany* (Penguin, 1971).
   (2) *Language and History in Early Britain* (Edinburgh University Press, 1953; Harvard University Press, 1954).

Jenkins, Stephen, *The Undiscovered Country* (Neville Spearman, 1977).

John of Glastonbury, *The Chronicle of Glastonbury Abbey*, ed. James P. Carley, trans. David Townsend (Boydell, Woodbridge, Suffolk, 1985).

Jolly, Eva, *The New Bath Guide* (Orlando Press, Bath, 1983).

Joyce, P. W., *Old Celtic Romances* (reissue by Talbot Press, Dublin, 1961).

Kendrick, T. D., *British Antiquity* (Methuen, 1950).

Keys, David, 'Academics shed new light on Druids' link with stones': news item in *The Independent*, London, June 21st 1988.

Kightly, Charles, *Folk Heroes of Britain* (Thames and Hudson, 1984).

Kraft, John, *The Goddess in the Labyrinth* (Åbo Akademi, Finland, 1985).

Lacy, Norris J., ed., *The Arthurian Encyclopedia* (Garland, New York, 1986; Peter Bedrick, New York, 1987; Boydell, Woodbridge, Suffolk, 1988).

Lancelot (medieval romance). See Wilhelm (1).

Lapidge, Michael, and Dumville, David, eds., *Gildas: New Approaches* (Boydell, Woodbridge, Suffolk, 1984).

Layamon. See Wilhelm (2).

Leir. The True Chronicle Historie of King Leir and his Three Daughters, in *Shakespeare's Library*, vol. 6 (Reeves and Turner, 1875).

Lewis, Lionel Smithett, *St Joseph of Arimathea at Glastonbury* (1922; revised edition, James Clarke, Cambridge, 1982).

Lloyd, John Edward, *A History of Wales* (Longman, 1939).

Loomis, Roger Sherman, ed., *Arthurian Literature in the Middle Ages* (Oxford, Clarendon Press, 1959).

Mabinogion:
  (1) Trans. by Lady Charlotte Guest, with the Story of Taliesin (2nd edition, Bernard Quaritch, 1877).
  (2) Trans., with introduction, by Gwyn and Thomas Jones (Dent, 1949).

Mack, Maynard, *Alexander Pope* (Yale University Press in association with W. W. Norton, 1985).

Mackenzie, Donald A., *Scotland: the Ancient Kingdom* (Blackie, 1930).

Malory, Sir Thomas, *Le Morte d'Arthur*: Caxton's text with modernised spelling, ed. Janet Cowan with introduction by John Lawlor, 2 vols (Penguin, 1969).

Maltwood, K. E., *A Guide to Glastonbury's Temple of the Stars* (1935; reissue, James Clarke, Cambridge, 1964).

Man, Myth and Magic, ed. Richard Cavendish, 7 vols (BPC Publishing, 1970–2).

Markale, Jean, *King Arthur: King of Kings*, trans. Christine Hauch (Gordon and Cremonesi, 1977).

Marples, Morris, *White Horses and other Hill Figures* (Alan Sutton, Gloucester, 1981).

Matthews, W. H., *Mazes and Labyrinths* (1922; reissue, Dover, New York, 1970).

Mirror for Magistrates, A, ed. Lily B. Campbell (Cambridge University Press, 1938).
  . . . *Parts added to A Mirror for Magistrates*, including John Higgins's contributions, ed. Lily B. Campbell (Cambridge University Press, 1946).

Moncreiffe of that Ilk, Sir Iain, *Royal Highness* (Hamish Hamilton, 1982).

Morgan, R. W., *St Paul in Britain* (1861; reprint by Covenant Publishing Company, n.d.).

Morris, John, *The Age of Arthur* (Weidenfeld and Nicolson, 1973).

Mort Artu (medieval romance), trans. by James Cable as *The Death of King Arthur* (Penguin, 1971).

'Nennius':
  (1) *Historia Brittonum*, with *Annales Cambriae*, ed. and trans. under the title *British History* by John Morris, in *History from the Sources*, vol. 8 (Phillimore, Chichester, 1980).
  (2) *Nennius's History of the Britons*, with Welsh genealogies and other additional matter, trans. A. W. Wade-Evans (SPCK, 1938).

Newstead, Helaine, *Bran the Blessed in Arthurian Romance* (reprint, AMS Press, New York, 1966).

Oman, Charles, *England before the Norman Conquest* (Methuen, 1938).

Parry, Thomas, *A History of Welsh Literature*, trans. H. Idris Bell (Oxford, Clarendon Press, 1955).

Perlesvaus (medieval romance), trans. by Nigel Bryant as *The High Book of the Grail* (D. S. Brewer, Cambridge, and Rowan and Littlefield, Totowa, New Jersey, 1978).

Piggott, Stuart:
  (1) *The Druids* (Thames and Hudson, 1968; Penguin, 1974 – page references are to the latter).
  (2) 'The Sources of Geoffrey of Monmouth', *Antiquity* XV, 1941.

Plutarch:
  (1) *Concerning the Face which appears in the Orb of the Moon*, ed. and trans. Harold Cherniss. In Plutarch's *Moralia*, vol. 12 (Loeb Classical Library. Heinemann and Harvard University Press, 1957).
  (2) *The Obsolescence of Oracles*, ed. and trans. Frank Cole Babbitt. As (1), vol. 5, 1936.

Prebble, John, *The Lion in the North* (Secker and Warburg, 1971).

Prose *Merlin* (medieval romance). See Wilhelm (2).

Queste del Saint Graal (medieval romance), trans. by P. M. Matarosso as *The Quest of the Holy Grail* (Penguin, 1969).

Rahtz, Philip, *Invitation to Archaeology* (Basil Blackwell, Oxford, 1985).

Rees, Alwyn and Brinley, *Celtic Heritage* (Thames and Hudson, 1978).

Renfrew, Colin, *Archaeology and Language* (Jonathan Cape, 1987).

Rhys, John, *Celtic Folklore*, 2 vols (Oxford, Clarendon Press, 1901).

Rolleston, T. W., *Myths and Legends of the Celtic Race* (Harrap, 1911; reissue, Constable, 1985).

Ross, Anne, *Pagan Celtic Britain* (Routledge and Kegan Paul, 1967; Cardinal, 1974 – page references are to the latter).

Rutherford, Ward, *The Druids and their Heritage* (Gordon and Cremonesi, 1978).

Sackville, Thomas, and Norton, Thomas, *Ferrex and Porrex* (otherwise *Gorboduc*), in Sackville's *Works*, ed. Reginald W. Sackville-West (John Russell Smith, 1859).

Sargent, H. N., *The Marvels of Bible Prophecy* (Covenant Publishing Company, 1938).

Scott, John, *The Early History of Glastonbury*: i.e. *De Antiquitate Glastoniensis Ecclesiae* by William of Malmesbury and interpolators, with introduction and translation (Boydell, Woodbridge, Suffolk, 1981).

Sheldon, Gilbert, *The Transition from Roman Britain to Christian England* (Macmillan, 1932).

Sir Gawain and the Green Knight (medieval romance). See Wilhelm (1).

Sitwell, Edith, *Bath* (Faber, 1932).

Slover, Clark H.:
  (1) 'Glastonbury Abbey and the Fusing of English Literary Culture', *Speculum*, April 1935.
  (2) 'William of Malmesbury and the Irish', *Speculum*, July 1927.

Snell, F. J., *King Arthur's Country* (Dent, 1926).

Spencer, Hazelton, *Shakespeare Improved* (Harvard University Press, 1927).

Spenser, Edmund, *The Faerie Queene*, ed. A. C. Hamilton (Longman, London and New York, 1977).

Stewart, R. J.:
(1) *The Mystic Life of Merlin* (Arkana, 1986).
(2) *The Prophetic Vision of Merlin* (Arkana, 1986).

Stuart-Knill, Sir Ian, *The Pedigree of Arthur* (Kingdom Revival Crusade, Sidmouth, Devon, 1977).

Suite du Merlin (medieval romance). See Wilhelm (2).

Tatlock, J. S. P., *The Legendary History of Britain* (University of California Press, 1950).

Thom, Alexander, *Megalithic Lunar Observatories* (Oxford, 1971).

Thomas, Charles:
(1) *Exploration of a Drowned Landscape* (Batsford, 1985).
(2) 'Tintagel Castle', *Antiquity* LXII, September 1988.

Todd, Ruthuen, *Tracks in the Snow* (Grey Walls Press, 1946).

Tolstoy, Nikolai, *The Quest for Merlin* (Hamish Hamilton, 1985).

Vickery, A. R., *Holy Thorn of Glastonbury*: West Country Folklore Series No. 12 (Toucan Press, Guernsey, 1979).

Voyage of Bran, The, trans. Kuno Meyer and Alfred Nutt, 2 vols (David Nutt, 1895–7).

Wace. See Wilhelm (2).

Wade-Evans. See 'Nennius' (2).

Weston, Jessie L., *From Ritual to Romance* (Cambridge University Press, 1920; Doubleday, Garden City, N.Y., 1957).

Westwood, Jennifer, *Albion: a Guide to Legendary Britain* (Granada, 1985).

White, Richard B., 'Excavations at Aberffraw, Anglesey, 1973 and 1974', *Bulletin of the Board of Celtic Studies*, xxviii, May 1979.

Wilhelm, James J:
(1) . . . and Laila Zamuelis Gross, eds., *The Romance of Arthur* (Garland, New York, 1984). Includes translations of *Culhwch and Olwen*, Chrétien's *Lancelot*, and *Sir Gawain and the Green Knight*.
(2) ed., *The Romance of Arthur* II (Garland, New York, 1986). Includes translation of Béroul, and translated excerpts from Wace, Layamon, the Prose *Merlin*, and the *Suite du Merlin*.

William of Malmesbury. See Scott.

Wood, Ian, 'The Fall of the Western Empire and the End of Roman Britain', *Britannia* XVIII, 1987.

Zvelebil, Marek and Kamil V., 'Agricultural transition and Indo-European dispersals', *Antiquity* LXII, September 1988.

Index

Page numbers in italics refer to illustrations